IDEAS: Brilliant Thinkers Speak Their Minds

IDEAS

Brilliant
Thinkers
Speak
Their
Minds

Edited by
BERNIE LUCHT

Copy editing by Barry A. Norris

Cover photo: Creatas
Cover and interior design by Julie Scriver.
Printed in Canada.
10 9 8 7 6 5 4 3 2 1

Library and Archives Canada Cataloguing in Publication

Ideas: brilliant thinkers speak their minds / Bernie Lucht, editor.
Interviews and lectures first broadcast on the
CBC radio program Ideas.
ISBN 0-86492-439-9

1. Geopolitics. 2. World history. 3. Social history.
I. Lucht, Bernie, 1944- II. Title.

D20.I34 2005   909   C2005-904975-8

Published with the support of the Canada Council for the Arts and the New Brunswick Culture and Sport Secretariat. We acknowledge the financial support of the Government of Canada through the Book Publishing Industry Development Program (BPIDP) for our publishing activities.

Goose Lane Editions
469 King Street
Fredericton, New Brunswick
CANADA E3B 1E5
www.gooselane.com

Contents

IDEAS: Brilliant Thinkers Speak Their Minds

"The Best Ideas
You'll Hear Tonight"

"Ideas . . . The Best Ideas You'll Hear Tonight," intoned CBC announcer Ken Haslam. With those words, spoken in his cultivated baritone voice, Haslam launched the first episode of what was described as "the new look in CBC educational broadcasting," an hour-long show of "radio for the mind," to be heard each weeknight. It was Monday, October 24, 1965.

The program was the brainchild of two CBC Radio producers, Phyllis Webb and Bill Young. Webb was a West Coast poet who had always wanted to work in radio. She joined the CBC in 1964 and began producing a lecture series called *University of the Air*. In later years, she would win a Governor General's award for her collection of poetry, *The Vision Tree: Selected Poems*. Bill Young was an American who had come to Canada to study. In 1964, while he was doing graduate work in English at the University of Toronto, he was recruited to the CBC. His first job was to produce *The Learning Stage*, an adult education program with lectures and interviews on such subjects as theatre, film, music, travel and poetry.

Bill Young recalls attending a meeting at which producers were asked to consider amalgamating programs with similar mandates. The CBC needed to save money. *Plus ça change*. Webb was enthusiastic. She felt the lecture format of her program was too constraining and wanted to try doing something livelier. She and Young worked together on a proposal to merge *University of the Air* and *The Learning Stage* to create a new nightly program that would take the best of each series and present adult education on radio using a variety of approaches. They sent the proposal to CBC management, and it was accepted.

The new program was launched under the title *The Best Ideas You'll Hear Tonight,* but within months it was shortened to *Ideas.* Webb and Young hired a third person to work with them, a young woman named Janet Somerville. Somerville had been working on her master's degree in theology at the University of St. Michael's College in Toronto when she learned of the vacancy at *Ideas.* She jumped at the opportunity and applied. She didn't expect to get the job, and when she did, it was to her "absolute astonishment." The program also had a roster of freelance contributors. Among the best known were Timothy Findley, who became the show's literary editor, and Bill Whitehead, its science editor.

"Idea Number One for Monday," Haslam announced briskly, "Charles Darwin's Theory of Evolution," and the show began with a discussion about Darwin's 1831 trip to the Galapagos. Webb was disappointed with that first show and says the series got off to a "horrible start." Janet Somerville says it was "class-roomy" and "text-bookish." But the new series quickly found its feet. The second program was much better and eventually won an award.

What was happening in the world in 1965, the year *Ideas* went on the air? Lester B. Pearson was Canada's prime minister. After a bitter debate, the country adopted a new flag with the red maple leaf at its centre. Trans-Canada Airlines was renamed Air Canada. A failure at the Niagara Generating Station caused the Great Northeast Blackout in November, leaving twenty-five million people in Ontario and the eastern United States without power for up to twelve hours. Internationally, the colony of Rhodesia, now Zimbabwe, after months of threats, made a dramatic Unilateral Declaration of Independence under a white minority government led by Ian Smith. Lyndon Johnson began his second term as US president: he proclaimed the Great Society and committed the first combat troops to Vietnam. As the year progressed, Johnson would escalate the war in Vietnam to unprecedented levels. T.S. Eliot and Somerset Maugham died in 1965. The Grateful Dead, Jefferson Airplane, and Pink Floyd launched their musical careers. The Beatles started shooting their second film, *Help!*, and released the all-time favourite song, "Yesterday." American television premiered *Hogan's Heroes* and *I Dream of Jeannie*. *The Sound of Music* starring Julie Andrews was released and received an Oscar for Best Picture of the Year. 1965 was a busy year, and, oh yes, there was *Ideas*.

Ideas underlie every aspect of our lives. They shape how we think and speak about the world, how we behave, how we see ourselves, individually and in society. Ideas drive imagination; they determine how we conceive the past, the present and the future; they inform our political and social arrangements, our arts and culture, science, technology and religion, our personal relationships and beliefs.

Lister Sinclair, genius and polymath, an icon of Canadian culture and broadcasting, was the much-loved host of *Ideas* between 1983 and 1999. He described the purpose of the show elegantly and concisely: *Ideas,* he said, was about helping to "locate ourselves in the universe." Locating ourselves in the universe is the work of all of us, as we struggle to understand our individual lives and the world around us. It is an enormous task — vast, complex and neverending. In forty years of broadcasting, this task has been addressed by the thousands of thinkers who have appeared on *Ideas*. They have explored an array of subjects that span the range of human thought, imagination, knowledge and experience. They have been presented in documentaries, interviews, lectures, debates, panel discussions and public forums.

Ideas has also been a venue for experimentation. In 1967, as a Centennial project, the show commissioned Glenn Gould to create a documentary called "The Idea of North." Gould had long been intrigued by the North, which he described as an "incredible tapestry of tundra and taiga which constitutes the arctic and sub-arctic of our country." In 1967, very few Canadians had been there; for most people, the North was a mythical landscape, more dreamed about and imagined than experienced. In "The Idea of North," Gould brought together four people who had lived and worked there — a geographer, a sociologist, a government official and a nurse — to talk about the role the North had played in their lives. There was also a fifth character, Wally McLean, whom Gould had met during a train trip from Winnipeg to Fort Churchill. McLean was a surveyor, and as the train travelled north, he and Gould talked in what stretched into a day-long conversation. "I began to realize," Gould wrote, "that his relation to a craft, which has as its subject the land, enabled him to read the signs of that land, to find in the most minute measurement a suggestion of the infinite, to encompass the universal within the particular." Gould used Wally McLean as the narrator of the documentary.

"The Idea of North" was the first example of what Gould called "contrapuntal radio," in which several people are sometimes heard speaking all at once. Their voices were arranged like the parts for instruments in an orchestra — sometimes playing solos, sometimes duets, sometimes three or more together. Because of the way Gould combined the voices, working with the different timbres and rhythms of speech, you could follow what each person was saying and, through the overlapping voices, hear the interplay of related ideas. According to Lorne Tulk, the brilliant sound engineer who collaborated with Gould on "The Idea of North," Gould conceived the technique after discovering that the material he wanted to use was fourteen minutes longer than the hour-long format would permit.

"The Idea of North" was the first of three "contrapuntal radio" documentaries Gould produced over the course of a decade that became known as *The Solitude Trilogy*. The programs explored the theme of isolation — geographic, political, cultural and religious.

Ideas is the home of the annual Massey Lectures series. Named in honour Vincent Massey, the first Canadian Governor General, the Massey Lectures began in 1961, conceived as a venue where prominent thinkers could explore significant contemporary ideas for Canadian audiences. The first Massey lecturer was Lady Barbara Ward Jackson. Her lecture series, *The Rich Nations and the Poor*

Nations, became an early classic in the literature of the relationship between developing and developed countries. From 1961 until 1994, distinguished thinkers from both Canada and abroad delivered the lectures, among them Northrop Frye, John Kenneth Galbraith, Martin Luther King, Jr., R.D. Laing, George Grant, George Steiner, Claude Levi-Strauss, Jane Jacobs, Carlos Fuentes, Doris Lessing, Gregory Baum, Noam Chomsky, Ursula Franklin, Charles Taylor and Conor Cruise O'Brien.

In 1995, we decided to draw exclusively on the Canadian intellectual community for the Massey Lectures. Since then, they have been given by John Ralston Saul, Hugh Kenner, Jean Vanier, Robert Fulford, Michael Ignatieff, Janice Gross Stein, Margaret Visser, Thomas King, Ronald Wright and Stephen Lewis.

Today the Massey Lectures are the fruit of the collaboration of three institutions: the Canadian Broadcasting Corporation, Massey College in the University of Toronto, and House of Anansi Press. For most of their history, the Massey Lectures were recorded in the austere confines of a studio in Toronto, broadcast on the radio, and then published as a book. In 2002, hoping to expand their impact, we moved them out of the studio and into the energetic give-and-take of the public world. Since then, the Massey Lectures have been presented each autumn to packed auditoriums on university campuses across Canada. They are broadcast in November by the CBC and published by House of Anansi Press. The book is usually a national best-seller, and the Massey Lectures have become an annual highlight of Canadian intellectual life.

The question I am asked most frequently is, "Where do you get your ideas?" I'm usually at a loss for an answer. Science fiction writer Frederick Pohl said, in an interview recorded for *Ideas* in the late 1970s, that science fiction writers are often asked the same thing. He said they found this experience so common that a group of them got together to figure out what to say. They decided that whenever someone asked them, "Where do you get your ideas?" they would all say the same thing: "Schenectady."

So where do we get our ideas? *Ideas* is a production unit of ten full-time people. Nine of us work in Toronto; one works in Edmonton and is responsible for *Ideas* production from the three prairie provinces. We have half-time producers in Vancouver and Montreal, as well as contributing producers in other cities. We all get together twice a year — in February and June — to discuss what is on our minds, what is going on in the world, and what we think the show should be doing. We also read and discuss approximately two hundred proposals that come to us from freelance contributors all over the country. Taken together, the producers and freelance contributors, as well as the many listeners who give us suggestions, make up a large pool of people. They have diverse lives in different parts of the country. They have their antennae out, they observe the world, and they read the times. They have all kinds of concerns, interests and passions, and they represent both breadth and depth of thought in our country. We get our ideas from them.

I spend a lot of time thinking about what *Ideas* is trying to do. The first word that comes to mind is "eclectic." We try to make the show eclectic, in both the range of topics we choose and the ways we present them on air. A second word is "resonant." The best *Ideas* programs strike a chord. They help us recognize truths that may be felt but not yet articulated, the way good fiction or poetry does. The best *Ideas* programs draw on the character of our contributors to provide original perspectives and insight. My hope is that, hearing an *Ideas* show, a listener will say, "I never knew that," or, "I never thought about it that way before." I have always felt that the show should induce doubt in listeners' minds — doubt about previously held opinion, doubt about what we claim to know. Our world is constantly creating itself, it is constantly in motion, dynamic and complex, slippery and impossible to grasp.

Making *Ideas* programs is an exercise in excitement, struggle, frustration, discovery and joy: the excitement of having an idea that compels you to want to share it with others; the struggle of working through the idea, clarifying it, finding out what it is about and how to best express it; the frustration that you can't seem to get it right; the discovery of new territory as you work on the idea and your understanding of it deepens; and the joy of breakthrough, a Zen-like moment when things become clear, the piece comes together, and you look back and wonder what all the fuss was about.

I have been associated with *Ideas* for more than thirty years of its forty-year life — as a production assistant, producer and executive producer. I fell in love with the show while I was still at university and nursed an early ambition to work on it, though I was smitten first by television. As a grade ten student, I had watched the production of a television variety show in Montreal, where I grew up. It was a glorious experience: the singers, the music, the cameras, the boom microphones, the cables, the lights, the professional showmanship of performers and crews working together in precise co-ordination to produce an entertainment spectacle — the loud brashness of it all. The next week, I began a persistent campaign to get a job at the CBC. I was seventeen years old. I began to mercilessly harass a personnel officer at the CBC headquarters in Montreal. I went to his office. I filled out an application form. He did a short interview with me. He smiled at me indulgently and promised to call if anything turned up. I called him first. I would call again and again. I would show up at his desk. He must have grown mightily tired of it, but he was kind and put up with me. This went on for a couple of years.

In the summer of 1964, when I was nineteen, the door opened a crack and I got a summer job as a researcher on a CBC television program called *The Observer,* a nightly half-hour show of current events and commentary. In the years that followed, I made an unsuccessful attempt to do graduate work in political science while working early morning and late night shifts as a producer at Radio Canada International. I spent a year producing *Cross-Country Checkup.* Then I quit the CBC and went to Nigeria for two years as a CUSO volunteer teacher. While in Africa, I set my sights on *Ideas.* In the fall of 1971, I returned to Canada and arrived in Toronto at the show's door, welcomed by the executive producer of the time, a bespectacled and kindly man named Lester Sugarman.

My first job was to edit the raw studio recordings of that year's

Massey lecturer, James A. Corry, one of Canada's most distinguished political scientists and a former principal of Queen's University. Corry's topic was *The Power of the Law*. He was a naturally slow and thoughtful speaker, and as I listened to the tape of him speaking, I wanted him to talk faster. The urge to speed him up became uncontrollable, so I started cutting out pauses — between paragraphs, between sentences, between clauses and phrases within sentences, and sometimes between single words. This was laborious work. It required making thousands of edits on quarter-inch audiotape. These days we edit digitally, on computers, but until the late 1990s, it was all done by hand. This involved physically marking the tape, slicing bits out with a razor blade and sticking the ends back together with a special adhesive tape, making sure the edit was undetectable to the ear. It was a good idea to save the bits that were cut out, including breaths and pauses, just in case you needed to put them back. After Corry's Massey Lectures were broadcast, the show received comments from many people who said that they had enjoyed the lectures but were a bit puzzled: they had never heard Corry talk so quickly.

Ideas is where I have learned the crafts of radio production and journalism. I am grateful to have found mentors — too numerous to count or name, including many who never thought of themselves as mentors. They guided me — intellectually, professionally and personally — with kindness and toughness. The experience continues to be a privilege; it is a daily joy to work amongst brilliant and talented colleagues, to encounter some of the finest thinkers of our age and to foster intellectual delight in the minds of our listeners.

We have compiled the material for this book, *Ideas: Brilliant Thinkers Speak Their Minds*, to mark the fortieth anniversary of the show. Most *Ideas* programs are radio documentaries. Generally, documentaries do not translate well into print: they are made for the ear. So in pondering what to include in this book, we have decided not to use material that originally appeared in documentary form; it would be too fragmented and might not make sense on the page. We have chosen to focus on prominent thinkers who have appeared on the program during its first forty years, drawing primarily on lectures and extended interviews. The selections cluster around three main themes: societal values, how we govern ourselves, and navigating in the international community. These are contentious areas and have been significant amongst the show's concerns over the decades: democracy, dictatorship, the nature of the nation-state, the public good, ideology, utopianism, secularism, religion, peace and violence. Many of the questions that people were grappling with twenty, thirty and forty years ago are startlingly similar today, even in an environment that has radically changed. And while each thinker speaks from his or her specific experience in time, the themes and concerns still resonate.

The subtitle of this volume is "Brilliant Thinkers Speak Their Minds." *Ideas* has had the privilege of hosting some of the greatest minds in the world, but space allows us to revisit only a small number of them here. In deciding on the selections for this book, a balance between Canadian and international thinkers has been attempted, and each of the four decades that the show has been on the air has been represented as well as possible, given the changing nature of the broadcasts over the years and the varied access to materials. Fidelity to the content of the original broadcasts has remained vitally important; at the same time, it has been necessary to edit the presentations somewhat to offer a satisfying reading experience. Having presented these unique voices over the airwaves, we now present them to your mind's ear in the hope that they will make you say once again, "I never knew that," or, "I never thought about it that way before."

I would like to thank Susanne Alexander, Publisher of Goose Lane Editions in Fredericton, for her enthusiasm in embracing this project when she learned that CBC wanted to produce a book marking *Ideas'* fortieth anniversary. Particular thanks must go to Laurel Boone, Editorial Director of Goose Lane; she has been the backbone of the project, working many long hours under insanely tight deadlines to pull the book together. I also want to thank the following people at the CBC for their diligence in uncovering material in the archives and helping get it ready for publication: Barbara Brown, Ian Godfrey, Scott Heaney, Brent Michaluk, Alison Moss and Susan Young.

I want to express my special gratitude to all my colleagues at *Ideas* — the past and present members of the production staff and the freelance contributors who have worked on the show and continue to work on it today; whatever success *Ideas* has had is the result of their collective talent, imagination and hard work. Thanks also to the many people who have appeared as interviewees on the show over the years; they have generously given of their time and expertise. Ultimately, we do this work for our listeners, so it's most important to thank them as well: they keep us honest and they keep us going.

Finally, I want to thank Susan Crammond, my wife, for her sharp eye and sharp mind, and for being the love of my life.

Bernie Lucht
Toronto, July 2005

Apocalypses: Prophecies, Cults and Millennial Beliefs through the Ages

The 1999 Barbara Frum Lecture | EUGEN WEBER

Eugen Weber, a specialist in the history of France, is the author of a dozen books and the writer and narrator of a fifty-two-part PBS series, The Western Tradition. *Until his retirement, he held the Chair of Modern European History at the University of California in Los Angeles. Professor Weber says every era has prophesied that the end is nigh. Apocalyptic prophecies are attempts to interpret their times, to console and guide, to suggest the meaning of the present and the future. They relate fear to hope: tribulation and horror will usher in public and private bliss, free of pain and evil.*

EUGEN WEBER

When the University of Toronto invited me to deliver the Barbara Frum Lecture of 1999, they asked, appropriately enough, that it should be about *fin des siècles*, in the plural. The more I worried that particular bone, however, the less meat I found there was on it. Centuries, like the one happily just ending, appear to be a sixteenth century invention, a hesitant usage of the seventeenth century. The special attention focused on a century's end, with a halo of reference that we associate with the turn of the nineteenth century into the twentieth — this was a one-shot affair. Like our own century's tail end, that of the eighteenth century and of every other attracted no endist label, so that anyone tackling *fin des siècles* in the plural would have gathered a very sparse harvest.

And yet, ends and, along with ends, beginnings have played a large part in humanity's experience of itself, not least in that Judeo-Christian tradition that forms the backbone of western history, from Asia Minor to the Pacific shore. Hebrew history plunges its roots in the first five books of the Bible. The history of Christendom, in turn, is irrigated by the New Testament, which culminates in the Book of Revelation.

Apocalypse — the revelation or unveiling of the world's destiny and of mankind's fate — fascinated Jews and their Christian off-spring for at least the last two thousand two hundred years. And so I turned to this grand and more final version. I turned from *fin de siècle* to *fin du monde*, to the end of days. Christians and Jews knew or thought they knew how the world began, and they had a fair idea how it was supposed to end, although precise circumstances remained debatable. Knowledge of the end affects the turns and manner or progression to it. For a long time, Christian history developed along with prophecy, along with interpretation of prophecy within a destiny that had been foretold. Apocalypse, judgment and the thousand-year millennium that would follow Christ's Second Coming, or in some versions precede it, were major parts of this process, and they loomed vastly larger than calendar dates. Indeed, the measuring of worldly time was mainly relevant insofar as it served divine time. The Christian year began with Advent, the weeks that lead up to the Incarnation, the Passion, the Resurrection of Christ, and liturgically this is what it continues to do. What sometimes escapes notice is that the first familiar act celebrated at Christmas and at Easter is only an introduction to the climactic conclusion, when the long struggle between satanic darkness and divine light is at last resolved in the triumph of good over evil. One tends to think of Advent as leading up to the birth of Christ, but it culminates in his Second Coming, and that is what the rite and the lessons and the sermons of the rite are about: the judgment to come. And before it, the Son of Man coming in a cloud, with great power and glory, and the terrors that precede his coming, and the magic millennial interlude between his preliminary and his final victory over Satan. That is what generations were exposed to, one generation after another during hundreds and hundreds of years. That is what they grew up with, that is what they grew old regarding as history and as premonitory history, as real as the seasons were real and as sure. It entered the language, it entered the mindset, it entered the store of common resonances. It aroused great passion and great controversy, and when, after the seventeenth century, it gradually began to seep out of educated consciousness, it did so only partially and quite incompletely.

Matthew the Apostle recorded the words that Jesus uttered on the Mount of Olives about his Second Coming and the end of the world and the signs that were to announce these events: war and rumours of war, nation rising against nation, kingdom against kingdom, famines, earthquakes, plagues, false prophets, deception, hate, iniquity abounding, love waxing cold. And since very few times are without all or most of these things, Christ had drawn the logical conclusion. This generation shall not pass till all these things be fulfilled. And he urged his followers to watch and be ready. There was no knowing when the Lord would come, but he would come certainly and he would come very soon. Certainly, though, as the Church of Christ became less embattled and more institutionalized — a little like some universities — imminence seeped out and protraction percolated ecclesiastical thinking. Like death, judgment was only suspended. Judgment was deferred by a variety of interpretations and rationalizations. But a Christian world, however un-Christian it may have been in practice, was a less obvious candidate for closure than its unregenerate, pagan predecessor. It argued less forcefully for a catastrophe, for catastrophic abolition, and more for emendation, reformation, melioration.

Still, preparations for the Second Coming also involved defensive aggression against the forces of darkness. Stiff-necked Jews were cohorts of Antichrist who, in some versions, was to be born of the Tribe of Dan. The followers of Mohammed were the embodiment of Antichrist. Mongols, Tartars were the hosts of Gog and Magog, and interpretations of this order inspired the Crusades, which were not, or not only, about conquest and trade but about getting to Jerusalem in time for the Second Coming, or else to help these last days and the judgment along — conversion of the heathen, return of the Jews to Palestine preliminary to their conversion in the world's dusk, restoration of those holy places where the heavenly Jerusalem would logically replace its biblical and its present-day successor.

But, as you well know, the Jews did not play their part, which was to go back to Palestine, convert to the True Faith, rebuild the Temple and welcome the Messiah whom they once rejected. And this stubborn blindness of unregenerate Jews was going to exasperate true believers through the ages, was going to contribute to what we now call anti-Semitism, which persisted into the nineteenth and twentieth centuries, for all sorts of reasons, but not least because the Jewish conspiracy was part of Antichrist's campaign against Christ and against God.

Jews or not, however, the Crusades stumbled. The Temple was not rebuilt and Jerusalem substitutes proved carnal — all too carnal. Petrarch, like his contemporaries, identified papal Avignon with Babylon, and Rome was similarly identified. Popes and anti-popes denounced each other as Antichrists. Emperors and princes were similarly designated. You can see the Jews had a lot of competitors. There was little clarity and much menace about inter-Christian relations.

Dante assigns a conspicuous place in his Paradise to a visionary friar patronized by three popes in his twelfth-century lifetime and condemned by a fourth pope in the Lateran Council of 1215. That's Joachim of Fiore. Joachim argued from the corruption of the world around him to the imminence of Antichrist and of Armageddon and the final reign of the saints. Not Mary but the Great Whore ruled over the kings of the earth. At the end of the twelfth century, Richard the Lionhearted, on his way to the Third Crusade, asked to see Abbott Joachim and inquired about Antichrist. The holy abbot told him that the Son of Perdition had already been born in Rome and was now living in Paris and waiting to become pope. Not long after this, Joachim's younger contemporary, St. Francis of Assisi, would be identified with the angel of the Sixth Seal, of Revelations VI, when the sun became black, when the moon became red as blood and the stars of heaven fell onto the earth, for the great day of wrath was come, just before the servants of God were sealed and led before His throne.

Thomas of Solano was the first Franciscan to compose a biography of St. Francis, and it was also Thomas who rewrote the Church's Prayer for the Dead into the classic *Dies Irae*, "Day of wrath, of doom impending/David's word with Sybille's blending/Heaven and earth in ashes ending." One more instance of how, from William the Conqueror's Domesday Book, from *The Divine Comedy* to *Piers Ploughman* and Chaucer, apocalyptic references and apocalyptic images rerun through the Middle Ages, which is not surprising since so much of these times felt like the last times. Not least the fourteenth and fifteenth centuries, which were clearly cut out for the deadly apocalyptic Horsemen — war, famine, plague and death — and hell on earth and their retinue of visionaries and scourging flagellants, massacres, flaming pyres, mass burnings of beggars and vagabonds and witches like Joan of Arc and especially of Jews, who obstinately refused to see the light. "What people said," noted a Norman priest, "was that the world was ending."

And people were right, of course. The world kept right on ending. The art and the literature of the Renaissance — because I've now come to the Renaissance, being a very modern historian — bulge with reminders and predictions of apocalyptic prophecy, much as did those of the centuries preceding, which the Renaissance, of course, relegated to middle status — the Middle Ages. The fresco of Antichrist that Luca Signorelli painted at Orvieto and the nativity that Botticelli painted, with its explicit reference to apocalypse — works like these and others testify to the familiarity, to the popularity, of the theme. Even in the Sistine Chapel, pagan prophetesses rubbed elbows with their male Old Testament counterparts. In the Borgia apartments that Pinturicchio decorated, the mysteries of Osiris prefaced the mysteries of Christ. Clearly, the abomination of desolation stood in the holy place once again.

So no wonder that Savonarola, in Florence, identified the Borgia pope with Antichrist and preached about the world's ending being very close, with a French invasion of Italy compared to a second Deluge. But Savonarola did not get very far or last very long. Luther, who was fifteen when Savonarola sizzled at the stake, did much better. Whatever else the Reformation contributed to our history, it reaffirmed this coming end, and it etched two apocalyptic images very firmly into Protestant law: the pope as Antichrist and the Church as the Whore of Babylon. They and other evil powers were going to be overthrown by heavenly armies that would install the City of God on earth.

Now, some took this as a promise of divine realization, where the great horseman called Faithful and True comes to smite the nations and rule them with a rod of iron. Others saw it as an invitation to advance His coming and the binding of the great beast, the Devil, and the millennium to follow. One way or another, St. Paul had declared that in God's kingdom every rule and every authority and power would be destroyed. The end, or the millennium, or the new earth that followed the Second Coming, and the end of death and the end of hell, these would have no room for property or principalities and powers. And this was a vision that inspired not only millenarian rebels in the Middle and early Modern ages but pietists and cultists, religious or secular, Christian and socialist, to our own day. You can find it in hundreds of sects like that of the Doukhobors in Russia and in Canada, with their vegetarianism and pacifism and rejection of ungodly state and society, including schools and man-made laws. But you can also find it in violent and non-violent secularized eschatologies that mobilized millennial terminology to preach the passage from the era of necessity into the realm of freedom: the abolition of conflict — including class conflict — the end of oppression, the end of oppressors and of oppressed, the Kingdom of God without a god.

Prophecies of this sort have always been around, and prophecies tend to destabilize, and so princes and prelates, ready enough to use them when convenient, legislated against them. But another kind of prophecy just as enticing, just as destabilizing, also persisted. Whatever the warnings, first of Jesus and then of his church, men could not forebear from trying to discover the time of his return. Old Testament and New furnished intimations: there were signs to be found, there were lengths of time to be computed, all sorts of evidence for seekers to identify, to calculate the timetable of God's plan for the world and for its ending.

The missionaries whom Pope Gregory the Great sent to convert England at the end of the sixth century were part of Gregory's preparations for the coming end. The voyages that Isabella of Castille and Ferdinand of Aragon financed nine centuries later had a similar scope. Columbus was fascinated by the prospect of the end of the world approaching, but first, as explained in Matthew, the gospel had to be preached "in all the world for a witness unto all nations and then shall the end come." It was up to Columbus to help God's work along by carrying the message of salvation to those as yet unsaved and by providing the means, the goad, to free Jerusalem and to rebuild the Temple.

And it was up to his masters, too. Like other contemporary princes, Ferdinand and Isabella had been hailed as messiahs, and messianic expectations encouraged them to harry Jews and Muslims, trying to convert them, as they hoped to teach the heathen overseas, so as to create or to accelerate conditions for a Second Coming, and the gold of the Indies would finance the ultimate Crusade.

Now, that was one way in which fervent eschatological calculations affected the history of the world, but if you want to calculate right, you need to perfect your observations and your estimations. The coming of Arabic numerals and especially of the zero in the thirteenth century made calculation easier. You could promote yourself from counting on your fingers. And calculation could address itself, not to biblical clues alone, but to astrological clues as well.

Heaven was a screen where signs appeared by which God forewarned mankind. This orderly activity in the heavens anticipated greater or lesser disorder down on earth, and in 1572, when the Danish astronomer Tycho Brahe discovered a new star, he presented it as heralding the Second Coming. His near-contemporary, John Napier, of Merchiston, near Edinburgh, devised logarithms in order to simplify the complicated calculations needed for astronomy, but he valued logs chiefly because they speeded up his calculations of the number of the Beast.

Newton died in 1727, having written more than two million words about alchemy and hermetic law. We remember him as the patron saint of the Enlightenment, when astronomy broke its compact with astrology, when irrational beliefs were left to the lower classes and the sillies. Now, understanding the natural mechanisms of comets and of earthquakes did not extinguish fear of a God who could use secondary causes to execute His judgments. Earthquakes, but especially comets, continued a part of divine seismography and cosmology — signs, omens, warnings, quite possibly of last times — and they excited panicked fears, at least until the passage of Halley's Comet in 1910, when churches were crowded, when people danced in the streets the next morning because the world had not ended. I can't imagine what made them so jubilant.

So some believed in God and some did not. But humans have never lacked the capacity to accommodate two contradictory ideas in one mind. Working out the law of gravity and the Second Coming, calculating the course of comets and yet interpreting them in biblical and apocalyptic terms, reconciling natural science with what we now would call fundamentalism — all confirm that God works in mysterious ways. But they are only aspects of a wider propensity to notice only things that we want to notice. The enlightened belief that lives, societies, nations can sooner or later be brought under the rule of reason was no less mythological and became no less dogmatic than the Christian beliefs it tried to discard.

It could be that the aspirations of the Enlightenment were too demanding. At any rate, it looks as if the Enlightenment has been dimming while apocalyptic cultures are still with us, and so are the dissonances and the cross-purposes that divide them from secular minds. To take just one example among many, in the late 1850s, the first and last American war of religion was waged in Utah Territory when President James Buchanan sent the US Army, which is always busy putting the world to right, to impose the rule of law on the Latter-Day Saints, who were trying to build Zion by their own light. The administration in Washington was certain that most Mormons, and especially their oppressed womenfolk, would welcome the troops as saviours from religious bondage, and it was shocked when the soldiers were treated as hostile intruders.

A similar misunderstanding in the spring of 1993 cost the lives of seventy-three men, women and children and several federal agents near Waco, Texas. For the FBI, the people at Mount Carmel were hostages to be rescued from a mad prophet and a con man. For David Koresh and his Branch Davidians, the rescue that they wanted was from the government assailants. Davidians saw themselves as living in the Fifth Seal of Revelation, slain or about to be slain just before the great day of God's wrath. Federal agents represented Babylon, the evil system — I hardly dare say the Evil Empire — a system threatening and slaughtering God's anointed prophet and his true believers. And you can find similar cross-purposes in the sad sagas of the Doukhobors in Canada or in Jim Jones's holocaust in Guyana.

Now these and other similarly spectacular situations are only the media-worthy tips of a much greater iceberg. Six thousand — I can't believe it, but that's what the books tell me — six thousand new messianic movements have been identified in Africa between the 1940s and the 1970s, hundreds more in Japan and the Philippines, thousands of cargo cults and prophetic movements in New Guinea and Oceania. It would be tempting to dismiss these as the superstitions of backward peoples, or at least exotic ones, if we did not know that similar beliefs flourish in North America, where the rather bizarre menagerie of revelation, flying horses, multi-coloured scorpion locusts, demon frogs, and lots of dark dragons has simply been transmuted into extraterrestrial beings, flying saucers and cosmic radio signals, where apocalyptic prophecies sell by the million, where the birth of Israel in 1948 was taken as an even clearer milestone on the road to rapture than the atom bomb, where the Common Market was very quickly identified as an ally of the Beast, where the "Jewnited" Nations were soon recognized as satanic and new technologies as diabolic snares: television, computers — I agree with that — credit cards, ATMs, COM satellites, microchips and, of course, laser-readable price markers. In 1995, the Internet was associated with the Fourth Beast of the Apocalypse and Bill Gates with Antichrist. The manoeuvres of Antichrist have also been detected in Walkman stereos, MTV, Teenage Mutant Ninja Turtles. The Number of the Beast has been recognized in product codes, computer programs, licence plates, telephone prefixes, not to mention the nine-digit zip codes of the US Post Office, which, when added to the nine-digit number of our US social security system, add up to eighteen, obviously three times six: 666. And all that being so, one might well wonder why a motif and a motivating agency so strong and so pervasive has been so long ignored in recent times, especially by professional historians.

Just thirty years ago, Christopher Hill began his Riddle Lectures of 1969 with a similar remark — great minds think alike — that sheds light on my question. Historians — Hill calls us intellectual snobs and I hope he's right — have ignored the lunatic fringe that believed in the imminence of the end and the necessary preliminary of Antichrist, paying no heed to Milton, to Cromwell, to Newton, to so many others who shared a belief in the imminent end of the world.

Great historian of seventeenth-century England that he is, Hill saw the need to look with attention on beliefs of that time because beliefs influence and inflect action, as they encouraged Cromwell to readmit Jews to England in the hope of advancing the time of the Lord's return. Nevertheless, Hill's scholarship and his language characterized — and hence intellectually marginalized — the believers whom he studied as a "lunatic fringe." Now, that was not so until the seventeenth century — even until the eighteenth century — and many eighteenth- and nineteenth-century reformers would have counted among the lunatic fringe: Lord Shaftsbury, for example, and his friends, supporters of Jewish emancipation and of Zion, and abolitionists like Harriet Beecher Stowe. But there were lots of others like her who, in Britain, in North America, in France also, eventually brought the slave trade to an end.

Prophecies make very little sense to rational, modern scholars, and they embarrass advocates of a Christianity which in the past two hundred years has learned to present itself as a rational enterprise like any other. Before the eighteenth century ended, bowdlerized

Bibles had dropped most of Paul's Epistles and the whole Book of Revelation as "too incendiary." In the nineteenth century, the textual or higher criticism which a superintendent of Scotland Yard denounced as "a German infidel crusade" cleared most of the supernatural out of Christian beliefs or else explained it away. In 1925, one great student of Antichrist — and a German at that — Wilhelm Bousset, authoritatively declared that Antichrist's legend is now to be found only among the lower classes of the Christian community, among sects, eccentric individualists and fanatics. And, of course, university professors. In 1957, another very serious scholar, Norman Cohn, memorably assigned the apocalyptic tradition to the obscure underworld of popular religion.

So Christianity was being recast. Of course, it has been recast through the ages, but now its supernatural foundations were being meddled with, and reconstruction can shore up structures or weaken them — subtract one aspect of the supernatural and the edifice may crumble. In another few years, a very distinguished theologian like Karel Killie dismissed even belief in the afterlife as a corrupt form of theological expression, disseminated among the relatively poor and uneducated.

Now, if some don't think the way we, the educated, think, it must be because they are uneducated, poor or crackpots. They may, on the other hand, be sociologically all right and simply be mistaken, or they may not be mistaken at all. Condescension, at any rate, is surely not the right approach. History is not an exclusively rational process. It is not about exclusively rational processes. And anyway, one man's reason is another man's nonsense — ask your wife.

Which leaves us with the question of the reasons of unreason, or of what others dismiss as unreason, and of its survival and of the way it thrives, about all of which your guess is as good as mine, but I shall hazard some speculations because that's what I'm here for. Now, one can simply argue that the apocalyptic tradition survives because it is right and true, as we shall soon find out. Or one can argue that endism provides powerful compensatory fantasies of escape from grim reality. Escape — release by havoc, ruin, liquidation, devastation, annihilation — we pause to draw breath. But why should one grim prospect attract more than another? Perhaps because it responds to profound human aspirations: to avoid death, to believe that decay is only a prelude to resurgence and revival. Perhaps because apocalyptic tragedy and terror transcend the banality of the everyday, enhance our trivial human lives, suggest exhilarating deaths beyond the obvious shallows that surround us.

But there may be more. Dostoyevsky's *Crime and Punishment* demonstrates how easily the everyday banality that we call reality can be torn up by the eruption of evil. His *Brothers Karamazov* presents the triumph of Antichrist. It indicates how shortcuts to freedom will cut freedom short. Now, we call Dostoyevsky a "fantastic realist," and John of Patmos was that kind of realist also. It's not clear whether Dostoyevsky really believed in God, but he certainly believed in Antichrist, and it may be that Man can do without God but not without Antichrist, not without apocalypse. Apocalypse reconciles nihilistic rejection and ideological faith. It denounces suspect prophets who peddle alleged absolutes, and yet it still awaits the prophet or the witness with his monolithic, all-resolving message. Apocalypse is flexible, it's pessimistic and optimistic, it's annihilating and promissory, it spurs conflict and reconciliation separately or all at once, and it provides an escapist commitment. Politics is about how people make choices. Apocalyptic religion is about how people have no real choice, which means that it replaces the difficult problems of human politics with visions. It replaces the insuperable with the ineluctable.

Self-centered, self-fascinated, humanity is loathe to concede that we are not central to the cosmic scheme of things, and in this view apocalypse, however tragic, reassures. Time and space, it says, are about mankind's relation with God. They will end when mankind ends, but God doesn't want to face loneliness, and so mankind will be humankind, will be reborn in a new heaven and a new earth, where there shall be no more death, neither sorrow nor crime nor pain nor evil nor darkness, and only open gates.

Now, that must have been what Jacques-Bénigne Bossuet meant in his sermon on providence: "Look at human affairs in their course.

All is confused and mixed up. But view them in relation to the last and universal judgment and you'll see them shine with an admirable order." It had been said before, for now we see "through a glass darkly, but then, face to face."

Eugen Weber's lecture was broadcast on December 15, 1999.

Anarchism in the
Mid-Twentieth Century

GEORGE WOODCOCK

In the late 1930s, George Woodcock (1912-1995) belonged to a radical group of writers in London, England, that included Aldous Huxley, Herbert Read and George Orwell, and in their company, he became a poet, a pamphleteer, and a pacifist. Eventually, he became the most articulate spokesman for literary anarchism and a prolific writer of poetry, journalism, travel literature and history. In 1949, he returned to Canada, where he had been born, and settled in Vancouver. There he wrote Anarchism : A History of Libertarian Ideas and Movements *and numerous books and articles about the role of the arts in a free society. One of Canada's most influential men of letters, he founded* Canadian Literature *in 1959 and edited it for nearly twenty years.*

GEORGE WOODCOCK

Anarchism is a word about which there have been many confusions. For this reason, I must begin by defining what I mean by the word. But first of all, let's clear up some of the misapprehensions. Anarchy is very often mistakenly regarded as the equivalent of chaos, and an anarchist is often thought of as, at best, a nihilist, a man who has abandoned all principles and, at worst, a sinister bearded figure speaking broken English, who secretes a black and smoking bomb under a shabby opera cloak.

The Anarchists I'm talking about are men of elaborate principles who may, on a few occasions in the past, have had a little to do with bombs, but who have never hoped to compete in this direction with the nuclear scientists employed by the world's great powers. In other words, I am talking about anarchists as they are, rather than as they have been represented in the fantasies of cartoonists and journalists and politicians, whose favourite way of amusing their opponents is to accuse them of promoting anarchism.

What we are really concerned with is a cluster of words which, in its turn, represents a cluster of doctrines and attitudes whose principle uniting feature is the belief that government is both harmful and unnecessary. A double Greek root is involved — the word *arkon*, meaning a ruler, and a prefix *an*, indicating without. Hence, anarchy means the state of being without a ruler. By derivation, anarchism is the doctrine which contends that government is at the source of most of our social troubles and that there are viable alternative forms of voluntary organization. And by further derivation, the anarchist is the man who sets out to create a society without government.

That concept of a society without government is essential for an understanding of the anarchist attitude. In rejecting government, the true anarchist doesn't reject the idea or the fact of society. On the contrary, his view of the need for society as a living entity becomes intensified when he contemplates the abolition of government. As he sees it, the pyramidical structure imposed by a government, with power proceeding from above downwards, can only be replaced if society becomes a closely knit fabric of voluntary relationships. The difference between a governmental society and an anarchic society is, in his view, the difference between a structure and an organism. One is built and the other grows according to natural laws. Metaphorically, one can compare the pyramid of government with the sphere of society, which is held together by an equilibrium of stresses.

Anarchists are much concerned with equilibriums, and two kinds of equilibrium play a very important role in their philosophy. One is the equilibrium between destruction and construction, which dominates their tactics. The other is the equilibrium between liberty and order, which dominates their view of the ideal society. But order for the anarchist is not something imposed from above. It arises from self-discipline and voluntary cooperation.

The roots of anarchist thought are very ancient. Libertarian doctrines which argued that as a moral being Man can live best without being ruled existed among the philosophers of ancient Greece and among the heretical Christian sects of the Middle Ages. Elaborately argued philosophies that were anarchist in all but name began to appear during the Renaissance and Reformation periods, between the fifteenth and seventeenth centuries, and even more copiously in the eighteenth century, as events built up to the French and American revolutions which ushered in the modern age. But as an activist movement seeking to change society by collective methods, anarchism belongs only to the nineteenth and twentieth centuries.

Its fortunes have fluctuated greatly. There were times when millions of European and Latin American working men and peasants followed the black or black and red flags of the anarchists. There were also great writers who expressed in their novels and poems and in their other writings the essential viewpoints of anarchism. One of these was the Russian novelist Tolstoy who, in his last years, summed up a lifetime's observation of the activities of governments:

> I regard all governments as intricate institutions sanctified by tradition and custom for the purpose of committing by force and with impunity the most revolting crimes, and I think that the efforts of those who wish to reform our social life should be directed toward the liberation of themselves from national governments whose evil and, above all, whose futility is in our time becoming more and more apparent. Henceforth, I shall never serve any government anywhere.

And another was the poet Shelley, who gave an ideal form to the social condition which anarchists envisage as the goal of their efforts. He portrays the world after governments have come to an end and men are ruled only by the necessities that time inflicts upon them:

The loathsome mask has fallen, the man remains
Sceptreless, free, uncircumscribed, but man
Equal, unclassed, tribeless, and nationless,
Exempt from awe, worship, degree, the king
Over himself; just, gentle, wise; but man
Passionless — no, yet free from guilt or pain,
Which were, for his will made or suffered them;
Nor yet exempt, though ruling them like slaves,
From chance, and death, and mutability,
The clogs of that which else might oversoar
The loftiest star of unascended heaven,
Pinnacled dim in the intense inane.

* * *

Anarchism is something different from a dogmatic political orthodoxy. And it's also something different from the kind of tightly
organized, hierarchical structure with which we are familiar among
political parties whose aim is to seek power. When Anarchism existed as an identifiable movement, it had intellectual leaders but no
organizational leadership. It included within itself a variety of viewpoints on tactics and on the nature of the desirable society which
coexisted with a remarkable degree of mutual tolerance, rather like
the religious sects of India. Even then, it was the idea expressed
directly in action that was dynamic, rather than the movement. In
fact, even when Anarchism was strongest and most popular, even
when there were Anarchist organizations which numbered their followers in the millions, as the National Confederation of Labour did
in Spain, the organization was always a fragile and flexible frame
within which it was the power of spontaneous thought that seemed
important.

In essence, Anarchism is an anti-dogmatic and unstructured cluster of related attitudes, and this explains why it can flourish when
conditions are favourable and then, like a plant in the desert, lie dor-
mant for seasons and even for years, waiting for the rains that will

make it blossom again. In an ordinary political faith like communism or social democracy or even conservatism, the party is needed as a kind of church, a vehicle of the dogma. But Anarchism has always been rather like those mystic faiths that rely on personal illumination, and for this reason, it has never needed a movement to keep it alive. Many of its important teachers, were solitary men, dedicated individualists like William Godwin and Henry David Thoreau and Max Sterner. Those who granted the need for organization wanted it to be minimal, so that even Pierre-Josef Proudon, who was the intellectual founder and mentor of the Anarchist movement of the nineteenth century, warned his followers against any rigidity of thought or action and refused to countenance the suggestion that he had invented a system or that a party might be built up around his teachings.

With very few exceptions, the great Anarchist originators carefully avoided the trap of becoming infallible gurus. And it is significant that there has never been a single Anarchist book that has been put forward or accepted as a political gospel in the same way as Marx's or Lenin's or that of Chairman Mao. In fact, Anarchist writings like Kropotkin's or Herbert Read's or the essays of Paul Goodman, to give a few rather varied examples, retain their freshness and their appeal precisely because their intent is to awaken thought, not to direct it.

It is, in the last resort, this peculiarly unpartisan element in Anarchist thought that makes it resilient and durable and explains why the downfall of the movement in Spain with Franco's victory, though it certainly meant the end of the historical movement founded by Proudon and Bakunin, did not mean any more than a temporary eclipse of the Anarchist idea. Between 1939 and the beginning of the 1960s, Anarchism did not play a great part in the affairs of any country or in the thoughts of anyone but a few Libertarian intellectuals and a few aging veterans of the battles of the past. Yet, from the early sixties onward, there has been a decade during which the ideas of Anarchism have emerged again rejuvenated, have clothed themselves in action, have stimulated the young in age and spirit, and have disturbed the establishments of both the Right and the Left.

What has happened, indeed, is a kind of explosion of ideology which has carried the essential doctrines of anarchism and the methods associated with them far beyond the remnants of the old Anarchist organization. New kinds of movements have appeared, new modes of radical action have evolved, but they reproduce with a surprising degree of faith, even among people who hardly know what the word "anarchism" means or perhaps have never even heard of it, the same ideas on the defects of our present society and the desirable qualities for a better society that have been taught by the seminal thinkers in the Libertarian tradition, from Winstanley in the seventeenth century down to Herbert Read in the present age.

Let us turn now to the sequence of events. The Second World War, following on Franco's victory in Spain, completed the breakdown of Anarchism as an international movement. That process had begun as early as 1918. In Russia, after the October Revolution of 1917, the Bolsheviks regarded the Anarchists as among their most important rivals and eliminated them, but only after a long struggle during which large areas of the Ukraine were operated as a kind of Anarchist peasant community by a celebrated guerrilla leader known as Nestorenko, who finally fled to Western Europe in 1921 to escape destruction by Trotsky's Red Army.

The advent of Fascism in Italy and Nazism in Germany meant the end of Anarchism as a movement in both those countries, and by the time the German army had completed its conquests in Europe, the only Anarchists at large and active were in Britain, the United States, Switzerland and the more liberal of the Latin American states, of which Mexico was the most important. All the countries where mass Anarchist movements had once existed — Russia, France, Italy and Spain — were living under totalitarian regimes. The result was a situation that was quite new in terms of Anarchist history, for during World War II it was the English-speaking countries in which Anarchism demonstrated the greatest vitality, and the tradition was interpreted in completely new ways. The stimulus did not come from the Spanish and Italian and Russian refugees, who represented the movement created by Prudon and Bakunin and Kropotkin. It came, rather, from the intellectuals, and particularly from the writers who belonged to the Modernist movement and who learned their Anarchism as much from Oscar Wilde and William Morris as they did from the militants whose significance vanished as history eliminated their roles.

In England, the interim movement, as I choose to call it, because it really represents an interregnum between the Anarchism of the nineteenth century and contemporary Anarchism, was distinguished by the fact that it drew together, not only British writers and painters from the whole period between the 1920s and the 1940s, but also a considerable number of refugee artists from Eastern Europe and from France and Belgium. There were English painters like Augustus John and Russian Constructivist artists like Naum Gabo and Polish Expressionists like Yankel Adler. Herbert Read and John Cowper Powys represented the older writers, but Dylan Thomas was a declared Anarchist and so were Alex Comfort and Denise Levertov. In the United States, there was a similar tendency during the 1940s and the 1950s for Anarchism to escape from the traditions of Spain and of the nineteenth century International and to permeate intellectual and literary circles. In New York, intellectual Anarchism centered around Wyatt MacDonald and Paul Goodman, who was already relating traditional Libertarian doctrines to contemporary American problems of rural decay and urban chaos. In San Francisco, even during the early 1940s, a literary Anarchist movement arose under the leadership of the poet Kenneth Rexroth. Other poets, like Robert Duncan and Philip Lamantia and later Kenneth Patchen, became closely involved, and Anarchism eventually became one of the motivating philosophies of the Beat movement in California.

The fact that during the 1940s Anarchism became concentrated, like a seed germ, in the minds of a small group of English-speaking intellectuals led to some interesting theoretical developments. The most important related respectively to science and to education. Ever since Peter Kropotkin produced his important contribution to evolutionary theory, mutual aid, Libertarian theoreticians have attempted to relate their doctrines to whatever sciences of man seem to be currently important. Towards the middle of the present century, the place which biology had held in the speculations of Kropotkin and of his associates like Élisée Reclus, was assumed by psychology. Alex Comfort, long before he became the guru of geriatric sexology, wrote an extremely valuable Anarchist treatise on the psychology of power entitled *Authority and Delinquency in the Modern State*. The teaching of Erich Fromm made its appeal to the Anarchists of the 1940s and so did the heretical Freudian teachings of Wilhelm Reich, which related psychological repression to political repression and sought the origins of coercive power in neurosis, a doctrine very close to that of the classic Anarchists, who saw political coercion as a perversion of what they regarded as the natural law of social cooperativeness.

But perhaps the most important of the Anarchists to be influenced by modern psychological theory was Herbert Read, who drew copiously on the theories of Freud, of Adler and of Jung in his writings on the nature and the history of art and who also used them to support the other characteristic departure of Anarchist theory during the 1940s, which was an intensified recognition of the need for a new type of education that would enable men to accept and also to endure freedom. I use the word "endure" quite deliberately because, as the very title of Erich Fromm's book *Escape from Freedom* indicated, it had dawned upon Libertarians by the mid-twentieth century that freedom was an austere discipline whose advantages would not be immediately evident to the masses accustomed to state tutelage and the welfare society. Herbert Read believed that the educational system as it existed, with its emphasis on merely academic learning, prepared men for obedience, not for freedom. In his books, he argued that the schools should be transformed to educate the senses before they touch the mind and that the harmonious personality which resulted from education through art would not only live a more balanced individual life but would also be able to achieve, with a minimum of disturbance, the kind of peaceful transformation of society of which the Anarchists had long dreamed, a transformation in which people who were inwardly at peace, and therefore at peace with each other, could make equality and fraternity compatible with freedom.

When the war ended in 1945 and countries like Italy and France, which had formerly been Anarchist strongholds, were liberated, there was a kind of rattling of the bones in the movement which Bakunin had created. Old Anarchists met again, and there was an uneasy liaison between them and the British and American intellectuals who had extended Anarchist theory during the wartime period. There were even some international conferences, but the one which I attended at Bern in 1946 was a curiously spectral affair: a few old men and a few young poets gathering beside the grave of Bakunin to play Mozart in his memory and dream of repeating his achievement.

Neither Bakunin nor his movement was resurrected, yet the Anarchist idea, as distinct from the Anarchist movement, has certainly been born again, and the rebirth has taken place mainly outside the gallant but scanty groups of veterans who sought to recreate a tradition unfitted for our age. The crucial decade has been the 1960s. The 1950s, the decade of cautious careerist youth, had been a period of hibernation for Anarchist ideas, though they were kept alive by the Beat novelists and poets of the time. But as that decade ended, the idea seemed suddenly alive again. It developed in two different ways. First, there was the scholarly interest. Nowadays, in view of the wealth of available material, it seems astonishing that until less than twenty years ago, very little had been written on Anarchism in a spirit of scholarly enquiry. There were the apologies of the Anarchists and the diatribes of their opponents but very few objective studies of what Anarchism meant and what Anarchists had done. Two French scholars published the first volume of a history in 1949, but the remainder of the book never appeared and the first complete history of Anarchism ever written in English or any other language was my own *Anarchism*, which appeared in 1962. Other general histories followed, and also biographies of the more important Anarchist thinkers and activists, as well as reprints of their works, so that Anarchism during the 1960s became at least academically respectable.

But that was the Anarchism of the past, the classic thinkers, the historic movement that had been moribund since 1939. What began to emerge in the 1960s was an actual revival of Anarchism as a current of thought and an activist movement among young people, particularly intellectuals and students in many European and American countries. Often the name did not re-emerge. Often the dogma was diluted by other strains of radical thought. Rarely was there an attempt to re-establish continuity with a movement in the past, but the idea had re-emerged, clear and recognizable, and in countries as varied as Britain and Holland, France and the United States, it attracted adherents on a scale unparalleled since the days before the last world war. Like the New Left to which it was loosely related, the movement, which one might call Neo-Anarchism really, had double roots. It sprang partly from the experience of those who became involved in the civil rights campaigns in the United States as early as the mid-fifties and partly from the great mass protests against nuclear disarmament that were held in Britain during the early 1960s.

In Britain, the protest movement was developed by the Campaign for Nuclear Disarmament, and within the CND there appeared a more militant group called the Committee of One Hundred, in which Bertrand Russell was active, but which also included a number of Anarchist intellectuals who had become known in earlier decades, particularly Herbert Read and Alex Comfort. But apart from these links with classic Anarchism, there was within the Committee of One Hundred, as always happens when militant pacifism encounters a government irremediably bent on warlike preparations, a spontaneous surge of anti-state feeling, that is to say, Anarchist feeling, still unnamed. Arguments surfaced within the Committee of One Hundred in favour of methods advocated by the Anarchists. Groups dedicated to direct action and to exploring the implications of a society without war and violence, and hence without coercion, sprang up all over Britain. At the same time, the remnants of the Anarchist movement were revivified, and the Anarchists, in the new sense as well as the old, became a vocal and active element in British political life, few in comparison with the larger political parties but more numerous and more influential than they ever were in the England of the past. Where young British rebels in the 1930s were inclined to join the Communists, in the 1960s, they were likely to become

Anarchists. Note the change — becoming rather than joining — a change of heart rather than a party ticket. It marks a whole generational shift in the attitude to politics and also to life.

One of the most striking characteristics of the Neo-Anarchism that emerged in Britain and shortly afterwards in the United States during the aftermath of the civil rights movement was that, like so many modern protest movements, it represented mainly a trend among the young and especially among the middle-class young. In 1962, right at the beginning of the upsurge, a British Anarchist paper conducted an interesting survey of the occupations and class backgrounds of its readers. While past Anarchist movements had consisted mainly of artisans and peasants, with a few intellectual leaders recruited from the upper- and middle-class intelligentsia, the survey revealed that in Britain only fifteen percent of the Anarchists willing to answer questions about themselves belonged to the traditional groupings of workers and peasants. Of the eighty-five percent which remained, the largest group consisted of teachers and students, and there were also many architects, doctors, journalists and people working independently as artists and craftsmen. Even more significant was the class shift among the young. Forty-five percent of readers over sixty were manual workers, as against twenty-three percent of those in their thirties and ten percent of those in their twenties. Very similar proportions existed in Anarchist and near-Anarchist movements in most Western countries and, indeed, throughout the counterculture.

The new Libertarianism has been essentially a revolt, not of the underprivileged and certainly not of the skilled workers, who are busy defending their recent gains in terms of living standards, but of the privileged, who have seen the futility of affluence as a goal. Undoubtedly one of the factors that has made Anarchism popular among the young has been its opposition to the increasingly centralized and technocratic industrial cultures of Western Europe, North America, Japan and Russia. In this context, one of the principal mediating figures, though the orthodox Anarchists never accepted him, was Aldous Huxley. Huxley's pacifism and his early recognition of the perils of population explosion, ecological destruction and psychological manipulation, combined in a social vision that in many ways anticipated the preoccupations of the counter-culture during the 1960s and the early 1970s. Already, when he wrote during the 1930s, Huxley had presented the first warning vision of the kind of mindless, materialistic existence a society dominated by technological centralization might produce. In his foreword to the 1936 edition of *Brave New World*, Huxley revealed quite distinctly his Anarchist sympathies when he declared that the perils implicit in modern social trends could only be averted by switching over to radical decentralization and simplification in economic terms and to political forms that, as he put it, would be Kropotkinesque and co-operative. In later works, Huxley enlarged on his acceptance of the Anarchist critique of the existing order, and it was largely through these works of his, often taught in college English courses, that the Libertarian attitude was transmitted to the generation of the 1960s and welded onto their concern for environmental regeneration.

Even among movements of the counterculture which did not accept the title of Anarchism, such as many phases of student rebellion in America, Germany, France and Japan, Anarchist texts were read, and their arguments played a great part in shaping attitudes and action. Even in mood, in its insistence on spontaneity, on theoretical flexibility, on simplicity of life, on love and anger as complimentary and necessary components of social as well as individual action, Anarchism had a special appeal to a generation that rejected the impersonality of massive institutions and the pragmatic calculations of political parties. In terms of social organization, the Anarchist rejection of the state and the insistence on decentralism and grass-roots responsibility have found a strong echo in a contemporary movement which demands that its democracy be not representative but participatory and that its action be direct. The recurrence of the theme of workers' control of industry also shows the enduring influence of the ideas that Proudhon created and passed on to the *anarchos indicalis*.

The movement in which Anarchist ideas perhaps came most dramatically to the surface in recent years was the French uprising against de Gaulle in 1968. It was a largely spontaneous affair in which left-wing party leaders and trade union leaders had little control and in which something resembling the Anarchist scenario for a Libertarian revolution was actually enacted. The students occupied their colleges, they raised the black flag of the Anarchists on the Paris Stock Exchange, and they inspired the workers to strike and occupy their factories. For a few days, the power of General de Gaulle and the vainglorious nationalism he represented seemed to hang in the balance. It was by making a deal with his enemies in the army, in fact, that he survived long enough for the basic conservative forces in French society to reassert themselves.

What the events of Paris demonstrated, as events in Athens and Bangkok have since done, is that, in spite of all their sophisticated techniques of holding power, modern governments are almost as vulnerable as their predecessors and, in some respects, more vulnerable, since contemporary society has become such an elaborately interlocking structure of bureaucratic machinery that even a slight failure of function quickly becomes magnified in its effects. In such circumstances, the rebel becomes rather like the small state in a world seemingly dominated by nuclear superpowers. His ability to disturb the intricate balance gives him certain advantages, and there is no doubt that because of the dynamics of the situation, contemporary radicals have managed to change social attitudes and to induce retreats on the part of authority that would not have been likely even a decade ago.

But we have to bear in mind that these retreats are largely tactical. Nowhere has a spontaneous rebellion in recent years resulted in a radical change in the structure of power. Governments may have changed. The pattern of authority has not been fundamentally changed. A recognition of this fact has led many of the contemporary Anarchists to leave for the time being the matter of attacking the citadel of power directly, on the assumption that it may collapse of its own rigidity if they can change the attitudes of people at the grassroots level. The two most interesting examples of this approach, interesting largely because of their mutual contrasts, come from Holland and India. In Holland, which had a rather respectable tradition of

Tolstoyian pacifist Anarchism before World War II, there have been two Neo-Anarchist movements, the Provos in the 1960s and the Kabouters in the 1970s.

The difference between the two groups illuminates fairly well the differences that have emerged between the two decades in terms of tactical attitudes. Provo is a contraction of provocation, and it was precisely by provocation, in the form of noisy demonstrations, eccentric happenings, original forms of mutual aid, that the Provos set out to stir the people from a too-complacent acceptance of the welfare state into which Holland had transformed itself. The actions of the Provos were dominated by a spirit of originality, reminiscent of one of the anonymous posters that appeared in Paris during the rising of 1968. The society of alienation must disappear from history, that poster declared. We are inventing a new and original world. Imagination is seizing power. By using their imagination, the Provos sought to give the doctrines and tactics of rebellion a new twist, so that the despair of ever attaining a free society, which gnaws secretly at every Anarchist, became in its own way a weapon to be used in goading governments to show their true faces. The weak provoke, the strong unwillingly expend themselves. Having stirred the imagination of the Dutch, the Provos showed their difference from ordinary political parties by voluntarily disbanding. Three years later, the old members came together in a new group, the Kabouters — the Goblins — dedicated to working at the grassroots level through local administrations, and the effect which the acts of their predecessors had achieved in the minds of Dutch people were such that they were able in 1970 to elect five delegates to the forty-five-member Amsterdam city council.

In India, Anarchism has been a respected if not a very much implemented word ever since Gandhi described himself as an Anarchist and planned a decentralized society based on autonomous village communes. When India became independent, Gandhi's associates in congress abandoned his plan, since they wished to make of India a state with a great army and a vast bureaucracy on the British model. Nevertheless, some of his followers decided to develop his thoughts, and one of the most important Anarchistic movements in the contemporary world is Saudovaya, the movement led by Vinoba Bhave and Jayaprakash Narayan which has sought to make Gandhi's dream a reality by means of Gramdam, the ownership of land by autonomous communities. By 1969, a fifth of the villages of India had declared themselves in favour of Gramdam, and while much of this intent consists still of unrealized gesture, it does represent perhaps the most extensive commitment to basic Anarchist ideas in the contemporary world.

Anarchism, in summary, is a phoenix in an awakening desert, an idea that has revived for the only reason that makes ideas revive: they respond to some need felt deeply by people and, since the activists are always the tip of any social iceberg, by more people than overtly appear concerned. Anarchism's present popularity is part of the reaction to the monolithic welfare state, and already some of its proposals, like the greater involvement of workers in industrial control and a greater decisive say by people in matters that affect them locally and personally, are beginning to take shape as part of a general shift towards participatory democracy.

But up to now, there has been little progress towards using Anarchist conceptions in the wider organization of society. Yet it is not impossible that technology might offer some of the means to that end, for technology is itself neutral. There is, despite the gloomier prophets, nothing to suggest that a technologically developed society need be either centralized or authoritarian or ecologically wasteful, and one can, to give an example, conceive a time arriving when people in control of their technology might use electronic communications to inform themselves of all sides of a public issue and use the same means to make their will known and effective without intermediaries. In this way, the institution of the referendum, which is now so clumsy that it is rarely used, could be applied to all important decisions, and referenda could be adjusted to the particular constituencies actually affected by a decision. Democracy might then become direct and active again, as it once was, for the citizens at least, of ancient Athens. And if a live participatory democracy may not yet be the naturally ordered society of Anarchy, it would still represent the largest step that has ever been taken in that direction.

George Woodcock broadcast four lectures on the history of anarchy on December 10, 1973, December 12, 1973, January 1, 1974, and January 3, 1974. This selection includes Woodcock's introduction to the topic in the first broadcast and the fourth broadcast.

The Empty Society

Massey Lectures, 1966   PAUL GOODMAN

Paul Goodman, 1911-1972, described himself as an anarchist and a man of letters. He taught at universities and colleges including the University of Chicago, New York University, Sarah Lawrence College and the Experimental College of Black Mountain. A poet, novelist and writer of non-fiction, he authored several books on education, city life, children's rights, politics and the counterculture of the mid- and late-1960s, including People or Personnel, Compulsory Mis-Education, Communitas, *and* The Society I Live in Is Mine. *"The Empty Society" was delivered as the first part of the sixth annual Massey Lecture series in the fall of 1966.*

PAUL GOODMAN

During Eisenhower's second administration, I wrote a book describing how hard it was for young people to grow up in the corporate institutions of American society. Yet statistics at that time indicated that most were content to be secure as personnel of big corporations; a few deviated in impractical, and certainly unpolitical, ways, like being Beat or delinquent. The system itself, like its president, operated with a cheerful and righteous self-satisfaction. There were no signs of its being vulnerable, though a loud chorus of intellectual critics, like myself, were sounding off against it. We were spoilsports.

Less than ten years later, the feeling is different; it turns out that we critics were not altogether unrealistic. The system of institutions is still grander and more computerized, but it seems to have lost its morale. The baronial corporations are making immense amounts of money and are more openly and heavily subsidized by the monarch in Washington. The processing of the young is extended for longer years and its tempo speeded up. More capital and management are exported, interlocking with international capital, and more of the world (including Canada) is brought under American control. When necessary, remarkable military technology is brought to bear. At home, there is no political check, for no matter what the currents of opinion, by and large the dominant system wreaks its will, managing the parliamentary machinery to look like consensus.

Nevertheless, the feeling of justification is gone. Sometimes we seem to be bulling it through only in order to save face. Often, enterprises seem to be expanding simply because the managers cannot think of any other for use energy and resources. The economy is turning into a war economy. There are warnings of ecological disaster, pollution, congestion, poisoning, mental disease, anomie. We have discovered that there is hard-core poverty at home that is not easy to liquidate. Unlike the success of the Marshall Plan in Europe in the forties, it increasingly appears that poverty and unrest in Asia, Africa, and South America are not helped by our methods of assistance, but are perhaps made worse. There are flashes of suspicion, like flashes of lightning, that the entire system may be unviable. Influential senators refer to our foreign policy as "arrogant" and "lawless," but, in my opinion, our foreign and domestic system is all of a piece and is more innocent and deadly than that; it is mindless and morally insensitive. Its pretended purposes are window-dressing for purposeless expansion and a panicky need to keep things under control.

And now very many young people no longer want to co-operate with such a system. Indeed, a large and rapidly growing number — already more than five per cent of college students — use language that is openly revolutionary and apocalyptic, as if in their generation they were going to make a French Revolution. More and more often, direct civil disobedience seems to make obvious sense.

We are exerting more power and feeling less right — what does that mean for the future? I have heard serious people argue for three plausible yet drastically incompatible predictions about America during the next generation, none of them happy:

One: Some feel, with a kind of Virgilian despair, that the American empire will succeed and will impose for a long time, at home and abroad, its meaningless management and showy style of life. For instance, we will "win" in Vietnam, though such a victory of brute military technology will be a moral disaster. Clubbing together with the other nuclear powers, we will stave off the nuclear war and stop history with a new Congress of Vienna. American democracy will vanish into an establishment of promoters, mandarins, and technicians, though for a while maintaining an image of democracy as in the days of Augustus and Tiberius. And all this is probably the best possible outcome, given the complexities of high technology, urbanization, mass education, and overpopulation.

Two: Others believe, with dismay and horror, that our country is overreaching and is bound for doom, but nothing can be done because policy cannot be influenced. Controlling communications, creating incidents that it then mistakes for history, deceived by its own intelligence agents, our system is mesmerized. Like the Mikado, Washington is captive of its military-industrial complex. The way we manage the economy and technology must increase anomie and crime. Since the war economy eats up brains and capital, we will soon be a fifth-rate economic power. With a few setbacks abroad — for instance, when we force a major South American country to become communist — and with the increasing disorder on the streets that is inevitable because our cities are unworkable, there will be a police state. The atom bombs may then go off. Such being the forecast, the part of wisdom is escape, and those who cultivate LSD are on the right track.

Three: Others hold that the Americans are too decent to succumb to fascism and too spirited to remain impotent clients of a managerial elite, and the tide of protest will continue to rise. The excluded poor are already refusing to remain excluded, and they cannot be included without salutary changes. With the worst will in the world we cannot police the world. But the reality is that we are confused. We do not know how to cope with the new technology, the economy of surplus, the fact of One World that makes national boundaries obsolete, the unworkability of traditional democracy. We must invent new forms. To be sure, the present climate of emergency is bad for the social invention and experiment that are indispensable, and there is no doubt that our over-centralized and Establishment methods of organization make everybody stupid from top to bottom. But there is hope precisely in the young. They understand the problem in their bones. Of course, they don't know much, and their disaffection both from tradition and from the adult world makes it hard for them to learn anything. Nevertheless, we will learn in the inevitable conflict, which will hopefully be mainly non-violent.

I myself hold this third view: American society is on a bad course, but there is hope for reconstruction through conflict. It is a wish. The evidence, so far, is stronger than for either our empty success or for crack-up. My feeling is the same as about the atom bombs. Rationally, I must judge that the bombs are almost certain to go off in this generation; yet I cannot believe that they will go off, for I do not lead my life with that expectation.

Let me stop a moment and make another comparison. Thirty years ago the Jews in Germany believed that Hitler did not mean to exterminate them; "nobody," they said, "can be that stupid." So they drifted to the gas chambers and went finally even without resistance. Now the nuclear powers continue stockpiling bombs and pouring new billions into missiles, anti-missile missiles, and armed platforms in orbit. You Canadians, like us Americans, do not prevent it. Afterwards, survivors, if there are any, will ask, "How did we let it happen?"

I am eager, as well as honoured, to be talking to a Canadian audience on the state of American society, and especially to the

Canadian young. You people are not yet so wrongly committed as
we. Your land is less despoiled, your cities are more manageable, you
are not yet so sold on mass miseducation. You are not in the trap of
militarism. A large minority of you are deeply skeptical of American methods and oppose the unquestioned extension of American
power. Some of us Americans have always wistfully hoped that you
Canadians would teach us a lesson or two, though, to be frank, you
have usually let us down.

In this lecture on our ambiguous position, I shall have to talk a good
deal about style. To illustrate the current style of American enterprise, let me analyze a small, actual incident. It is perfectly typical,
banal; no one would raise his eyebrows at it, it is business as usual.

Washington has allotted several billions of dollars to the schools.
The schools are not teaching very well, but there is no chance that
anybody will upset the apple cart and ask if so much doing of lessons is the right way to educate the young altogether. Rather, there
is a demand for new "methods" and mechanical equipment, which
will disturb nobody, and electronics is the latest thing that every
forward-looking local school board must be proud to buy. So to cut
in on this melon, electronics corporations, IBM, Xerox, etc., have
hastened to combine with, or take over, textbook houses. My own
publisher, Random House, has been bought up by the Radio Corporation of America.

Just now, General Electric and Time, Inc., that owns a textbook
house, have put nearly forty millions into a joint subsidiary called
General Learning. And an editor of *Life* magazine has been relieved
of his duties for five weeks in order to prepare a prospectus on the
broad educational needs of America and the world, to come up with
exciting proposals, so that General Learning can move with purpose
into this unaccustomed field. The editor has collected and is boning
up on the latest High Thought on education, and in due course he
invites me to lunch, to pick my brains for something new and radical. "The sky," he assures me, "is the limit." (I am known, let me
explain, as a severe critic of the school establishment.) "Perhaps,"

he tells me at lunch, "there *is* no unique place for General Learning. They'll probably end up as prosaic makers of school hardware. But we ought to give it a try."

Consider the premises of this odd situation, where first they have the organization and the technology, and then they try to dream up a use for it. In the eighteenth century, Adam Smith thought that one started with the need and only then collected capital to satisfy it. In the nineteenth century, there was already a lot of capital to invest, but by and large the market served as a check, to guarantee utility, competence, and relevance. Now, however, the subsidy removes the check of the market, and a promotion can expand like weeds in a well-manured field. The competence required is to have a big organization and sales force and to be *in*, to have the prestige and connections plausibly to get the subsidy. Usually it is good to have some minimal relation to the ostensible function, e.g. a textbook subsidiary related to schooling or Time-Life related to, let us say, learning. But indeed, when an expanding corporation becomes *very* grand, it generates an expertise of its own called Systems Development, applicable to anything. For example, as an expert in Systems Development, North American Aviation is hired to reform the penal system of California; there is no longer need to demonstrate acquaintance with any particular human function.

Naturally, with the divorce of enterprise from utility and competence, there goes a heavy emphasis on rhetoric and public relations to prove utility and competence. So an editor must be re-assigned for five weeks to write a rationale. It is his task to add ideas or talking points to the enterprise, like a wrapper. The personnel of expanding corporations, of course, are busy people and have not had time to think of many concrete ideas; they can, however, phone writers and concerned professionals. Way-out radicals, especially, do a lot of thinking, since they have little practical employment. And since the enterprise is free-floating anyway, it is dandy to include, in the prospectus, something daring, or even meaningful. (Incidentally, I received no fee, except the lunch and pleasant company; but I did pick up an illustration for these lectures.)

In an affluent society that can afford it, there is something jolly

about such an adventure of the electronics giant, the mighty publisher, the National Science Foundation that has made curriculum
studies, and local school boards that want to be in the swim. Somewhere down the line, however, this cabal of decision-makers is going
to coerce the time of life of real children and control the activity of
classroom teachers. These, who are directly engaged in the human
function of learning and teaching, have no say in what goes on. This
introduces a more sober note. Some of the product of the burst of
corporate activity and technological virtuosity will be useful, some
not — the pedagogical evidence is mixed and not extensive — but
the brute fact is that the children are quite incidental to the massive
intervention of the giant combinations.

I have chosen a wry example. But I could have chosen the leader
of the American economy, the complex of cars, oil, and roads. This
outgrew its proper size perhaps thirty years ago; now it is destroying
both the cities and the countryside and has been shown to be careless
of even elementary safety.

Rather, let me turn abruptly to the Vietnam War. We notice the
same family traits. Whatever made us embark on this adventure, by
now we can define the Vietnam War as a commitment looking for a
reason, or at least a rationalization. There has been no lack of policy
statements, rhetorical gestures, seemingly manufactured incidents,
and certainly plain lies; but as the war has dragged on and grown, all
these have proved to be mere talking points. Ringing true, however,
has been the fanfare about the superb military technology that we
have deployed. The theme is used as a chief morale builder for the
troops. In the absence of adequate political reasons, some have even
said that the war is largely an occasion for testing new hardware and
techniques. It is eerie to hear, on the TV, an airmen enthusiastically
praise the split-second scheduling of his missions to devastate rice
fields. Such appreciation of know-how is a cheerful American dispo-
sition, but it does not do much credit to him as a grown man.

Yet what emerges most strikingly from our thinking about and
prosecution of the Vietnam War is, again, the input-output account-
ing, the systems development, and the purely incidental significance
of the human beings involved. The *communiqués* are concerned

mainly with the body count of V.C. in ratio to our own losses, since there is a theory that in wars of this kind one must attain a ratio of five to one or ten to one. According to various estimates, it costs $50,000 to $250,000 to kill one Vietnamese, hopefully an enemy. Similarly, the bombing of civilians and the destruction of their livelihood occur as if no human beings were involved; they are officially spoken of as unfortunate but incidental. (The average indemnity for a civilian death is $34.) We claim that we have no imperialist aims in Vietnam — though we are building air bases of some very heavy concrete and steel — but evidently old-fashioned imperialism was preferable, since it tried to keep the subjugated population in existence, for taxes and labour.

At home, correspondingly, college students are deferred from the draft because they will be necessary to man the professions and scientific technology, while farm boys, Negroes, and Spanish Americans are drafted because they are otherwise good for nothing. That is to say, the war is not regarded as a dread emergency, in which each one does his bit, but as part of the ongoing business of society, in which fighting and dying are usual categories of the division of labour. But this is bound to be the case when twenty per cent of the gross national product is spent on war (using a multiplier of two); when more than half of the gross new investment since 1945 has been in war industry; and when much of higher education and science is devoted to war technology.

The Americans are not a warlike or bloodthirsty people, though violent. The dehumanizing of war is part of a general style of enterprise and control in which human utility and even the existence of particular human beings are simply not a paramount consideration. Great armaments manufacturers have said that they are willing and ready to convert their capital and skill to peaceful production when given the signal; this seems to mean that it is *indifferent* to them what they enterprise. Studies of American workmen have shown that they take their moral and aesthetic standards not from family, church, friends, or personal interests, but from the organization and style of work at the plant. I think that this explains the present peculiar situation: other nations of the world regard our behaviour in the Vietnam War with a kind of horror, whereas Americans sincerely talk as if it were a messy job to be done as efficiently as possible.

This brings us to a broader question: What do we mean by technical efficiency in our system?

Corporate and bureaucratic societies, whether ruled by priests, mandarins, generals, or business managers, have always tended to diminish the importance of personal needs and human feeling in the interest of abstractions and systemic necessities. And where there has been no check by strong community ties, effective democracy, or a free market, it has not been rare for the business of society to be largely without utility or common sense. Nevertheless, modern corporate societies that can wield a high technology are liable to a unique temptation; since they do not exploit common labour, they may tend to exclude the majority of human beings altogether as useless for the needs of the system and therefore as not quite persons.

This has been the steady tendency in America. The aged are ruled out at an earlier age, the young until a later age. We have liquidated most small farmers. There is no place for the poor, e.g., more than twenty million Negroes and Latin Americans. A rapidly increasing number are certified as insane or otherwise incompetent. These groups already comprise more than a majority of the population. Some authorities say (though others deny) that with full automation most of the rest will also be useless.

There is nothing malevolent or heartless in the exclusion. The tone is not like that of the old exploitative society, when people were thrown out of work during the lows of the business cycle. For humane and political reasons, even extraordinary efforts are made to shape the excluded into the dominant style, so they can belong. Even though the system is going to need only a few per cent with elaborate academic training, all the young are subjected to twelve years of schooling, and forty per cent go to college. There is every kind of training and social service to upgrade the poor and to make the handicapped productive members of society. At high cost of effort and suffering, mentally retarded children must be taught to read, if only "cat" and "rat."

But a frank look shows, I think, that for most, the long schooling is a way of keeping the young on ice; the job training is busy work; and the social services turn people into "community dependents" for generations. Much of the anxiety about the "handicapped" and the "underprivileged" is suburban squeamishness that cannot tolerate difference. What is *never* done, however, is to change the rules of the system, to redefine usefulness in terms of how people are, and to shape the dominant style to people. This cannot be done because it would be inefficient and, indeed, degrading, for there is only one right way to exist. Do it our way or else you are not quite a person.

Inevitably, such self-righteous inflexibility is self-mesmerizing and self-proving, for other methods and values are not allowed to breathe and prove themselves. Often it would be cheaper to help people to be in their own way or at least to let them be; but anything in a different or outmoded style has "deviant" or "underprivileged" written on it, and no expense is spared to root it out, in the name of efficiency. Thus, it would have been cheaper to pay the small farmers to stay put if they wished. (Anyway, in many situations, it is not the case that small farming and local distribution are less efficient than the plantations and national chain grocers that have supplanted them with the connivance of government policy.) It would be far cheaper to give money directly to the urban poor to design their own lives, rather than to try to make them shape up; it has been estimated that, in one area of poverty in New York City, the cost per family in special services is more than $10,000 a year; and anyway, to a candid observer, the culture of poverty is not inferior to that of the middle class, if it were allowed to be decent, if it could be, in Péguy's distinction, *pauvreté* rather than *misère*. Very many of the young would get a better education and grow up useful to themselves and society if the school money were used for real apprenticeships, or even if they were given the school money to follow their own interests, ambitions, and even fancies, rather than penning them for lengthening years in increasingly regimented institutions; anyway, many young people could enter many professions without most of the schooling if we changed the rules for licensing and hiring. But none of these simpler and cheaper ways would be "efficient"; the clinching proof is that they would be hard to administer.

Also, *are* the people useless? The concept of efficiency is largely, maybe mainly, systemic. It depends on the goals of the *system*, which may be too narrowly and inflexibly conceived; it depends on the ease of administration, which is considered as more important than economic or social costs; but it depends also on the method of calculating costs, which may create a false image of efficiency by ruling out "intangibles" that do not suit the method. This source of error becomes very important in advanced urban economies, where the provision of personal and social services grows rapidly in proportion to hardware and food production and distribution. In providing services, whether giving information, selling, teaching children, admitting to college, assigning jobs, serving food, or advising on welfare, standardization and punch cards may seem to fulfill the functions, but they may do so at the expense of frayed nerves, waiting in line, bad mistakes, misfitting, and cold soup. In modern conditions, the tailor-made improvisations of fallible but responsive human beings may be increasingly indispensable rather than useless. In the jargon of Frank Riessman, there is a need for "sub-professionals." Yet the mass-production and business-machine style, well adapted to manufacturing hardware and calculating logistics, will decide that people are useless anyway, since they can theoretically be dispensed with. It is a curious experience to hear a gentleman from the Bureau of the Budget explain the budget of the War on Poverty according to cost-benefit computation. He can demonstrate that the participation of the poor in administering a program is disadvantageous; he can show you the flow chart; he cannot understand why poor people make a fuss on this point. It is useless to explain to him that they do not trust the program (nor the director) but would like to get the money for their own purposes.

Abroad, the Americans still engage in plenty of old-fashioned exploitation of human labour, as in Latin America; yet the tendency is again to regard the underdeveloped peoples as not quite persons, and to try to shape them up by (sometimes) generous assistance in our own style. For example, one of the radical ideas of General Learning, the subsidiary of General Electric and Time, Inc., is to concentrate on electronic devices to teach literacy to the masses of children in poor countries; we must export our Great Society. Our enterprisers are eager to build highways and pipelines through the jungle, to multiply bases for our airplanes, and to provide other items of the American standard of living, for which the western-trained native political leaders have "rising aspirations." Unfortunately, this largesse must often result in disrupting age-old cultures, fomenting tribal wars, inflating prices and wages, and reducing decent poverty to starvation, causing the abandonment of farms and disastrous instant urbanization, making dictatorships inevitable, and drawing simple peoples into Great Power conflicts. And woe to them if they do not then shape up, if they want to develop according to their local prejudices, for instance, for land reform. They become an uncontrollable nuisance, surely therefore allied with our enemies, and better dead than Red. In his great speech in Montreal, Secretary McNamara informed us that since 1958, eighty-seven per cent of the very poor nations and sixty-nine per cent of the poor nations, but only forty-eight per cent of the middle income nations, have had serious violent disturbances. The cure for it, he said, was development, according to the criteria of our cash economy, while protected from subversion by our bombers. How to explain to this arithmetically astute man that he is not taking these people seriously as existing?

A startlingly literal corollary of the principle that our system excludes human beings rather than exploits them is the agreement of all liberals and conservatives that there must be a check on population growth, more especially among backward peoples and the poor at home. We are definitely beyond the need for the labour of the "proletariat" ("producers of offspring") and the Iron Law of Wages to keep that labour cheap. Yet I am bemused by this unanimous recourse to a biological and mathematical etiology for our troubles. Probably there *is* a danger of world overpopulation in the foreseeable future. (The United States, though, is supposed to level off at three hundred million in 2020, and this would not be a dense population for our area.) Certainly with the likelihood of nuclear war there is a danger of world-underpopulation. However, until we institute more human ecological, economic, and political arrangements, I doubt that population control is the first order of business, nor would I trust the Americans to set the rules.

In this lecture, I have singled out two trends of the dominant organization of American society: its increasing tendency to expand meaninglessly, for its own sake, and its tendency to exclude human beings as useless. It is the Empty Society, the obverse face of the Affluent Society. When Adam Smith spoke of the Wealth of Nations, he did not mean anything like this.

The meaningless expansion and the excluding are different things, but in our society they are essentially related. Lack of meaning begins to occur when the immensely productive economy over-matures and lives by creating demand instead of meeting it; when the check of the free market gives way to monopolies, subsidies, and captive consumers; when the sense of community vanishes and public goods are neglected and resources despoiled; when there is make-work (or war) to reduce unemployment; and when the measure of economic health is not increasing well-being but abstractions like the gross national product and the rate of growth.

Human beings tend to be excluded when a logistic style becomes universally pervasive, so that values and data that cannot be standardized and programmed are disregarded; when function is adjusted to the technology rather than technology to function; when technology is confused with autonomous science, a good in itself, rather than being limited by political and moral prudence; when there develops an establishment of managers and experts who alone license and allot resources, which deludes itself that it knows the only right method and is omnicompetent. Then common folk become docile clients, maintained by sufferance, or they are treated as deviant.

It is evident that, for us, these properties of the empty society are essentially related. If we did not exclude so many as not really persons, we would have to spend more of our substance on worthwhile goods, including subsistence goods, both at home and abroad; we would have to provide a more human environment for the children to grow up in; there would be more paths to growing up and more ways of being a person. On the other hand, if we seriously and efficiently tackled the problems of anomie, alienation, riot, pollution, congestion, urban blight, degenerative and mental disease, etc., we would find ourselves paying more particular attention to persons and neighbourhoods, rather than treating them as standard items; we would have a quite different engineering and social science; and we would need all the human resources available.

Certainly we would stop talking presumptuously about the Great Society and find ourselves struggling, in the confusing conditions of modern times, for a decent society.

The chief danger to American society at present, and to the world from American society, is our mindlessness, induced by empty institutions. It is a kind of mesmerism, a self-delusion of formal rightness, that affects both leaders and people. We have all the talking points but less and less content. The Americans are decent folk, generous and fairly compassionate. They are not demented and fanatical, like some other imperial powers of the past and present, but on the contrary rather skeptical and with a sense of humour. They are not properly called arrogant, though perhaps presumptuous. But we have lost our horse sense, for which we were once noted. This kind of intelligence was grounded not in history or learning, nor in finesse of sensibility and analysis, but in the habit of making independent judgments and in democratically rubbing shoulders with all kinds and conditions. We have lost it by becoming personnel of a mechanical system and exclusive suburbanites, by getting out of contact with real jobs and real people. We suddenly have developed an Establishment, but our leaders do not have the tradition and self-restraint to come on like an establishment. Thus, we are likely to wreak havoc not because of greed, ideology, or arrogance, but because of a bright strategy of the theory of games and an impatient conviction that other people don't know what's good for them.

"The Empty Society" was broadcast on October 31, 1966.

On Religion and Language

NORTHROP FRYE

Presented by DAVID CAYLEY

Northrop Frye (1912-1991) was one of Canada's most distinguished men of letters. His first book, Fearful Symmetry, *published in 1947, transformed the study of the poet William Blake, and over the next forty years he transformed the study of literature itself. Among his most influential books are* Anatomy of Criticism *(1957),* The Educated Imagination *(1963),* The Bush Garden *(1971), and* The Great Code *(1982).* Northrop Frye on Shakespeare *(1986) won the Governor General's Award for Non-Fiction. A professor at the University of Toronto, Frye gained an international reputation for his wide-reaching critical vision. He lectured at universities around the world and received many awards and honours, including thirty-six honorary degrees.*

NORTHROP FRYE

I think my religious background really did shape almost everything, gave me the mythological framework that I was brought up inside of, and, as I know from experience, once you're inside a mythological framework, you can't break out of it. You can alter or adapt it to yourself, but it's always there.

The Bible is, to me, the body of words through which I can see the world as a cosmos, as an order, and where I can see human nature as something redeemable, something with a right to survive. I think if I didn't read the Bible and were confronted with all these dire prophecies about the possibility of the human race disappearing from the planet, I would be inclined to say, "Well, the sooner the better."

A lot of people, some very unlikely people, say that they feel that it's language that uses man rather than man that uses language, and I have a great deal of attraction to that view. It's partly because central to my whole thinking is, "In the beginning is the Word."

DAVID CAYLEY

In the early 1980s, Northrop Frye published a book on the Bible and literature called *The Great Code*. The title came from the English poet and painter, William Blake. "The Old and New Testaments," Blake said, "are the great code of art." Frye read Blake as a student in the early 1930s, and the encounter was formative. Blake taught Frye to see the Bible as the imaginative framework within which our entire civilization took shape, to see it as the source of the basic repertoire of images and stories out of which literature is made, to see it as the Great Code. This became the seminal idea in Frye's literary criticism. In book after book, he insisted that literature, like the Bible, reveals the structure of the human imagination — what's within us rather than what's out there in the world. "In a sense," Frye wrote in his introduction to *The Great Code*, "all my critical work has revolved around the Bible."

Frye's immersion in the Bible began in childhood. His family were Methodists, an evangelical Protestant church that had broken away from the Church of England in the eighteenth century and that in Canada eventually merged with the Presbyterians and Congregationalists to form the United Church. Methodist teaching stressed the authority of scripture and the importance of personal conversion. Frye's grandfather was a circuit-riding preacher, and Methodism permeated the milieu in which he grew up. He thinks today that it still colours his overall approach to things.

NORTHROP FRYE

I think Methodism is an approach to Christianity which puts a very heavy emphasis on the quality of experience. That is one reason why I have always tended to think in terms of, first, a myth which repeats itself over and over again through time, and then secondly the experience which is the response to it. Nothing that happens in history is unique. Everything is part of turning cycles and mythical repetitions. Everything in experience is unique, and I think it is because of the emphasis on the uniqueness of experience which I acquired so early that I realized that the other half of this was this mythological pattern.

DAVID CAYLEY

The emphasis on experience in Methodism — can you contrast that with other approaches to Christianity that might show its nature?

NORTHROP FRYE

Well, the Catholic approach, for example, is very much more doctrinal, and you learn a structure of doctrine and you step inside it, and that structure of doctrine performs instead of the myth. In Methodism, you listen to the stories of the Bible, and Presbyterians used to say that's the reason why Methodist ministers moved every two years, because the structure of doctrine in Methodism was totally exhausted long before then.

DAVID CAYLEY

Frye always retained Methodism's nondoctrinal approach to religion, but he quickly rejected the fundamentalist side of his family's beliefs. It happened when he was walking to high school in Moncton one day, he told an interviewer years later. "And just suddenly," he said, "that whole shitty and smelly garment of fundamentalist teaching I'd had all my life dropped off into the sewers and stayed there." The punishing father God, the post-mortem hell, the unpardonable sins — all this, he concluded, was "a lot of junk." But characteristically, he also realized that it would be a waste of time to get stuck in a rebellious reaction. Instead, he decided he'd accept from religion only what made sense to him as a human being. The rest he'd simply leave alone. This meant rejecting the sentiments of Cardinal Newman's famous hymn, "Lead Kindly Light," where God, says Newman, leads us, and deciding to steer by his own star.

NORTHROP FRYE

My attitude to freedom has always been the opposite of Newman's "Lead Kindly Light," where he says, "I love to choose and see my path" and calls that pride. Well, I always wanted to choose and see my path and was convinced that that was what God wanted too, and that if I went on with this "lead thou me on" routine I would run into spiritual gravitation and fall over a cliff.

DAVID CAYLEY

Frye's path led him first to the University of Toronto. As a boy of seventeen, he enrolled at Victoria College, the university's Methodist college. After his graduation, he went on to study theology at neighbouring Emmanuel College, Victoria's theological faculty. This would prepare him for the ministry, and in the summer of 1934, he set off for Saskatchewan's parched Palliser triangle as a student minister. For five months, he ministered to the congregations of Stone, Stonepile and Carnagh, travelling between them on a horse as old as he was called Katy.

NORTHROP FRYE

I remember something that I found later in a Canadian critic, I think it was Elizabeth Waterston, where she spoke of the prairies as the sense of immense space with no privacy. And I found that on top of Katy, who naturally stimulated one's bladder very considerably, and realizing I couldn't get off in that vast stretch of prairie, because everybody was out with opera glasses, you see, watching the preacher on top of Katy.

DAVID CAYLEY

You really were observed to that extent?

NORTHROP FRYE

Well, one was. I mean, that was what people did. They all had spy-glasses. They weren't doing it with any malicious sense. It was just that their lives were rather devoid of incident. Naturally, they liked to see who's going along.

DAVID CAYLEY

That was just a summer, I think.

NORTHROP FRYE

That was a summer, yes. I thought the people were wonderful. Again, I realized that this wasn't the thing I would be good at.

DAVID CAYLEY

Was it difficult to decide whether or not to seek ordination?

NORTHROP FRYE

Yes, it was difficult for me. And I consulted a friend whose judgment I had a great respect for, Hal Vaughan — he died recently — and he asked me what my difficulty was. And I said, "Well, various people, including Herbert Davis, a very civilized man, have pointed out that it might be embarrassing later on if I had a professional connection with the church." And he said, "Well, isn't that your answer?"

DAVID CAYLEY

You mean, if it's embarrassing, then you should go ahead?

NORTHROP FRYE

Yes.

DAVID CAYLEY

Frye was ordained in 1936. He already knew that his vocation was teaching and writing, not the active ministry, and through the years he has appeared more often at a lectern than in a pulpit. But he still regards himself very much as a minister of the United Church.

NORTHROP FRYE

I used to describe myself as a United Church plainclothes man — that is, that I was in effect somebody who was attached to a church, but most undergraduates are instinctively agnostic and rather rebellious about churches and about religious institutions generally. And I have always used a very secular attitude in order to, in effect, win the confidence of people, not because I want to catch them in a trap later, but precisely because I want them to understand that there isn't any trap.

DAVID CAYLEY

Frye's secular attitude is evident in his writings. His perspective is the literary critic's, never the theologian's. Nevertheless, he has reacted hotly when people have misinterpreted his anti-doctrinaire approach. Once he was asked in public to comment on a reviewer's claim that he'd written *The Great Code* as an ex-Christian. "I can't express my opinion of those sentences in a language that I think is appropriate to them," he responded. "The United Church of Canada, of which I am an ordained clergyman, would be surprised to hear that I am an ex-Christian."

Frye's relationship to the Bible is the foundation of all his work as a literary critic. It was hearing the echoes of the Bible in English poetry that made him aware that literature always belongs to a mythological universe that gives it its fundamental forms and images, and the Bible has given him his personal bearings as well.

NORTHROP FRYE

The Bible is, to me, the body of words through which I can see the world as a cosmos, as an order, and where I can see human nature as something redeemable, something with a right to survive. Otherwise you're left with human nature and physical nature. Physical nature doesn't seem to have very much conversation. It's a totally inarticulate world. Human nature is corrupt at the source because it's grown out of physical nature, and it has various ideals and hopes and wishes and concerns, but its attempt to realize these things is often abominably cruel and psychotic. And I feel there must be something that transcends all this, or else.

DAVID CAYLEY

Or else?

NORTHROP FRYE

Well, or else despair. Why keep this miserable object, humanity, alive on this planet when it's doing nothing but pollute it?

DAVID CAYLEY

Frye learned to see the Bible as a cosmos from William Blake. As a boy, Frye had already rejected a fundamentalist reading of the Bible which made it a prop for authoritarianism and repression. Blake showed him another way, an imaginative reading which saw the Bible as the manifesto of human dignity and creative freedom, not the dictation of a tyrannical God. To Blake, God and the human imagination were ultimately identical. In his later writings, he spoke of "Jesus, the imagination." What this imagination is, neither our senses nor our reason can tell us. They can only observe and compare. "None, by travelling over known lands, can find out the unknown," Blake says. The imagination must be revealed by what he called "the poetic genius." The Bible is this revelation. The alternative is the worship of nature and ourselves as natural beings, which Blake called "natural religion."

NORTHROP FRYE

Natural religion, for him, was what the Bible calls "idolatry." It means finding something numinous in nature, in the physical environment, and the Bible says that there are no gods in nature, that nature is a fellow creature of man, and that, while one should love nature, you actually get your spiritual vision through human society, and then you see nature as it is. But all the gods that people have pretended to find in nature are, in effect, devils — that is, they're projections of the wrong side of man's natural origin.

DAVID CAYLEY

Blake's contemporaries sanctified nature. Blake asserted that mental things alone are real. Whether the sun appears to us as "a round disc of fire" or "an innumerable company of the heavenly host," he says, depends on who's looking, not on what's objectively there. Reality is something that we make in perceiving it, and we can't understand what we haven't made. Our capacity to do this is what Blake called "vision."

NORTHROP FRYE

He meant the capacity to live with one's eyes and ears in what he called the spiritual world. It was not a world of ideas, it was not a Platonic world. It was the physical world in its organized form. He says spirits are organized man. He also says spirits are not cloudy vapours or anything fuzzy, they are organized and minutely articulated beyond anything the physical world can produce. In other words, it was his world of poetry and painting. Vision, for him, was, as I say, the ability to hear and see in that world.

DAVID CAYLEY

This was not a world that had an independent existence.

NORTHROP FRYE

Oh, no.

DAVID CAYLEY

Not a Platonic world.

NORTHROP FRYE

This is the world as it really is, not the world as our lazy minds and senses perceive it.

DAVID CAYLEY

The Bible, to Blake, was the source of this visionary seeing. "Why is the Bible more entertaining and instructive than any other book?" he once asked, and answered, "Because it is addressed to the imaginations. The whole Bible," he says, "is filled with imaginations and visions from end to end. It is within the figures of the Bible that the imagination awakens and expands. They become the reader's chariots of fire. We build Jerusalem by recreating the divine forms of the imagination. The Bible is the model, the arts are the means."

This was the view that Frye first encountered in Blake and adopted as his own. Soon after he began teaching at Victoria College in 1939, he began to offer a course on the Bible which continues to this day. He also had the idea of doing a book on the Bible, and friends encouraged him in it, almost from the beginning. But, for years, he was primarily taken up with his writings on "the secular scripture," as he once called literature. He finally got around to the Bible in the late seventies, and *The Great Code* was published in the early eighties with the subtitle, "The Bible and Literature."

NORTHROP FRYE

I didn't want to write a book called "The Bible as Literature." What I wanted to do was to deal with the entire narrative and imagery of the Bible and the impact that it has made as a totality on literature, and that was why the word "and" was extremely important to me.

DAVID CAYLEY

So it's not a strategic disclaimer to fend off charges that you're poaching in theological territory.

NORTHROP FRYE

Well, it was partly that as well. I wanted to make it clear that I was dealing with the Bible's relation to literature, and the fact that it was written mostly in literary language, and that it was neither an aesthetic literary approach to the Bible nor a doctrinal one.

DAVID CAYLEY

Frye does not consider the Bible "as" literature. He puts it in a category of its own, for which he uses the Greek term *kerygma*, meaning "proclamation." But he does recognize that the Bible is made of the same figures as any other literary work. "People are unlikely to get to the centre of the Bible," Frye says, "unless they are willing to pass through the shadowy world of literary imagination, with all its fictions, illusions and suspended judgments."

To understand the Bible, Frye says, we have to understand the kind of language it's written in. And so he begins *The Great Code* by distinguishing three different phases of language, which are, roughly: mythic or poetic language, logical or dialectical language and, finally, descriptive or scientific language. The Bible is expressed almost entirely in the primitive language of myth and metaphor. Logical language appears first with Greek philosophy, and only much later does descriptive language come on the scene.

NORTHROP FRYE

In ordinary speech, we use words to represent things outside the structure of words, but as a technique of writing that is a fairly late development because it depends on technology, really. You can't write history until you have historiography and archives and documents, and you can't do science until you have a machinery for experimentation, and you can't write descriptively in any sort of mature or fully developed way until you've established these things. Consequently, I wouldn't put descriptive language as a continuous form of prose much earlier than about the seventeenth century.

DAVID CAYLEY

What is happening before that?

NORTHROP FRYE

What is happening before that is, first of all, the logical language developed out of Plato, and more particularly Aristotle, where the criterion of truth is in the integrity of the verbal structure rather than in its relation to something outside.

DAVID CAYLEY

And how is mythic thinking contrasted with this logical thinking?

NORTHROP FRYE

Mythic thinking is the earliest of all, the most primitive form of thinking. Consequently, the illusion turns up in every generation that it's something that'll be outgrown, but we always find that if you try to outgrow mythical thinking, you end up by rehabilitating it. And mythical thinking proceeds metaphorically in a world where everything is potentially identifiable with everything else. Gods, for example, are linguistically metaphors. That's how they start out. You have a sea god or a gun god or a war god, where two things are being identified within a supposed personality.

DAVID CAYLEY

And it's your view that that form of thinking is ultimate, a boundary for us.

NORTHROP FRYE

I think it's where the use of words begins, and I think it's where the use of words is likely to end.

DAVID CAYLEY

The language of the Bible is metaphoric, not philosophical or descriptive. This means that the Bible neither reasons about reality nor points at something outside of itself, like a work of history. It comes to us, like any literary fiction, as a self-contained world of words.

NORTHROP FRYE

There is nothing that we get from Christianity except a body of words, and they become transmuted into experiences. You start out with the notion that if you have a body of words, they must point to an event. So, in the beginning, God did something, and the words are the servo-mechanisms which tell us what he did. But the Gospel of John doesn't begin that way. It just says the word came first. You've got a body of words and nothing else. You create the events yourself. God said, "Let there be light," and there was light. The word comes first, the event follows. Verbalizing consciousness precedes the physical existence.

DAVID CAYLEY

There are words before there are things.

NORTHROP FRYE

There are in Genesis, certainly.

DAVID CAYLEY

Words, for Frye, are powers, and as we recreate the world in their light, they use us as much as we use them. When we use words to describe a world "out there," they divide our reality. If we use them metaphorically, they can be healing powers.

NORTHROP FRYE

My growing interest in the Bible has led me to a growing interest in the way that nouns, the world of things, block movements. It's partly the screw-up of language because the scientist, for example, is trying to describe processes in space-time, and ordinary language has to twist that into events in time and things in space. And they're not going on there. One of the most seminal books that I've read is Buber's *I and Thou,* and Buber says we all are born into a world of "its." Everything is a solid block of thing, this and that, and so forth. Consequently, when we think of "God," we think of a grammatical noun, and you have to get used to the notion that there is no such thing as "God," because God is not a thing. He's a process fulfilling itself. That's how he defines himself: I will be what I will be. Similarly, I am more and more drawn to thinking in terms of a great swirling of processes and powers rather than a world of blocks and things. A text, for example, is a conflict of powers. A picture is not a "thing," it's a focus of forces.

DAVID CAYLEY

When Frye began teaching his Bible course at the University of Toronto, his so-called "mythological" approach scandalized the campus fundamentalists. "Myth" was a word they preferred to apply to other people's religions. Like many Christians, they wanted to believe that there is a substratum of historical truth in their Bible. The quest for the historical Jesus has been perennially popular. Modern Protestant theologians have even spoken of "de-mythologizing" the Bible, as if myth were an archaic husk that could be stripped away to reveal a kernel of theological truth. In Frye's view, the Bible itself condemns such undertakings. The Bible contains history, but only as the raw material of myth, and its view of evidence would make any historian blush. This can be seen quite clearly in a traditional way of studying the Bible called typology.

NORTHROP FRYE

The Christian Bible consists of an Old Testament and a New Testament, and the relation between them from the Christian point of view is that everything that happens in the Old Testament is a type of something that happens in the New Testament. And so you get this tennis game view of evidence. How do you know that the Old Testament is true? Because it's fulfilled in the New Testament. How do you know the New Testament is true? Because it fulfills the prophecies of the Old Testament. And after the Resurrection, we're told that the disciples confronted the risen Jesus and said, "We find this resurrection very hard to understand," and he simply said, "Search the scriptures and you'll find that the Messiah has to rise from the dead." And that's the only evidence that the writers of the Gospels are interested in. They are not biographers. The one criterion they subject themselves to is that what happens to Jesus in the account must fit what the Old Testament said would happen to the Messiah. Typology is really a view of history which says that history is going somewhere and meaning something.

DAVID CAYLEY

And the meaning appears in the future.

NORTHROP FRYE

Yes. All our ideologies today are typological in the sense that they're all donkey's carrots — that is, they pull you forward to something that's to be fulfilled.

DAVID CAYLEY

The Bible's typological structure yields a philosophy of history which the modern secular world interprets in terms of continual progress and improvement. Progress, in our modern sense, is an idea foreign to the Bible itself, but it is a reflection of the value the Bible places on the future. Even where the original ideas have been transformed, the Bible colours the western tradition and produces what is distinctive in it.

NORTHROP FRYE

The difference between the biblical religions and, say, the oriental religions, is that in Buddhism you have a compassionate Buddha, and in Jesus you have a compassionate Jesus, but he's also a Jesus that confronts and condemns the world. It is a more militant conception, more thrown on the will and less thrown on enlightenment. That is, the crucifixion of Jesus is something that goes on every day. It goes on in El Salvador, it goes on in Vietnam, it goes on here. And that condemnation of the world by the fact that it tries to kill God, and is always trying to kill God, is what seems to be distinctive in the biblical religions.

DAVID CAYLEY

Why is the biblical, Hebraic tradition revolutionary? Why do you call it a revolutionary tradition?

NORTHROP FRYE

Well, I call it revolutionary because the Old Testament comes out of a people that was never any good at the game of empire. It was always on the underside, the side oppressed and placed in bondage by more powerful kingdoms like Egypt and Assyria and Babylonia. So the central thing in the Old Testament is the liberation of an enslaved people — in other words the Exodus — and that goes on repeating through the return from Babylon. And in the New Testament, it is again a struggle between Christ and the world in which the world wins, to the extent that Christ is crucified and dies and is buried. But, of course, the central thing is the Resurrection: God can't die.

DAVID CAYLEY

What does the eye-ear dialect in the Bible have to do with its revolutionary cast?

NORTHROP FRYE

The metaphor of the "ear" — of the voice of God, God speaking
— suggests an invisible God who nevertheless enters into you and
becomes a part of you, and the "eye" always retains a sense of the
objective, the thing "over there." In a polytheistic religion like the
Greek one, you have to have visual symbols like statues in order to
distinguish one god from another, but if you don't have the problem
of distinguishing among gods, if there's only one, then it's a reduc-
tion of that god to see him as an object.

DAVID CAYLEY

Does the word also become a command in a different sense?

NORTHROP FRYE

It has often taken the form of command, yes. The word of command
in an ordinary society is the word of authority, which is in that whole
area of ideology and rhetoric, and that kind of word of command has
to be absolutely at a minimum. It can't have any comment attached
to it. Soldiers won't hang themselves on barbed wire in response to a
subordinate clause, and if there's any commentary necessary, it's the
sergeant-major's job to explain what it is, not the officer's. Now that
is a metaphor; it's an analogy of the kind of command that comes
from the other side of the imagination, what has been called the
kerygmatic — the proclamation from God. And that is not so much
a command as a statement of what your own potentiality is and of
the direction in which you have to go to attain it. But it's a command
that leaves your will free, whether you follow it or not.

DAVID CAYLEY

For Frye, God is not an objective being who compels our obedience.
God is a human identity towards which we grow, the word of God
a statement of our potential. God only acts and is in existing beings,

Blake says. Reality is not something fixed forever, it is something we make. Literature, Frye has always said, deals with the conceivable, not the real, with what can be made true rather than what is true now. The important question about the Bible is not whether we believe it, but what actually happens when we enter into its imaginative forms. Like literature, it is a vision to be tested rather than believed, and this testing is what Frye calls faith.

NORTHROP FRYE

Faith is, according to the New Testament, the *hypostasis* of hope and the *elenchos*, the proof or evidence of the unseen. I would translate that approximately as meaning that faith is the reality of hope and the reality of illusion.

DAVID CAYLEY

The reality of illusion?

NORTHROP FRYE

Yes.

DAVID CAYLEY

You put it rather paradoxically. Illusion is something that is not real by definition.

NORTHROP FRYE

That's right. For most people, it's the schoolboy's definition. Faith is believing what you know "ain't so." I have no use for that kind of faith, and I don't think the New Testament does either. Faith can only be achieved through experience. Say the Wright brothers start to wonder if a heavier-than-air machine can actually get off the ground. Everybody says that's impossible, that's an illusion. They get the damn thing off the ground. That's faith. It's not an objective body of propositions, because the author of Hebrews, after he's given his definition of faith, goes on and gives examples from the Old Testament and, he says, by faith these people did certain things. They weren't talking about a trinity with three persons in one substance, and anybody who doesn't believe in the identity of the substance or the difference of the persons is this and that. If the Gospel says that faith can move mountains, it's not good just saying I have faith that that mountain shall not be there the next minute, and of course it stays there. So obviously, you have to keep on working at your conception of faith until it becomes more precise and heads in the direction of realization. The important thing is that it does work. It's a process of turning into reality what has been either a matter of hope or a matter of illusion.

DAVID CAYLEY

The Great Code is a study of the Bible's overall narrative pattern. Frye finds this pattern to be the characteristic U-shape of comedy. The book begins well, with the Creation, quickly runs into complications with the expulsion of Adam and Eve from the Garden of Eden, and ends in re-creation with the Resurrection of Jesus and the promise of a new Heaven, a new Earth and a new tree of life in the Book of Revelation. The same pattern is repeated over and over again in miniature in the individual stories of the Bible. Israel captive, Israel delivered. Jonah swallowed by the whale, then disgorged. The same images recur and build towards the unification of the entire book in the comprehensive personality of Jesus.

Frye finds an epitome of the Bible's overall shape in the Book of Job. The familiar story concerns a wager between God and Satan over the loyalty of Job. God delivers Job into Satan's hands. His property is taken, he's afflicted with boils, and his friends claim that he must have done something wrong or this would never have happened. Finally, God reveals a vision of the Creation to Job. Above is the uncorrupted world, where the morning stars sing together. Below are the great beasts, Behemoth and Leviathan, in whose bellies we live. Job is reconciled to God. "I have heard of thee by the hearing of the ear," he says, "but now mine eye seeth thee," and his property is restored and increased. It's a story which Frye says can be read in two diametrically opposed ways. Bernard Shaw, for example, saw it as a story in which God first betrays Job, then bullies him into submission with what Shaw called "an ignoble and impertinent tirade."

Blake, who illustrated the book in a wonderful set of engravings, saw the story as Job's deliverance from an ego-centred consciousness into an enlarged vision. Frye reads the book as Blake does.

NORTHROP FRYE

Blake looks at Job as a kind of spiritualized version of the story of the Fall in Genesis. That is, you start with Job doing his moral duty and therefore not being quite on the upper limit of what human beings can achieve, so he falls into Satan's world. Satan is young and vigorous, God is old and imbecile, and Satan takes over and dominates the world, until Job goes through the vision of the morning stars singing together, in plate fourteen, and the vision of Leviathan and Behemoth in plate fifteen. And the new Creation and consequently a renewed God, who is, among other things, the divinity in Job himself, takes over.

DAVID CAYLEY

You've called the Book of Job an epitome of the Bible.

NORTHROP FRYE

Yes.

DAVID CAYLEY

What does that mean? How does it epitomize the whole Bible?

NORTHROP FRYE

Well, it seems to me that Job begins with, as I say, a spiritualized form of Genesis. It ends with a spiritual form of Apocalypse or Revelation. And in the middle comes this vertical contact between God and man, of which the New Testament has a different version. It sees that contact as existing in Jesus. But imaginatively and mythically, it's in the Book of Job.

DAVID CAYLEY

What's the difference between the two readings of the book you've given, by way of a conception of God?

NORTHROP FRYE

Well, the reading which I disagree with, which makes God a bully who forces Job into agreeing with the justice of his ways, is the objective God who is sitting up there in the sky and is linguistically a noun — that is, he's an object that never changes. And all he does is to say, look what I did in the remote past, I created this wonderful world. As I see it, the opening of the story with Satan in God's court depicts God as shifting the centre of action to Satan, who brings about all these disasters. Job then is driven to assert the dignity of human beings. If I've done so and so, then it's all right, but I haven't, therefore there's a problem. At that point, God moves in on it, and the new Creation which he displays to Job is the old Creation again, but it's something in which Job now participates. It's something that engages Job as an actor, as an experiencer. That means that God himself has become a principle of action and experience. He has transformed himself from a noun in Job's mind into a verb in Job's spiritual body.

DAVID CAYLEY

The Book of Job ends with an apocalypse, a word meaning literally "an uncovering," a revelation of how things really stand. Frye sees the same dynamic in literature, which he calls a human apocalypse — man's revelation to man, the arena in which we divide what we want from what we don't want. Usually, Frye rejects either/or choices. What we exclude, he says, will only ambush us somewhere farther down the road. But he does accept the Bible's apocalyptic either/or.

NORTHROP FRYE

The only either/or dialectic that I'm interested in is the apocalyptic one, which moves towards a separation of a world of life from a world of death, not a separation of the good from the evil. I don't believe in that. In ordinary life, the good/evil distinctions are hopelessly tangled. Jesus has another parable on the wheat and the tares in which he says there's no use trying to root out the weeds from the grain in this world, and when you make choices, when you make decisions, you're always moving towards an apocalyptic vision of something that doesn't die and throwing off the body of the death that you want to be delivered from. So that the final separation of life and death has to be in the form of an imaginative vision, which is what literature expresses and what the critic tries to explain.

DAVID CAYLEY

Literature is apocalyptic because it distinguishes what human beings actually care about from what they merely belong to by birth or by circumstances. Comedy shows us the world we want, tragedy the world we don't. Whichever it is, literature, for Frye, must be rooted in what he calls primary concern.

NORTHROP FRYE

Man is a concerned being. I think that's one way of defining the conscious animal. And as I went on, I tended to see a distinction between the primary concerns of man as an animal — that is, food and sex and property and freedom of movement — and his secondary concerns, which are religious belief, political loyalties and everything ideological. And it seems to me that literature has a profound and, well, primary connection with primary concerns and that that is what distinguishes it from ideology and rhetoric of all kinds. You can learn a great deal about the ideological or religious structure of a society from novels like Flaubert's or Zola's or Tolstoy's, but in the work of fiction they have to be subordinated to making love and making a living and getting on with your life, the questions of survival. And if there's one thing clear about the late twentieth century, it is that it's an age where primary concerns have got to become primary, or else. I mean, food and sex and freedom of movement and property, in the sense of what is proper to individuality, are the primary concerns. We must come to terms with those.

DAVID CAYLEY

The Bible reflects primary concern. Jesus was a teller of tales, not an ideologue. He preached the power of the present moment, the kingdom of Heaven in a mustard seed, later echoed in Blake's eter-

nity in a grain of sand. This is what Frye thinks the Bible gives us
— a real present.

NORTHROP FRYE

The present doesn't exist in ordinary experience. It's always a never-quite, and it keeps vanishing between the past and the future. The Bible, while it doesn't raise so abstract an argument, nevertheless makes it clear that reality is a matter of a real present, a "now" which exists, and a real presence, a real "here" in space, because in space, things are just as alienated as they are in time. "Now" is the centre of time, but there's no such time as "now," ordinarily. "Here" is the centre of space, but there's no such place as "here." It's always a "there," even if you're pointing to your own backbone. And to me, the words "eternal" and "infinite" do not mean time and space going on and on without ever stopping. They mean the reality of now and the reality of here.

DAVID CAYLEY

What makes the reality of now and the reality of here is vision, the power to see in the light of eternity, which is the world as it always and never is. The Bible is the source of this vision for our culture. We forget it, Frye says, at our peril.

NORTHROP FRYE

I think that forgetting the Bible is on a par with forgetting the rest of our cultural heritage, and I have always maintained that when you lose your memory you become senile, and that's just as true of a society as it is of an individual.

DAVID CAYLEY

Do you see this as a senile society in that sense?

NORTHROP FRYE

Well, there's a lot of senility about, yes.

DAVID CAYLEY

Frye's answer is characteristic. He notes the reality of growing senility, but humorously, in passing. He doesn't dwell on it, brood about it, berate others about it. His eyes remain fixed on a better possibility and on his obligation to try and realize it. He makes a statement of his faith in the conclusion to his book *Creation and Recreation*, published in 1980. "If we could transcend professed belief," Frye says, meaning essentially ideology, "and reach the level of a world-wide community of action and charity, we should discover a new creative power in man altogether, except that it would not be new, but the power of the genuine word and spirit, the power that has created all our works of culture and imagination and is still ready to recreate both our society and ourselves."

This combined interview and documentary was broadcast on March 5, 1990, as the first part of the series The Ideas of Northrop Frye.

The Secular Messiahs

Massey Lectures, 1974 | GEORGE STEINER

George Steiner was born in 1929 in Paris. After studying in France, the United States, and England, he became an editor at The Economist. *He has taught at Princeton, Oxford, Harvard, the University of Geneva, and Cambridge University. Steiner has received honours and awards in the United States, France, Belgium, and England. Although he has written major works of fiction, translation, politics, and autobiography, he is best known in the field of comparative literature and literary criticism. "The Secular Messiahs," the first part of the fourteenth series of Massey Lectures, was delivered in the fall of 1974.*

GEORGE STEINER

The conjecture which I want to put forward in this lecture is a very simple one. Historians and sociologists agree — and after all we should sometimes believe them, too — that there has been a marked decline in the role played by formal religious systems, by the churches, in Western society.

The origins and causes of this decline can be variously dated and argued, and, of course, they have been. Some would locate them in the rise of scientific rationalism during the Renaissance. Others would assign them to the skepticism, to the explicit secularism, of the Enlightenment, with its ironies about superstition and all churches. Still others would maintain that it was Darwinism and modern technology during the industrial revolution which made systemic beliefs, systematic theology, and the ancient centrality of the churches so obsolete. But the phenomenon itself is agreed upon. Gradually, for these very complicated and diverse reasons, the Christian faiths (may I emphasize this plural) which had organized so much of the Western view of man's identity and of our function in the world, whose practices and symbolism had so deeply pervaded our daily lives from the end of the Roman and Hellenistic world onward, lost their hold over sensibility and over daily existence. To a greater or lesser degree, the religious core of the individual and of the community degenerated into social convention. They became a kind of courtesy, an occasional or perfunctory set of reflexes. For the very great majority of thinking men and women — even where church attendance continued — the life-springs of theology, of a transcendent and systematic doctrinal conviction, had dried up.

This desiccation, this drying-up, affecting as it did the very centre of Western moral and intellectual being, left an immense emptiness. Where there is a vacuum, new energies and surrogates arise. Unless I read the evidence wrongly, the political and philosophic history of the West during the past one hundred and fifty years can be understood as a series of attempts — more or less conscious, more or less systematic, more or less violent — to fill the central emptiness left by the erosion of theology. This vacancy, this darkness in the middle, was one [aspect] of "the death of God" (remember that Nietzsche's ironic, tragic tonality in using that famous phrase is so often misunderstood). But I think we could put it more accurately: the decay of a comprehensive Christian doctrine had left in disorder, or had left blank, essential perceptions of social justice, of the meaning of human history, of the relations between mind and body, of the place of knowledge in our moral conduct.

It is to these issues, on whose formulation and resolution society and individual life depend for coherence, that the great "antitheologies," the "meta-religions" of the nineteenth and twentieth centuries, address themselves. These are very awkward terms and

I apologize for them. "Meta-religion," "anti-theology," "surrogate creed" — they are awkward but also useful tags. Let me try and pull them together in this lecture by using a general term. I want to propose to you the word "mythology."

Now, in order to qualify for the status of a mythology, in the sense in which I am going to try and define it, a social, a psychological, or a spiritual doctrine or body of thought must fulfill certain conditions. Let's have a look at these. The body of thought must make a claim of totality. That sounds very simple-minded, and in a way it is. Let me try and sharpen the idea. What do we mean by its being total? It must affirm that the analysis which it puts forward of the human condition — of our history, of the meaning of your life and mine, of our further expectations — is a total analysis. A mythology, in this sense, is a complete picture of "man in the world."

This criterion of totality has a very important consequence. It allows, it invites, if the mythology is an honest and serious one, disproof or falsification. A total system, a total explanation, falls down when and where a substantive exception, a really powerful counter-example, can be produced. It is no use trying to patch up a little corner here or adding a bit of glue or string there. The construct collapses unless it is a whole. If any of the central mysteries, sacramental mysteries, of Christianity or of the life of Christ or his message were to be totally disproved, it would be no good trying to do a quick repair job on one corner of the structure.

Secondly, a mythology, in the sense in which I am using the word, will have certain very easily recognizable forms of beginning and development. There will have been a moment of crucial revelation or diagnostic insight from which the entire system springs. This moment and the history of the founding prophetic vision will be preserved in a series of canonic texts. Those of you who are interested in the Mormon movement will easily recognize my image: an angel appearing to the founder of the whole movement and handing to him the famous golden plates, or the Mosaic law. There will be an original group of disciples who are in immediate contact with the master, with the founder's genius. Soon some of these disciples will break away into heresy. They will produce rival mythologies or sub-mythologies. And now watch something very important. The orthodox in the great movement will hate such heretics, will pursue them with an enmity more violent than that which they vent on the unbeliever. It's not the unbeliever they're afraid of — it's the heretic from within their own movement.

The third criterion of a true mythology is the hardest to define. A true mythology will develop its own language, its own characteristic idiom, its own set of emblematic images, flags, metaphors, dramatic scenarios. It will breed its own body of myths. It pictures the world in terms of certain cardinal gestures, rituals, and symbols. As we proceed, I hope this will become entirely clear.

Now consider these attributes: totality, by which I simply mean the claim to explain everything; canonic texts delivered by the founding genius; orthodoxy against heresy; crucial metaphors, gestures, and symbols. Surely the point I am making is already obvious to you. The major mythologies constructed in the West since the early nineteenth century are not only attempts to fill the emptiness left by the decay of Christian theology and Christian dogma. They are themselves a kind of *substitute theology.* They are systems of belief and argument which may be savagely anti-religious, which may postulate a world without God and may deny an afterlife, but whose structure, whose aspirations, whose claims on the believer are profoundly religious in strategy and in effect. In other words, when we consider Marxism, when we look at the Freudian or Jungian diagnoses of consciousness, when we look at the account of man offered by what is called structural anthropology, when we examine all these from the point of view of mythology, we shall see them as total, as canonically organized, as symbolic images of the meaning of man and of reality. And when we think about them we will recognize in them, not only negations of traditional religion (because each of them is saying to us, look, we don't need the old church any more — away with dogma, away with theology), but systems which at every decisive point show the marks of a theological past.

Allow me to underline this. It is really the centre of what I'm trying to say, and I hope it is quite clear. Those great movements, those great gestures of imagination, which have tried to replace religion in the West, and Christianity in particular, are very much like the churches, like the theology, they want to replace. And perhaps we would say that in any great struggle one begins to become like one's opponent.

This is only one way, of course, of thinking of the great philosophic, political, anthropological movements which now dominate so much of our personal climate. The convinced Marxist, the practising psychoanalyst, the structural anthropologist will be outraged at the thought that his beliefs, that his analyses of the human situation, are mythologies and allegoric constructs directly derivative from the religious world-image which he has sought to replace. He will be furious at that idea. And his rage has its justification.

I have neither the wish nor the competence to offer technical observations, for example, on the Marxist theory of surplus value, on the Freudian account of the libido or the id, on the intricate logistics of kinship and linguistic structure in Lévi-Strauss's anthropology. All I hope to do is to draw your attention to certain powerful, recurrent features and gestures in all these "scientific" theories. I want to suggest to you that these features directly reflect the conditions left by the decline of religion and by a deep-seated nostalgia for the absolute. That nostalgia — so profound, I think, in most of us — was directly provoked by the decline of Western man and society, of the ancient and magnificent architecture of religious certitude. Like never before, today at this point in the twentieth century, we hunger for myths, for total explanation: we are starving for guaranteed prophecy.

The mythological scenario in Marxism is not only expressly dramatic, but is also representative of the great current of thought and feeling in Europe which we call romanticism. Like other constructs of social utopia, of secular, messianic salvation, which follow on the French revolution, Marxism can be expressed in terms of historical epic. It tells of the progress of man from enslavement to the future realm of perfect justice. Like so much of romantic art, music, and literature, Marxism translates the theological doctrine of the fall of man, of original sin, and of ultimate redemption into historical, social terms.

Marx himself suggests an identification of his own role with that of Prometheus. Isn't it interesting, and in a way unsurprising, that when Marx was a young man, the last thing he was planning to do was to write a major critique of political economy? Rather, he was working on an epic poem about Prometheus. And you can guess how the later scenario works. Bearing the destructive but also cleansing fire of truth, i.e., the materialist-dialectical understanding of the economic and social force of history, Prometheus/Marx will lead enslaved humanity to the new dawn of freedom. Man was once innocent, he was free of exploitation. Through what dark error, through what sombre felony did he fall from this state of grace?

This is the first of our theoretic problems, and it its one of extreme difficulty. In each of the great mythologies or substitute religions we are looking at together, the nature of the original sin remains obscure or problematic. How did slavery arise? What are the origins of the class system? Marx's answer remains peculiarly opaque. Perhaps I can explain why. Like almost every post-romantic, particularly German, he was obsessed with the magnificence of ancient Greece. He regarded the ancient Greek culture as the crown of man — artistically, philosophically, poetically, even in some ways politically. He knew full well about slavery and about the primitive development of Greek economy. So how could he reconcile his belief in the economic conditions of human well-being with what he knew of ancient Greek history? The answer is that he was too honest to lie about it and he never reconciled them. With one breath he speaks of the total excellence and eternal supremacy of ancient Greece, and with the next breath he tells us that the whole of human history is a great march forward into freedom and progress. We know from Marx that it is only with feudalism, and with the evolution of feudalism into mercantilism and, later, capitalism, that his epic diagnosis becomes confident. But the early writings, the famous 1844 manuscripts, show how explicitly theological was his image of the lost condition of man's innocence. I want to quote here, because unless one goes back to these profoundly moving pages, it is difficult to believe that we are listening to Marx and not, for example, to Isaiah. He's describing what this kingdom of innocence, this garden of perfect justice was like: "Assume," says Marx, "assume man to be man and his relationship to the world to be a human one. Then you can exchange love for love. Then you can exchange trust only for trust." This is a fantastic vision of the proper state of human society. Instead, says Marx, man carries about on his very mind and body the lasting emblem of his fallen state. And what is that emblem? It is the fact that man is exchanging money instead of love for love and trust for trust. I quote again: "Money is the alienated ability — or perhaps I should translate genius or capacity — of mankind." Money is the alienated "mankindness" of man — a dreadful condemnation when we think of the earlier vision of true innocence.

Now this sense of a distant catastrophe, of a cosmic disgrace — and may I put a hyphen in the word, a dis-grace, a falling from grace — comes through to us with vivid terror in the Marxist vision, as it does in Coleridge, in the "Ancient Mariner," or in Wagner's "Ring." Press more closely for definition, for historic location. Ask where did this horrible thing happen? What did we do wrong? Why have we been thrown out of the Garden of Eden? I don't think you really get a good answer. No less than Rousseau, Blake, or Wordsworth, Marx adopts almost unconsciously the romantic axiom of a lost childhood of man. Turning to the wonders of the Greek poets whom he loved so much; turning, as we have seen, though perhaps unconsciously, to the language of the prophets, Marx speaks, and I quote again, of "the social childhood of mankind where mankind unfolds in complete beauty." And when we ask again, with mounting impatience, What is the fall of man? What sin did we commit?, Marxism does not really reply.

But there can be no doubt about the visionary messianic character of what it says about the future. If it does not answer our burning question about the original catastrophe, it is only too eager to tell us everything about the day after tomorrow, about the withering away of the state, and of mankind's blessed existence in a world without class, without economic oppression, without poverty, and without war. It is in the name of this promise that generations of radical and revolutionary idealists have sacrificed their lives. It is to bring about this Edenic consummation — I do want to use the word Edenic because I think it's the only right one — of man's historical destiny, that untold suffering has been visited on dissenters, heretics, saboteurs. It is because even the most brutal totalitarianism could be construed as a necessary stage of transition between class conflict and utopia that rational men and women were prepared to serve Stalinism.

One would like to pause here and give considerable detail, because this is surely one of the clues to the mystery of why it should be that many of the most valuable young men and women in past generations, in the face of the most overwhelming evidence about the concentration camps, about perhaps the most brutal police state ever established, about the Asiatic Caesarism of Stalin, nevertheless continued to serve, to believe, and to die. If one wishes to understand the phenomenon of this kind of behaviour, it can only be in the light of a religious and messianic vision, of the great promise which says you shall wade through hell up to your eyeballs if necessary because you are on the destined, the prophetic way to the resurrection of man in the kingdom of justice. It is just because the millenarian scenario of the redemption of man and of the establishment of the kingdom of justice on earth continues to grip the human spirit (having long survived its theological premises) that every experiment in hope fires the imagination far beyond the political facts. What do I mean by experiments in hope? All of us have our own list. When I think of my own students in Cambridge in England, I have a calendar of the great moments of inner hope for them — the Prague spring before the Dubcek regime was crushed by Soviet counteraction; Chile and the Allende government; the seeming miracle of the overthrow of reaction in Portugal and in Greece. The facts are never a counter-argument. If we were to open our newspaper tomorrow morning and hear that the Portuguese coup had been a fraud, or that it was really financed by sinister forces of the right, or that it was being overthrown, there would be grief and bitterness. But then hope would find another scenario, because we are dealing with a religious, with a theological force.

I think we recognize in the history of Marxism each of the attributes which we cited as characteristic of a mythology in the full theological mould. We have the vision of the prophet and the canonic texts which are bequeathed to the faithful by the most important apostle. Witness the whole relation between Marx and Engels; the posthumous completion of the *Kapital*; the gradual publication of the early sacred texts. We find a history of ferocious conflict between the orthodox heirs to the master and the heretics, an unbroken family of fission from the time of the Mensheviks to Trotsky and now to Mao. Each time (and this is the theological scenario), a new group of heretics breaks away; and it always says, look, we have the real message of the master; listen to us, the sacred texts have been corrupted, the Gospel is in our keeping; don't listen to the church at the centre. How familiar all this is to students of the history of Christianity. Marxism has its legends, it has its iconography, by which I mean the standard pictures of Lenin, the whole history of Lenin's life in millions of stories, tales, operas, films — even ballet. Marxism has its vocabulary. Marxism has its emblems, its symbolic gestures, just like any transcendent religious faith. It says to the believer, I want from you a total commitment. I want from you a total investment of conscience and person into my keeping. And in exchange, as does a great theology, it offers a complete explanation of man's function in biological and in social reality. Above all, it offers a contract of messianic promise concerning the future.

Personally, I must express the belief — perhaps I could put it more strongly and sadly — I must express the conviction that both the Marxist explanation of the human condition and its promise as to our future state have been illusory. The Marxist analysis of history has shown itself to be one-sided and often grossly in violation of evidence. Crucial Marxist predictions have simply been unfulfilled, and I don't think one needs to be a technical or professional economist to know how wildly wrong Marxism has been about, for example, the pauperization of the working class or the prophecy made over and over again of the imminent cataclysmic collapse of capitalism. Remember the endless prophecies of the early Christians about the coming end of the real world, first in the year 1000, then in the year 1666. Today one hears of extremist sects in the mountains of California looking at their mystical calendar. Over and over we find this mechanism of saying, look, we know the end is almost in sight and that the new Jerusalem will descend upon us from the heavens.

Marxism, too, has predicted over and over the apocalypse of its enemies and the coming of the classless, perfect society. So on grounds
of prophecy as well as on grounds of history, it has failed. Worse,
where it is in power it has not brought liberation but bureaucratic
terror. Already the Marxist program for mankind is beginning to
assume aspects of historical decay. Already we are beginning to look
back at the great house of belief and conviction, starting up in the
mid-nineteenth century, changing our world, of course — as do these
great religious mythologies — but being eroded itself and crumbling
at many of its vital points. Marxism, too, is beginning to look today
like one of the great, empty churches.

But let us not deceive ourselves as to the tragic and pervasive
force of this failure, if failure indeed it be. What was at stake was
no mere technical critique of certain economic institutions; it is not
over theoretical questions of investment, division of labour, or trade
cycles that generations of men and women fought, died, and killed
others. The vision, the promise, the summons to total dedication
and a renewal of man were, in the full sense, messianic, religious,
theological. Or to borrow the title of a celebrated book, it is "a God
who failed."

"The Secular Messiahs" was broadcast on November 4, 1974.

Dictatorships and Democracies

RONALD WINTROBE

It has been said that, in a dictatorship, everything that's not forbidden is compulsory, and as for democracies, Winston Churchill said, "Democracy is the worst possible political system, except for all the others." There is a little bit more to it than that. Ronald Wintrobe is professor of economics at the University of Western Ontario. His work is mostly about political and bureaucratic behaviour from an economic point of view, and he is the author of The Political Economy of Dictatorships.

RONALD WINTROBE

Much of the world still lives today, as always, under dictatorship, but we know very little about a lot of these regimes. How much do we really know about how Saddam Hussein's Iraq functions? How much do we know about Mobutu's Zaire? How much do we know about Deng Xiaoping's China? We don't know very much about these regimes, partly because they're closed and information on what's happening there is hard to get, partly because dictatorship is so disliked and feared.

And so most research in politics has been about how they arise, with the view that, once we understand how dictatorships arise, we can prevent further instances. But there's not much research that takes a general point of view on how they behave. What research has been done along that line typically uses the idea that dictatorships operate by command: policies are decided at the top, by the dictator and a small group of his advisers, and then they're imposed on a hapless population. The population acquiesces through fear of the dictator's repressive apparatus or through brainwashing, thought control and indoctrination. These techniques are either not successful, in which case they don't explain how these regimes survive when they do survive, or, if they are successful — techniques of brainwashing and indoctrination — they're not well understood by social science. And so there is little evidence for the point of view that says dictatorships operate this way, and it is not as illuminating as it might be.

I'm an economist by profession. Economists tend to use, as a working assumption, the idea that people are rational, that they're more or less selfish and that they're competitive. By rational, I just mean that, whatever their goals are, they try to achieve them as best they can, and they're always alert to opportunities to achieve them a little better. Well, today I want to see how far we can get, using these same assumptions about people and using those assumptions about both the ruler and the people under his rule, in understanding dictatorship. I'll try to understand a little bit about how they work politically, a little bit about their economies, and what kind of policies we should adopt towards dictatorships. My primary purpose is to understand dictatorship, but I think this way of thinking also sheds a little bit of light on the workings of democracy.

A good place to start is to have some sympathy for the dictator and for his position. I define a dictatorship simply as a regime where the ruler is self-appointed and there is no legal procedure for removing him. Someone who rules under circumstances like that, where there is no procedure by which he can be removed, obviously has enormous power over his subjects — much more than a democratic ruler does. This makes the population afraid of him, and they're afraid to criticize him or his policies. But the fact that the population is afraid of him, in turn, breeds fear on his part towards the population, because he has no idea what they're thinking and planning, and he suspects that what they are thinking and planning is his assassination. So the more the ruler rules by repression and the more his repressive apparatus stifles dissent and criticism, the less he knows how much support he has among the population, and the more reason he has to be afraid.

Here's an example: it's a confidential dispatch from his secret service to Mobutu, the ruler of Zaire. Around the time that this dispatch was sent, roads under Mobutu's regime had deteriorated to about sixty per cent of what they were when the Belgians left; gross national product had fallen by thirty per cent, as Mobutu was looting the regime. Naturally he wanted to know what was going on in the hinterland, and so he had a secret service, which was the direct inheritor of the Belgian secret service, report to him and give him confidential information as to what was happening. And this is a direct quote from one of the dispatches: "The situation is calm. All the people work in joy, doubling their energies, thanks to the generosity of your regime." Now, did this make Mobutu feel more secure or less?

Jon Elster, the political philosopher, talks about this problem. He calls it the "Hegelian master-slave dialectic." The master can't simultaneously enjoy his absolute power and draw satisfaction from the recognition that the slave offers him. The problem has been known since ancient times. And there's a dialogue — apparently the only ancient dialogue written on the subject of tyranny — by Xenophon, called "Hiero" or "Tyrannicus," in which the tyrant complains about his life to Simonides, a sympathetic poet, who was also an economist. And the tyrant complains bitterly. He says he has no friends; everyone says he or she is his friend, but are they, really? His love life doesn't work out because, although many women want to sleep with him, he doesn't know why. He suspects it's because he's the tyrant. His life is governed by fear. He fears the crowd, he fears the men guarding him, and most of all, he fears his relatives.

Another way to see the point is to compare the dictator's situation to that of a democratic leader. The prime minister of Canada operates in a system where the press criticizes him every day; there are insulting cartoons printed about him on the editorial pages; an independent judiciary is free to rule his policies unconstitutional; opposition parties attack him daily during Question Period; and independent polls reveal just how popular or unpopular he is with the public. The dictator typically dispenses with all of these institutions, and because of that, he gains a freedom of action that's unknown to any democratic leader.

But there's a cost: he has no way of knowing how popular he really is or how successful his policies really are. So the Communist leaders in China only found out how unpopular collectivizing agriculture was when they abandoned it. The Chilean dictator Pinochet was supremely confident that he would win the 1988 plebiscite on his rule, and he was shocked when he lost. So the general proposition is that the typical dictator is less secure in office than a democratic leader and that the most likely personality characteristic of a dictator is paranoia. And many of the great dictators of human history have been consumed by this form of anxiety, including, apparently, Stalin and Mao Zedong.

So the implication, if dictators are rational, is that while all dictators rule by repression and use the instrument of the police and the courts to stamp out opposition to their regime — jailing, torturing and even executing people they think are opposed to them — successful dictators, ones who stay in office for a reasonable period of time, don't rule by repression alone. They also try to accumulate support or loyalty among the population, and especially among those groups who are powerful and who have some power to destabilize the regime. The simplest way to obtain the support or loyalty of a group is to overpay them, pay them more than they're worth. So military regimes gain the support of military personnel by paying them excessive wages. Dictatorships which are backed by workers gain their support by paying them wages in excess of what they would otherwise earn. So in South Africa, for example, by the practice known as "job reservation," the apartheid regime reserved certain classes of jobs for white workers, who, as a consequence, made much more than they ever would have had black workers been allowed to compete for those jobs, and, as a result, unskilled white workers were strong supporters of the apartheid regime.

The same principle works for every group in the population. You can obtain the support of capitalists by giving them monopoly privileges, which other rulers might not give them. You can obtain the support of particular regions by locating manufacturing facilities there, even when they really should be located somewhere else. You can obtain the support of ethnic groups by reserving special privileges for them. Of course, these practices are not unknown in democracy. In the United States, the word that was invented to describe them is "pork-barrel politics," and they're widely decried as a failure of democracy.

But if democracy sometimes appears to be a pork barrel, dictatorships are warehouses of pork, temples of pork. Typically you see only one side of this. In the former Soviet Union, the typical image of the regime was the empty stores that you saw everywhere, caused by the rationing and the fact that goods were always in short supply. There were always shortages in the Soviet Union. What you didn't see were the special shops where goods were reserved for people in the *nomenklatura*, the higher-ups, the people who were important in the regime and who had to be accommodated. One side of the picture you saw was that there's nothing for the average person to buy. The other side you didn't see was the special shops, the special system of hospitals and all the other privileges reserved for those whose loyalty was important. While there's always a class of people who are repressed under a dictatorship, there is also, in any successful regime, another class: the overpaid. As far as the people in the middle are concerned — and this is the sad part — they can side with either group. They can be made to side with the repressed if they feel that they themselves might become victims of the repression. They can also side with the overpaid if they feel the dictator's policies are going to be good for them.

And so even though most of the population loses certain civil liberties under a dictatorship, and even though they do not have the right to express and criticize the regime the way they would like, the fact that they are repressed does not mean that dictatorships are not popular. In fact, sometimes it appears that the more repressive the regimes were, the more popular they became! All the evidence we have indicates that Hitler was very popular. Communism's comeback in eastern Europe indicates how popular communism was at one time. When it became unpopular, the regimes fell.

Of course, some dictators are more popular than others — we don't want to say they're equally popular — and one key to how successful the regime is and how popular it can become is how the economy performs. Let's turn to this question of whether dictatorship is good for the economy or can be good for the economy. There's a lot of work which addresses this issue: which is better for the economy, democracy or dictatorship? One reason is that there's always some dictatorship or set of dictatorships that appears to perform better, economically speaking, than the democracies. In the 1930s, this threat, this authoritarian threat, came from Hitler's Germany and Stalin's Russia, and everyone wondered, was it possible for democracies to imitate the performance of societies like that? In our own time, there have been some enormous success stories among the dictatorships: Pinochet's Chile, South Korea under the generals and, most spectacularly, communist China.

But before you leap to the idea that dictatorships necessarily perform better than democracies do, remember there's a huge class of other regimes: Papa Doc's Haiti, Mobutu's Zaire, the last fifteen or twenty years of the former Soviet Union, when the regime's economic performance was very, very bad. And a quick glance around the economic systems of dictatorship immediately shows that there's very little that you can say in general about what the economic system looks like under a dictatorship. You have all kinds. Think of the regime in Haiti. Compare that to the regime in the former Soviet Union, compare that regime to the economy of South Korea or Pinochet's Chile, and you see that political dictatorship is compatible with all kinds of economic systems. And at that level, there are no generalizations about the dictator's economy. But there's one thing you can say if you compare dictatorships to democracy, which is that dictatorships are much more capable of decisive action than democracies are. Whether the action's good or bad, dictatorships are much more capable of it. If a dictator wants to raise taxes, if a dictator wants to go to war, if he wants to take tough measures against crime, he can do these things. He may face some opposition among his advisers, but in general he's free to do what he wants.

Democracies, on the other hand, are often mired in inaction. Democratic politicians are often afraid to act because essentially they feel there is no consensus in the society as to what they should be doing. As soon as they see that there's no consensus — there may be a consensus, for example, that something should be done, like there is about the deficit, but there's no consensus as to what should be done — under these circumstances, democratic politicians often prefer to do nothing. They don't want to take the risks of creating enemies among important groups in the population and losing their support, so they cloud their statements in ambiguity, they pretend to be on all sides of the issue, and they take very little in the way of decisive action. The result is that people often become cynical, and they lose trust in politicians. The more they do that, the more they make it even harder for politicians to act decisively in a democracy. And so it sometimes seems that, while there is freedom to speak in a democracy, very often no one is listening. The politicians do not act on the demands that are made on them constantly by the citizens.

I suggest that this inaction problem of democracy is the chief basis for what I like to call "the allure of dictatorship": the capacity of the dictator to take decisive action is what attracts people to the notion of dictatorship. The classic example is Weimar Germany, in the early 1930s. There was an enormous unemployment problem from the Depression, which hit Germany particularly hard, and there was a huge problem of political violence in the streets, on both the left and the right, and the politicians under Weimar didn't want to do anything to solve either of those problems. Hitler promised decisive action to curb political violence, and he also promised a job for every German.

Whether the actions of dictators are good for the economy or not depends partly on whose interests they serve — that is, whose loyalty the dictator is buying. Here you can get some odd results. The communists in the former Soviet Union took power in the name of the workers. They abolished private property in the means of production and promised to make the worker's life better than it ever could be under capitalism. Well, without markets, there was no way that the regime could find out what people wanted or really needed economically. By taking over the economy, in a sense, the dictatorship there created a dictator's dilemma on the side of the economy, as opposed to the polity. Without capitalists or their agents as managers, there was no solution to how to run enterprises, except, so it seems, the solution that was eventually adopted, which was to create a massive bureaucracy, operated by and under the control of the Communist Party.

Now, bureaucracies are not inherently inefficient: the Microsoft Corporation is a giant bureaucracy, by all accounts, and runs extremely well. But they have a central flaw, which is that if they're not shaken up periodically, they tend to ossify. This is what happens in private firms, and they need to be shaken up periodically via some sort of takeover. It happens in the bureaucracy of democratic governments, which need to be shaken up by the election of a new political party. The only instrument available under communism for this purpose was the party purge. And the party purge was used to shake up the bureaucracy most ruthlessly and infamously by Stalin. But the result of that process seemed to be that the process was only complete when those who did the purging were themselves purged, so the liquidators, under Stalin, eventually had to be liquidated themselves in order to complete the process. In the end, they were counted among its victims, something which is not uncommon in societies where there is no rule of law. This problem with the purge, this uncertainty as to what is going to happen once the process gets started, essentially was seen as the central problem under communism. After Stalin's death, there was no one around with the necessary ruthlessness and self-confidence to start this process going in a major way, and the system ossified until Gorbachev came along and tried to shake it up with *perestroika* and *glasnost*. In the end, the system collapsed.

For all these reasons, I see the future of labour-oriented dictators and labour-oriented dictatorships as a bit bleak. They face a
fundamental problem: if they're going to raise wages, then they're
going to make it unprofitable for people to invest in these regimes,
and they're going to get into all the difficulties — of who is going to
take the place of the investor — that communism did.

Capital-oriented dictatorships, on the other hand, have a reasonably bright future. The best example in the last few years is South
Korea. Under that system, money wages were kept low, workers were
given very few rights. The result was that investment was profitable,
and the injection of capital from investors raised the productivity
of labour. And the strange result was that, in the long run, regimes
run for the benefit of capital were highly beneficial to labour from
the economic point of view. So, over the fifteen years 1970 to 1986,
real wages in South Korea tripled. The system is bad for the workers
politically — it takes away their rights and it's inhumane. But from
the point of view of economics, it's been beneficial to them, and in
that sense, such regimes have some future.

Another interest group that dictatorship can operate for is the
military. Now, you might think, well, military regimes, should be
among the most stable and successful of dictatorships. After all, if
the military are good at one thing, it's got to be repression, and if
dictatorships are run by repression, then the military ought to be
the best at this kind of task. The funny thing is that military dictatorships tend to be short-lived. On average, they last less than three
years. They're unstable, and they often end most ignominiously by
handing over power to a civilian regime.

This seems odd. How can we explain this? There's a big literature
on this topic. Start with the idea that the military are self-interested.
Their main objective in taking over the regime is to raise the military budget and to raise the pay scale of the military. And we have
overwhelming evidence that this in fact is what military regimes do.
There's nothing odd about this. Capitalist dictatorships operate in
the interests of profits, labour-oriented dictatorships try to raise wages. So there's nothing odd about the fact that military regimes like to
raise the pay of the military. The funny thing is that when they raise

the pay of the military, since the way they rule is by repression, what they do is to raise the costs of the main instrument that they are using to govern. Suppose, for example, that the military regime doubles the pay of every military and police person in the regime. It now costs twice as much to repress the population as before, and so the regime loses its comparative advantage in governing. And once the rulers see this happening, once they've obtained the wage increases, then the rational thing to do is hand the regime over to civilians, having obtained suitable guarantees of immunity from prosecution and having obtained some guarantee that they will in fact keep their increases in wages and budgets. And so this is what you see.

The main purpose of all these regimes is economic, and they are run for a particular group. These are not the purest and the most dangerous form of dictatorship, which is essentially rule by a single individual, beholden to no interest group and not motivated by economic concerns. On theoretical grounds, it's easy to see why this is the most dangerous type: the smaller the number of people in the governing coalition, the less the need to compromise with anybody else on the objectives of the regime; and the smaller the number of people in the governing coalition, the more the people in that coalition will be willing to engage in actions that impose enormous costs on everyone else, simply because the smaller the number of people in the governing coalition, the more people there are out there to impose the costs of your policies upon. Of all the regimes you can think of, the most dangerous are those in which power is held by a single individual, possibly because he's charismatic, and in which that individual plays off different groups and is beholden to no particular group. These regimes are the most dangerous.

Well, thinking of the dangers of dictatorships brings us to the question: what should we do about them? That is, what policies should be followed by democratic regimes interested in promoting freedom? Obviously, this has been an important question in political science, and there was some very well-known work by Jeane Kirkpatrick, a political scientist who became ambassador to the United Nations under Ronald Reagan. Kirkpatrick's thought that the key to policy was that there were two kinds of dictatorships, what she called "traditional autocracies" and "totalitarian dictatorships." Totalitarian dictatorships are regimes like the Nazis or the communists, characterized by massive government intervention into the life of the society. Traditional autocracies, or what I will call "tin-pot" dictatorships, denoting their small-scale ambitions, are single-person regimes which really exist in office to collect the fruits of office — the Mercedes Benzes, the palace, the Swiss bank account and so forth — led by rulers like the Shah of Iran, Noriega of Panama, Ferdinand Marcos of the Philippines, regimes in which the main objective of the dictator is to collect money for himself, as much as possible.

Well, Kirkpatrick argued that there should be a double standard. She didn't like tin pots — her traditional autocracies — but there were two positive things about them. First of all, they were pro-US, on the whole. Second, while they were repressive, she felt they weren't nearly as repressive as communist regimes. And she felt that the US, in acting to destabilize, for example, the Shah of Iran or Somoza of Nicaragua, only resulted in destabilizing these autocrats, and the result was a much worse regime in terms of repression. And so, she argued, there should be a double standard: the US should not worry too much about repression under tin pots and concern itself mainly with fighting totalitarian regimes. Well, if you ask what her underlying model is, it seems clear the two regimes are differentiated mainly on the grounds of the level of repression. Traditional autocracies don't repress very much; totalitarian regimes are very repressive. And in this way of thinking, that's the only way of distinguishing them.

Now, in my way of thinking, dictators don't rule by oppression alone. They use two instruments to build power: repression and loyalty. You can translate her framework into mine by assuming that, under tin-pot regimes, the level of repression is low and so is the level of popularity. Totalitarian regimes tend to be both highly repressive and highly popular. Now, as soon as you do that, you see that there's another category that Kirkpatrick ignores, a category I call tyrannies — regimes where the level of repression is high but they're very unpopular. Political scientists who tried to test Kirkpatrick's theory found that many of the regimes that she labelled "traditional autocracies" and suggested were not very repressive turned out, on measures of repression, like the numbers jailed or the numbers tortured and so on, to be every bit as repressive as totalitarian regimes. And so the world didn't divide up neatly into the good dictators and the bad dictators the way she wanted.

What policies should be followed once this wider categorization of dictatorships is established? Let's suppose that we in the West, in the free countries, are only interested in reducing repression. The weapons in our arsenal are things like trade agreements, aid packages, sanctions and pressure to observe human rights. Now think about a typical tin-pot dictator like Ferdinand Marcos and ask: should we give aid to a person like that? Remember that a tin pot is a person whose only goal is to consume as much as possible. In Marcos's case, the main purpose of his consumption seemed to be to buy jewellery and shoes for his wife, Imelda. What limits his consumption? Well, the constraint is that he has to stay in power, so he can't spend so much money on jewellery and shoes for her that he actually runs the danger of losing office. But as long as he's secure in office, any extra money he gets he uses to buy shoes for her. So think of him that way. Should we give him aid? There are only two possibilities. In the first case, he is secure in office, and, according to his diary, which has been published in a book called *Delusions of a Dictator,* there was a point at which he felt that way. Well, if he's secure and we give him aid, he doesn't need to spend it on anything else, because he feels secure in office, so he takes all the aid money and buys some more shoes for Imelda. The aid has no effect on the level of repression under the regime; it just goes into his bank account. In that case there's obviously no point in giving him aid. On the other hand, suppose he's in danger of being deposed. Then, if you give him aid, he's going to use that money to repress the population in order to prevent being deposed, and the aid is counterproductive. So it seems that in neither of these cases would we want to give aid to a guy like Marcos.

On the other hand, suppose that the aid given is tied to a human rights constraint, and the package is that the constraint gets progressively tighter over time. We give him the aid, but we insist that, as time goes on, human rights improve steadily under the regime. If he wants the aid, in that case, he has some incentive to take the money and use it to promote the welfare of the people — let's say by promoting economic growth — because if he does that and the economy improves and the people support him more, then he can afford to relax repression, stay in office and still buy just as many, or perhaps more, shoes for Imelda as before. Thus the policy will work.

Now consider the other type of regime: totalitarian regimes or tyrannies. These rulers are uninterested in consumption. Stalin and Hitler weren't in power to live well. Their main interest in life was power. And let's suppose that, in these kinds of regimes, the leaders try and get as much power over the population as possible. Should we trade with them? Should we give them aid? Suppose we do. Suppose there is no human rights observance in the package, just a deal on trade of the kind that we've been making with communist China. Suppose that, as a result of the trade package or the aid package, economic growth under the system improves.

What that does is give the tyrant or the totalitarian an opportunity to accumulate more power by raising repression. He will grab this opportunity in the same way that a businessman who is already rich will grab an opportunity to make more money. These regimes like to have as much power as possible. If the economy improves, that removes the constraint on repressing the population; if they have more support, they can now afford to increase the level of repression higher than before, and this is what will happen. This is how I interpret what happened under Hitler or Stalin. The more popular they were, the more opportunities they took to put the screws to all those elements in the population whose absolute loyalty was uncertain. In the same way, enormous growth and even the introduction of free markets in communist China hasn't resulted in the slightest improvement in human rights there. In this case, the policy of trade with a totalitarian or a tyrant is actually counterproductive. If your goal is to lower the level of repression under the regime by trading with it or giving it aid, well, you've actually increased it.

Again, if you couple the aid or trade package with an insistence on human rights observances which get steadily more stringent over time, then the policy will work in the right direction. If the trade or aid is given and the economy improves, then in order to keep the trade agreement or keep receiving the aid, the regime knows it has to improve its human rights record. In these regimes, even more so than with tin pots, it is absolutely necessary that dealings should be coupled with an insistence on human rights observance if what you're after is to lower the level of repression under the regime.

One final point on policy. Sanctions are not just the opposite of aid or trade. There are a number of problems with sanctions that you don't have with aid or trade agreements. The first is the thing that we can see currently with the Helms-Burton Act — namely, unless everyone adheres to the sanctions, they just open up opportunities for businessmen who are not part of the sanctioning country to come in and pick up the business. Second, these sanctions can easily be perverse. They can stimulate nationalistic feelings in the country being sanctioned — it's an effect called the "rally-round-the-flag effect" — and in that sense tighten the regime's hold on its people. And finally, sanctions tend to isolate the regime from western influence, and in that sense they can also be perverse. Aid or trade agreements don't have any of these problems. And so I suggest that there is a single standard which can be used in dealing with any dictatorship. It is to trade with or aid them, provided the aid or trade is coupled with an emphasis on the observance of human rights under the regime.

Let me come just for a moment to one last issue, one last policy question. Who is responsible? After the dictatorship falls, who should be held responsible for the crimes against humanity committed by the regime? It's possible that more has been written on this subject than on any other. The general idea in a lot of what has been written is that dictatorship is ruled by orders. The people who tend to commit the crimes under the regime are people at the bottom. These people at the bottom only committed these crimes because they were ordered to do so by the people at the top. Consequently, no matter how heinous the crimes committed by the regime may be, it becomes very difficult to hold anyone in the regime except those at the top morally or criminally responsible for them, since everyone in the regime was just following orders. The classic analysis of this issue is that presented by Hannah Arendt in her famous book on the trial of Adolf Eichmann, which is called *Eichmann in Jerusalem*. Arendt's concepts, which have entered common parlance, of "bureaucracy as the rule of nobody" and "the banality of evil," are all based on a theory of how these regimes operate. The theory is the one I just outlined — namely, in these regimes, orders are given by people at the top, and the people at the bottom simply follow these orders. That is the way these regimes work, so it becomes hard to find anyone guilty. The same question has arisen repeatedly since then: who is responsible for the deeds committed by the Stasi in East Germany, and by secret police everywhere in eastern Europe and the former Soviet republics? Who should be prosecuted for the disappearances in Argentina or the killings in Chile? Should the government of the new majority in South Africa prosecute the perpetrators of government violence under apartheid? If so, is the defence "I only acted under orders" credible? In all these cases, the questions that arise here, the issues, are identical to those that arose in the Eichmann case.

It's worth dwelling a little bit on Eichmann because we know a lot about him by now. We know that he occupied desk 4B4 in the SS. He was chief of Jewish affairs under Hitler from 1933 to 1939. He organized the expulsion of Jews from Germany and Austria. After that he had the administrative responsibility for organizing their deportation to the concentration camps. Thus Eichmann was the transport coordinator of the "Final Solution to the Jewish Question." Arendt portrayed him as the perfect bureaucrat, and he presented himself that way at the trial. His defence was that he only acted under superior orders. At one point — apparently one of the climactic moments of the trial — he actually stepped out from behind the glass booth to defend himself with an organization chart. He said things like, "Officialese is my only language." He argued that he couldn't be held responsible for the executions because, while it is true that his office did deliver the victims, his office had no responsibility for delivering the gas to the camps. Therefore, how could he be responsible for what happened?

Did he really only follow orders? Is there any evidence for this in his case, or in the cases of Chile, Argentina or South Africa? So far as criminal behaviour is concerned, the kind of evidence that would support this defence is evidence that those who refused to take part in crimes against humanity were themselves subject to severe punishment: if you refused to engage in things like this, something terrible happened to you. There is not a shred of evidence like this in any of these cases.

I suggest that there's an alternative explanation of the willingness to take part in crimes like this, which has nothing to do with the command model, nothing to do with the idea that bureaucracies work by orders. The alternative explanation rests on two simple ideas. First, people are rational, they're normal, and most of the time they're looking out for their self-interest. Second, bureaucracies don't run on the basis of orders. Bureaucrats compete with each other. In any bureaucracy, like the University of Western Ontario, they compete with each other by being entrepreneurial and finding ways to do things which advance the goals of those people at the top. The more they do that, the more they get the privileges offered by the regime: promotions, extra perquisites and so on.

There's a lot of evidence that the Nazi bureaucracy was extremely competitive. Let's look at Eichmann just a bit. It's true, he had the office of chief of Jewish affairs in Berlin, but there was another chief of Jewish affairs in Munich. Other agencies also competed — in fact, there was fierce competition to handle parts of the Final Solution among the Foreign Office, the army commanders in the East, the higher SS and the police leaders. These people were always interfering, always trying to organize a piece of the Final Solution for themselves. And Eichmann is constantly complaining about their interference, their meddling, how they're trying to steal his business and so on. The reason they all competed so fiercely for a piece of the action in this case was simple: everyone knew that solving the Jewish Question was a top priority for the Nazi leadership. Anybody who showed entrepreneurship or cleverness or invented new ways of doing it could expect to do very well under the regime. If you look at Eichmann himself, he hatched all kinds of schemes. He initially got his promotion because he invented a system of forced emigration, which speeded up the process of deporting Jews in the early stages. That's what got him promoted to lieutenant-colonel. Later, he had wilder ideas, like establishing a Jewish state in Poland. He was a very entrepreneurial person. And so it's obvious he didn't just follow orders.

Was he guilty? Take two cases. Suppose that, instead of being employed by the SS, he had been self-employed — he had owned a transportation company. And rather than a title, a salary and prospects for promotion, which is what he had, he had been a private operator and had had the opportunity to bid against other private operators for a contract which would send millions of people to their death. The lowest bidder or the one who promised to kill the most people for a fixed sum would get the contract. The others wouldn't get the contract. They might get some other contract. But in any case, nothing would happen to them. Well, if that's the incentive, I suggest it's easy to find a person like that guilty. The other argument or the other possibility is this: suppose that a gun was held to Eichmann's head and possibly to the heads of members of his family, and he was told, "Either you engage in these activities or we'll execute you and your family." Then, in that case, I think, you might find it hard to find him guilty. But that case is no reflection on what went on in the Nazi regime, and I suggest it is no reflection on what happened in South Africa, in Chile or in eastern Europe, because bureaucracies just don't run that way. These people no more operated according to orders than the owner of a firm does when he responds to the "demands" of the marketplace in order to make money.

To conclude, let me emphasize that regimes like the Nazi one tend to bring out the worst in people, and to say that Eichmann could have been normal and rational doesn't mean that he's the same as everybody else. There is a self-selection process in a dictatorship where the worst tend to rise to the top. But the fact that bad people tend to rise to the top in these regimes doesn't mean they're not normal, doesn't mean they're not rational, and doesn't mean they're not responsible for what they do. I've tried to show in this lecture that making this general assumption about people — that they're rational, that they're normal — is a good way to understand dictatorship and provides a good guide to the kinds of policies we should adopt in dealing with these regimes.

"Dictatorships and Democracies" was broadcast on November 7, 1996.

Community and
Its Counterfeits

JOHN McKNIGHT
Moderated by
DAVID CAYLEY

To what extent should governments intervene in social problems? Contemporary western societies generally assume extensive government intervention. Demands for social services have come to exceed by far the capacities of public budgets, resulting in what is widely recognized as "the crisis of the welfare state." But the typical response has been a policy debate that focuses on setting ceilings or streamlining services. The fact that social services monopolize the definition of welfare is rarely questioned.

John McKnight has questioned that definition of welfare. He believes that, beyond a certain intensity, the professionalization of care, counsel, and consolation turns citizens into clients, and paid services degrade and often destroy abilities which already exist within the community. He has worked with communities and neighbourhoods throughout Canada and the United States, as well as directing the program in community studies at Northwestern University in suburban Chicago.

JOHN McKNIGHT

Culture, at least in the more traditional sense, is a set of learnings about how we as a people can persevere or survive in this place. Modern institutions are not about that question. They are new machines redefining us, not as a people in a place, but as individuals in a system.

I think one of the things that's happened in modern society is that we think more and more that institutions make people, that you will be trained, that out of the training and management of your life you will become who you are. I see very little discourse or consideration about the question: what is the gift of each person here? Is a gift something that is of your nature, rather than something that you develop out of your experience?

I often buy presents for Christmastime through catalogues, because I don't like to shop. And so I'll put these, as I buy them through the year, on a shelf. And a visitor who looked in the closet where I had all these things stacked up on the shelf said, "What's all this junk?" I said, "That's not junk, those are gifts." And the visitor, who's a very wise person, said to me, "Oh no, that's just junk. A gift isn't a gift till it's given."

My grandmother, I think, had a lot of influence on me, because one day — she was an Irish American — one day, probably when I was five or six years old, in her kitchen, she looked at me and said, "You know, you have a gift." And I said, "What?" I think maybe I thought she was going to give me a gift. And she said, "Blarney." And I think she was trying to tell me about a talent I had been given.

I was raised in a family of people who call themselves "Covenanters." There aren't many of them in the world — I think there are maybe three or four thousand in the United States, and in Northern Ireland and Scotland there may be five or six thousand more. They are the remnants of the formation of the Presbyterian Church in Scotland, back in the 1680s, but they were the extremists: they were the people who were unwilling to compromise with the British Crown. They made a covenant to resist the Crown and to say the head of their church was Jesus Christ and not the king. There were a bunch of compromises made by the other resisters or dissenters, but the Covenanters didn't compromise, and so they stood in rebellion and fought the English in some hopeless skirmishes; in Scotland you can see the little monuments to the places where the English descended on them in their prayer meetings and killed them all.

Finally they fled to Northern Ireland, and then some of them came to the United States. Those were the people who are my ancestors on my father's side and had a great influence, I think, on me. They were a saving remnant, the people of Zion. So we were raised with the view that there were three or four thousand people in the United States who knew the truth; then there were the others.

And by the time I left my family I think I was pretty well convinced that the institutions of society were not something that were to be honoured, were to be respected, were going to guide anybody in the right direction; it was from our community and our families and our faith that our guidance would come.

The first thing that struck me when I went to university — I went to Northwestern University — the first day the thing that struck me was, learning from a person who I just happened to be given as a roommate, that the university had a discriminatory policy that would let in only black people who were athletes, and it had a quota on the number of Jewish people they would admit. And the motto of this university is: "Whatsoever things are true, think on these things." So I come to this institution that has this motto on its lintel and find that it is just systematically denying the gifts of people who are black or who are Jewish. That confirmed, right off, what I had been told was the truth. And so I think that's probably the beginning of a story.

DAVID CAYLEY

John McKnight's story, as it unfolded, was about community organizing, first at Northwestern as a student and then, after three years in the Navy, with the Chicago Commission on Human Relations, the city's first civil rights organization. Later he would work for the American Civil Liberties Union, the Kennedy administration's pioneering Equal Employment Opportunity Office, and the US Commission on Civil Rights, as its midwestern director. Then, at the end of the sixties, he found himself unexpectedly transplanted to academia.

JOHN McKNIGHT

Northwestern University received a major grant from the Ford Foundation to start an urban centre in 1969. As the centre cities were burning across the United States, the Ford Foundation gave money to universities to try to give them an incentive to apply their knowledge, expertise, to the solution of city problems. They gave money to a lot of universities, and Northwestern was one of them. An old friend of mine was the person who was to create this new centre with this Ford Foundation money. It allowed him to bring a lot of faculty members in, but he thought there should be at least one person with real-world experience, in terms of the realities of cities and their lives. He had been a professor of mine when I was an undergraduate, and I had kept in touch with him all these years, so in a very unusual move they came to me with my bachelor's degree and said, would you come to this centre and we'll make you a professor, a full professor. And so I was made a tenured professor at the university by a stroke of the pen, and I've been there ever since.

But it was very clear that my purpose in being there was to be the connection between the demands and realities of the city and its life and the university and its resources. That has been a very happy fit for me because I don't think my background would allow me to be a full-time traditional academic.

And then as time passed I began to develop a little clarity on my own part as to a particular kind of focus that I might have, other than being the connector, and that focus evolved into what we now call the Program in Community Studies. It is an effort to understand how local communities solve problems. And I think that's pretty much what we've come to be known for.

DAVID CAYLEY

How would you define the word *community?*

JOHN McKNIGHT

You know, if you go to a sociology department and you ask that question of the faculty, you'll never leave. But my experience is, put in academic terms, applied, so that when you ask me the question, what is the community?, I probably hear "where is it?," and there the answer is: in your mind. And in the mind of every other person in Canada it's a different place. To some people it's a feeling, to some people it's relationships, to some people it's a place, to some people it's an institution.

So, while that word is used a lot, it is certainly not very functional if what you're trying to do is to think about anything that is applied and manifest. So I've had to come to creating a definition of community that is useful for our purposes, and that community is the space where citizens prevail.

DAVID CAYLEY

John McKnight found what he considered to be the most pertinent description of this space in the writings of Alexis de Tocqueville. De Tocqueville was a young French aristocrat who visited the United States in 1831 and 1832, journeying as far west as Green Bay, Wisconsin, and as far south as New Orleans. He noted on his travels how the young republic differed from the Old World and then, on his return to France, set down his impressions.

JOHN McKNIGHT

That book, *Democracy in America*, is, I think, the most useful book I know to help understand who we are. And he says, if I can summarize him in a rather gross form, that he came here and he found a society whose definitions and solutions were not created by nobility, by professionals, by experts or managers, but by what he identified as little groups of people, self-appointed, common men and women who came together and took three powers: the power to decide there was a problem, the power to decide how to solve the problem — that is, the expert's power — and then the power to solve the problem. These little groups of people weren't elected and they weren't appointed and they were everyplace, and they were, he said, the heart of the new society — they were the American community as distinct from the European community. And he named these little groups "associations." Association is the collective for citizens, an association of citizens. And so we think of our community as being the social space in which citizens in association do the work of problem-solving, celebration, consolation, and creation — that community, that space, in contrast to the space of the system with the box at the top and lots of little boxes at the bottom. And I think it is still the case that the hope for our time is in those associations.

DAVID CAYLEY

Associations, in de Tocqueville's view, expressed the spontaneous and voluntary character of the new society, the way in which Americans, without common traditions, could still make common cause. And this is what John McKnight wants to underline in de Tocqueville's account: the idea of a social space in continuous creation by its citizens, who claim, by the very fact of their citizenship, authority and responsibility in this space. And where such a space exists, McKnight says, associations will naturally tend to proliferate according to the gifts of the citizens.

JOHN McKNIGHT

The best community — it will be imperfect, it can't be fixed beyond this — is one in which all kinds of methods create all kinds of situations in which each of us finds relationships where our gifts are recognized and magnified. In my hometown, the newspaper printed a list of associations that the editor knew about — this is a town that has thirteen hundred people — and the list is eighty-one, and I know there are a lot more than that.

Now, why are there so many of these little associations in such a little town? Well, I think the reason for that is that they keep proliferating until all the ways that we appreciate each other, almost the mathematical possibilities for clusters of appreciations, get uniquely magnified and celebrated in these kinds of groups. And I think that leads to rich and diverse communities that recognize the specialness of people and provide all kinds of ways for them to express their spirit and to find other people who give expression to the spirit in the same way.

DAVID CAYLEY

John McKnight defines community as the space in which citizens associate in their own individual and collective interests. He believes this space to be mainly threatened by institutionally defined social programs with the power to establish authoritative definitions of need. Needs are, in effect, the resources of the services sector of contemporary economies — what iron ore is to the steel industry, needs are to those who propose to meet them. A hundred years ago, ninety percent of those who worked produced tangible goods and only ten percent what economists call "services." Today the situation is nearly reversed: a declining minority is employed in industry and agriculture, while the majority produces services of some kind. The perverse consequence, according to John McKnight, is that for this new economy to grow, problems must proliferate.

JOHN McKNIGHT

We have now, in a funny way, an architecture of industrial systems that manufactures and delivers services so that people can be paid for doing work that isn't goods-producing. So we're involved in, actually, a humorous but tragic kind of never-ending search for new needs in people, because systems that grow have to find new needs and impute them to people, and the problem with that is it is always at the cost of diminished citizenship. So that as these systems of service colonize your life and my life — saying that we are bundles of needs and there are institutionalized services there to meet the needs to make us whole, to make us real — what we become is less and less powerful. Our capacity as citizens and our gifts get lost and forgotten, so that there is, I believe, a relentless struggle between associational ways and system ways, and what we have seen in our time is the ascendance of systems over associations.

DAVID CAYLEY

Making the damage which follows from this ascendance visible has been one of John McKnight's central preoccupations. In the summer of 1989, in the American journal *Social Policy*, he published an article called "Do No Harm," in which he tried to establish the seemingly simple but utterly disregarded principle that social interventions have side effects. For this purpose he borrowed from medicine the idea of iatrogenesis — literally, physician-caused harm.

JOHN McKNIGHT

The idea of iatrogenesis is long established in medicine. In fact, there's a famous piece of lore in medicine that it was some time around 1910 or 1911 that medical skills developed to the place where it was more likely that a doctor would help you than hurt you if you showed up at a doctor's office. Prior to that time, the odds were that you were going to be worse off rather than better off. This is even institutionalized in the famous drug manual, the *Physicians' Desk Reference* every doctor has, which lists all of the drugs and then shows with each all of its negative effects. There's always a cost associated with the benefit. In fact, the famous Eli Lilly, who founded a major drug company in the United States, started out creating patent medicine, and on the labels of all his medicines, back in the early days — this is the 1800s — it said, "A drug with no side effects is no drug at all."

This idea, which is so deeply embedded in the premier service, medicine, is almost non-existent in all of the other helping services. You won't find the idea that a social worker's help might hurt more than help, or that a psychologist's or a psychiatrist's interventions have a necessary negative side effect. Like Eli Lilly's drugs, like every drug we have today — there is no drug in the PDR that doesn't have negative side effects. If you go to the other helping professions and you ask, "Now tell me, if you intervene in the following way, what are the probable negative side effects of that?" you will find a blank look. If you go to universities that prepare people for these professions, and say, "What studies are there on the negative side effects of the interventions of these helping services, what do they show us are the negative effects?" you will find a blank look — a non-researched area. So we began to raise the question: what are the negative effects of what you're doing?

DAVID CAYLEY

John McKnight and his colleagues eventually concluded that there were four such effects that could be described as universal and inevitable. He recognized, of course, that there were infinitely more particular or local effects that might sometimes occur. But these four, he argued, would always occur.

JOHN McKNIGHT

The first is that into the person's being or life comes an intervention that focuses upon deficiencies rather than capacities, and there are all kinds of effects that flow from that that are negative. We know that if one surrounds any individual with messages and experiences that are always saying, "What's important about you is what's wrong with you," that will have a powerful, depressing, disillusioning, and degrading effect upon that person. If we say to a kid when he gets up every morning, "You know what? You're no damn good!" what will happen to the kid? So the first cost is the necessary degradation of the individual's self-concept by the messages of deficiency, wrongness, brokenness, and need that the helper brings.

The second negative side effect has to do with what happens to the community's economy and the individual's economy. Every time we decide on a service intervention we're making an economic decision. Every time, in fact, you decide to buy a service intervention you are *de facto* deciding not to buy something else, including income for people whose primary problem is lack of income.

So the second great iatrogenetic effect is that we have decided so often in favour of the service intervention that we have now taken the majority of all public investments in the poor and given it to non-poor people, who are called "servicers."

The third effect has to do with the fact that each time we say, in a local community — and it's especially true in a low-income community — we need more services, we need more agencies, we need more systems, we need more outreach, we are making a decision that the neighbourhood's indigenous associations, leadership, and capacities are inadequate to solve the problem — in that trade-off we are always diminishing the community's powers by investing in the system's powers.

The fourth negative effect has to do with the fact that it is possible that a particular intervention has more benefit than cost. However, because one intervention works does not mean that six other interventions, each of which independently might seem to work, will give you a seven-times-more-powerful intervention. In fact, the aggregation of these interventions may negate the positive benefits.

Now, we can understand that in a metaphorical sense. I live in a neighbourhood where there are some trees. But if you said to me or any of my neighbours, "Do you live in a forest?" we would say, "No, we don't live in a forest." "But you have trees." "Yes, but we don't live in a forest." A forest is a place where there are enough trees that *they* define the environment. We all know when we walk into a forest because what is growing in a forest is different than what is growing in my neighbourhood — the density of the trees creates a different ecology, there are different animals, so that the very same elm trees, if there are enough of them, will create a new world, a new environment, a new ecology.

So it is with services. You can have one service alone, but when you get enough services intervening in a person's life, you will create a forest of services. So aggregating services around people creates new environments that will guarantee deviant behaviour by the people who receive the services, even though any one of them may look justified in and of itself.

DAVID CAYLEY

These are the four harms which John McKnight considers to be structural, in-built effects of human service interventions: people will become known by their deficiencies, not their gifts; money will tend to be put at the discretion of those offering service, rather than of those defined as "in need"; active citizenship will retreat in the face of professional expertise; and services will aggregate to form total environments. These effects, McKnight believes, are so widely overlooked because of the compelling rationale for human services.

The good that human services claim to provide is care, and care is normally an expression of love. The result is that the underlying political and economic structure of services is hidden by what John McKnight once called "the mask of love," a mask which deceives the benefactors and the beneficiaries alike.

JOHN McKNIGHT

Good intention, I think, is the most dangerous explanation for an action that there is. We ought never, ever to think that, because somebody has good intentions, says they care, is doing something for a good motive, that is any indication *at all* that in fact what they do will be good for others, for themselves, or for society. Almost every crime, I think, in society that is a societal crime is done by people who had good intentions. The great, great tragedy of the service industry is the blindness, the mask it wears, the blinding mask it wears, because of its belief in its good intentions.

DAVID CAYLEY

One of the inevitable side effects which John McKnight assigns to social services is the replacement of community capacities. Knowledge vested in professionals disappears from communities; confidence withers in the face of professional mystique; eventually communities lose the vital functions which sustain them as communities. And this loss, John McKnight believes, extends right down to the level of the family.

JOHN McKNIGHT

Families are the primary associations in a society, and just as other associations are under assault by our systems, so families are just one more manifestation, I believe, of the same thing. And you can see it and I can see it and all of us can see it in our own lives. If you have a family, a group of people, intimate, closely bound to each other, and you ask of them: "What do they do? They are of the same blood, but why do they stay together, this little group?" Well, it is a good question. Why would they stay together if their health is in a doctor, their knowledge is in a teacher, their mental stability is in a psychiatrist, their conflict resolution is in a lawyer, their family conflict is in a social worker, their meals are in a McDonald's?

What is this thing called a family? What *does* it do? It really doesn't do anything. A family that is a collection of clients has no purpose other than procreation. Human social organizations persevere because they perform functions. There's always a motive, a reason, a cement, something that keeps those people together, and we have always said kinship keeps people together as a cement.

But I think we've radically overestimated the cement if it is nothing more than blood, because what we know is that blood was a primary way of identifying those for whom we would take mutual responsibility and those with whom we would be able to make a way and make a life. And now those people don't have these mutual functions. Nothing's left but the hopeful power of love or romance or care. I think relationships grow out of function, that ultimately love grows strong on the basis of people who have worked together, who have suffered together.

I think of my grandparents on my mother's side, my Irish American grandparents. I can hardly think of anybody that I knew who I thought loved each other more. I never saw them touch each other, but I never saw them apart from each other, and I never saw them doing anything but making a life, a way, a home, an enterprise together. They had so understood each other's gifts, they had so worked them together and magnified them and grown powerful together, and each day in that way their affection grew, that when I knew them as old people, the love was impenetrable, and divorce could never have cut its way through that bond.

DAVID CAYLEY

John McKnight explored the issue of how families and communities lose their vital functions when he gave the fourth annual E.F. Schumacher Lecture in 1984. He called his lecture "John Deere and the Bereavement Counsellor," and in it he considered the suggestive analogy between the two figures of his title. John Deere was the blacksmith from Grand Detour, Illinois, who in 1837 invented a new tool, a steel plough capable for the first time of busting tough prairie sod. With this new tool, the Great Plains were tamed for agriculture. But the settlers, as they moved westward, often left behind them deserts of depleted soil, which later arrivals had to learn to husband and regenerate.

Bereavement counselling, McKnight claimed, is a tool with comparable effects on the human ecology: it cuts into the weave of community life as surely as Deere's plough sheared the tangled grasses of the prairie, and it leaves behind a social desert.

JOHN McKNIGHT

How did communities deal with tragedy before bereavement counsellors and psychological therapists descended on us when a tragedy came? They came together and sat with each other, and they cried together, they held hands, they wept on each other's shoulders, they remembered stories of other suffering and told those stories to each other, they sang songs that had been a part of the memory of their people forever about tragedy and about the meaning of life in the face of tragedy, and they said the seven hundred prayers that they knew that called for God to help them through this time, this people, this people together, and they lit some incense, and they sat in silence, and then they got up and they had a man with a mask of the devil, and they danced with the devil and scorned and laughed at him, and then they came together and they had a great meal, and they laughed and they drank and they cried. And all of that was what we did.

But now we are "enriched" because instead of that we have a person with a master's degree in bereavement counselling from the University of Minnesota who can come to our home and sit with us and put inputs into us that will help us process our grief, like a sausage-making machine processes sausage. We are impoverished by that service if it ever replaces our prayers, our songs, our tears, our hands.

DAVID CAYLEY

But does it ever precisely replace them, or is there always a gap? I mean, a bereavement counsellor, had he or she appeared a generation earlier, would have met incredulity. We know how to grieve. The need must first appear plausible. The bereavement counsellor will say, "Yes, it's very well for you, McKnight, to vaporize about community and all the wonderful things that used to happen, but in fact, lonely, isolated people need my service."

JOHN McKNIGHT

Ah. And I can assure you you're correct. I actually had the honour of meeting the first master's-degree-certified bereavement counsellor in the United States of America. This is about fourteen years ago, and I met her at the University of Minnesota. And that was exactly what I was wondering. They think they're meeting a need. Where in Canada or the United States would I find anybody who, when asked the question, "Do you need a bereavement counsellor?" would say, "Yes"? They would not have heard of one, they wouldn't know what one did, and it might be hard to imagine.

So the bereavement counsellor I met had to figure out some place to begin the work of introducing this new service in a society that didn't really see a need, and exactly the people you're talking about are the people that the bereavement counsellor picked: "Oh, we understand *you've* got a family, it still functions, these relationships are there, but there are lonely widows in nursing homes who just lost their husbands and they have nobody; they need my service."

And I think the way the progression goes is: they find those people who are the most defenceless and un-understanding and underprivileged, and introduce their services there. And then they approach the institutions of society — the United Way, the government, or foundations — and say, "You should pay me to provide my bereavement services to this poor lonely widow." If they're successful in that, they get this institutionalized as a service.

Then they will build out from there, and they will say, "We have done studies that show how kinship grieving is all right, but there are seven stages of grief, and our studies show that the grief process in the strongest of kinship groups involved in the traditions of solace only reaches the first three stages of grief, but there are four later stages of grief that our research has discovered, and we meet those four stages of grief. You may not be underprivileged, and you may have a full family, and you may have a community that provides you solace and support, but our research shows that there are four additional stages of grief that will not be affected by this, and you've got that need. There's something wrong with you, David: you have four stages of unprocessed grief, and let me tell you, we have just got the government to agree in its social insurance to fund grief counselling, so not only can the community not deal with all of your grief and we can, but you're paying for it, and if you don't use it, you're just wasting your money. So call us in, David, because you need *us*."

And when you call a bereavement counsellor in, and your Aunt Mary calls to say, "David, I'd like to come over this afternoon," because she's a part of the solace of your community, you say, "Aunt Mary, I'd love to have you come over, but the bereavement counsellor is here. Could you come over this evening?" And Aunt Mary comes to know *the real truth,* which is: the real solace is the solace you pay for, and hers is just sort of a tawdry, shabby, second-rate thing. And that's right, because she has been replaced by a bereavement counsellor. And that's the way it works.

DAVID CAYLEY

John McKnight sees community and social service as bound in the relationship mathematicians call "inverse proportion": their sum is constant, so as one waxes, the other must wane. And he believes that where consolation or other social supports are absent, the question must always be, where is the community? Not, where is the bereavement counsellor? Justifying bereavement counselling on the basis that there is no consoling community, even though it may in some cases be true, will also ensure that no community regenerates. Consolation will warp towards a standard cultivated in graduate schools, and a professional grouping will appear with a vested interest in damping down or denying community capacities.

But though Aunt Mary and the bereavement counsellor may be

alternatives, it is clear that the consolation each offers is of a very different kind. Community responses to life's vicissitudes differ from institutional responses: they cannot be managed in the same way, nor can they be certified or guaranteed. Community responses rest on character and ingrained virtue, things which can vary, waver, and fail. This may be one of the reasons, John McKnight supposes, that communities have yielded before the utopian promise of a system that cares, and cares unfailingly to the highest professional standard. Regeneration of community, therefore, depends on our abandoning the fantasy that our highest hopes can be transformed into effective techniques. John McKnight calls it "the belief that people can be fixed."

JOHN McKNIGHT

There are all kinds of people called "developmentally disabled" — some people will label these folks as "mentally retarded" people — who are in institutions and group homes, who were born with a set of gifts and capacities and a set of limits. If you go and look at what's being done with a lot of these people, you will find forty-year-old people with whom professionals are working, and they're teaching them how to tie their shoes. And if you say, "How's he coming along?" "Well, he can't tie his shoes." "How long do you think people have been trying to teach him how to tie his shoes?" "Well, I've only been here four years and we, you know, we do this getting-ready-for-community-life practice here twice a week, so I don't know, but probably, with the people before me, maybe twenty years."

"Oh, twenty years teaching this man how to tie his shoes. But if he ever learns how to tie his shoes, then, am I correct," I say to the professional, "then he'll be ready for community life and he can come out with us in the community?" "Yeah, that and a few other things."

Now, that man will live in the womb of professionals until he dies; he'll never be born to the community, because they are going to fix somebody who is unfixable, and in the course of that deny his gifts to community. It's a *terrible* trade-off! But most people in the community probably believe that he needs to be fixed. Now, they believe he needs to be fixed because somebody came into the community and said they could fix him — because there was a time when nobody thought he needed to be fixed because nobody proposed to fix him. So in that sense the possibility of saying, "Yes, you never will be able to tie your shoes or read" is the door to community and the recognition of the gifts. All of community life is like that.

There is nothing that is fixable in perfection. I think it comes with human nature that we are not finally going to be fixed. And so I think I start with that premise, that to the degree that all of the society is committed to and invested in fixing people, it creates huge and increasingly burdensome and increasingly tyrannical institutions intervening in the lives of people, when what we needed was a community that saw their gifts and said, "Those gifts need to be given."

We have wonderful possibilities in society if we're willing to fail to be gods, if we give up the idea that we can create institutions and systems that will fix everything, that will be the modern gods, that will make us whole, make us real, make us all those things. That's when life will come alive and communities will grow: when we see the wonderful possibilities of failing to be God.

"Community and Its Counterfeits" was the first of a three-part series broadcast on January 3, 10 and 17, 1994.

The Public Good in Canada

MICHAEL BLISS

What is good for society at large? Until recently, most Canadians agreed that we ought to do and pay for certain things together — as benefits (not free but shared) of national, provincial and local citizenship. Things like elementary and secondary education, roads, libraries, clean water, policing, public radio, and that icon of Canadianness over the past four decades, medicare. How many businesses should we collectively be in? Or should almost everything be an individual matter with an individual price tag, rather than a collective or common or public concern?

University of Toronto professor Michael Bliss is one of Canada's best-known historians and the author of Right Honourable Men: The Descent of Canadian Politics from Macdonald to Mulroney. *Professor Bliss spoke at St. Francis Xavier University in Antigonish, Nova Scotia, at a conference on the public good, in honour of Senator Allan McEachen, for twenty-seven years a member of Parliament, whose cabinet portfolios included labour, health, external affairs and finance.*

MICHAEL BLISS

My job as a historian is to begin to look at where we've been and to study our country's concept of the public good, as it were, by looking through the rear-view mirror, which, as Marshall McLuhan once

said, is the way that on modern expressways you see what's coming
up on you.

What did we think of as the public good in the half-century after
World War II? How did we try to realize it? And, as we study the
rear-view mirror, how and how often did we go off the road?

At a conference celebrating the forty years in public life of Senator Allan McEachen we might begin by quoting the first sentence
that Mr. McEachen uttered in the House of Commons as the rook-
ie MP for Inverness-Richmond, Nova Scotia. He gave his maiden
speech on February 15, 1954, starting his career in Parliament with
these words: "Mr. Speaker, in rising to take part in this debate on
unemployment, I am conscious of the concern any degree of unemployment causes honourable members in the House and the people
of Canada generally."

MPs didn't use the phrase "right on" in those days, but *we* might,
for we all know how consistently Canadians have seen unemployment
to be an enemy of the public good in the last half of the twentieth
century. When Canada first developed national employment surveys
during the early 1930s, at the height of the Great Depression, they
revealed a ghastly situation, with more than twenty-five per cent of
the workforce looking for jobs. The Great Depression was as searing
for Canada as it was for the United States, and afterwards even the
loosest notion of the public good included the idea that there must
never be another period of such widespread unemployment and human suffering. Never again. Never again such hard times.

But weren't hard times — like winter, like storms on the ocean,
like layoffs at the plant — simply facts of life? There was a lot of
fatalism in the 1930s, especially by those people who saw the Depression as part of the business cycle — a downturn, a setback,
a glutting of markets that would end once the balance of supply
and demand was righted. Given time, the classical economists had
taught us, markets would always clear because of the self-adjustments
brought about by the invisible hands of economic self-interest. Intervene directly in the marketplace and you might create distortions
that would make things worse. In other words, you might interfere
with the economic good being promoted by the activities of the free

market. So, in this traditional world view, the best way to promote the public good was by a hands-off, *laissez-faire* policy. Roll with the punches, and eventually Old Man Depression would tire himself out and go away.

"I belong personally to the school of thought which affirms that, with our new understanding of the causes of depression, there will not occur in Canada in the future the kind of depression that afflicted us in the thirties," the member for Inverness-Richmond told the House of Commons in 1954. Allan McEachen announced that he was a Keynesian, and in his remarks he celebrated the revolution in economic thinking wrought by John Maynard Keynes and his disciples, who argued that free markets did not necessarily find equilibrium at full employment and that there existed "certain established and recognized measures by which assistance can be given to the economy in its momentum toward full employment."

The Keynesian revolution, which had arrived in Canada by the late 1930s and was spelled out clearly in the 1945 White Paper on Employment and Income, represented a profound commitment not to roll with the punches but instead to fight back, by using the visible hands of economic managers to prod, stimulate, and goad modern economies towards full employment. There would be no more closing of the eyes, no more *laissez-faire,* no more fatalism; the national government would now actively promote this basic public good.

In his maiden speech the Cape Breton MP also instanced the work of another British social theorist, Sir William Beveridge. You will remember that the Beveridge report to the Churchill government, delivered during the height of World War II, became the blueprint for the post-war completion of the British welfare state, a set of programs that provided cradle-to-grave security for all Britons as a right of citizenship.

The idea of security from extreme hardship as a public good, to be supported by the state, wasn't new in the 1940s, and it hadn't been invented by the Canadian CCF in the 1930s. It had in fact originated in the 1880s, in Bismarck's Germany. Great Britain was well on its way towards a welfare state by 1914. In the mid-1930s, Franklin D. Roosevelt's New Deal administration had put the United

States far ahead of Canada in its commitment to this version of the public good. The operation of the war economy became a very important model of the use of the visible hand of state power to deal with pressing national problems. No one believed that market forces could adjust quickly or equitably enough to support a total war effort. Between 1939 and 1945 the government of Canada, like that of most belligerents, implemented a thoroughgoing program of war socialism, involving controls on wages and prices, foreign exchange, imports and exports, rationing, progressive and at times confiscatory taxes, the allocation of labour, and ultimately conscription for overseas service.

Victory in 1945 seemed to vindicate the workings of our very active, very visible political hands (except perhaps in the matter of conscription). If we could use these policy tools to achieve the public good of defeating fascism in wartime, could we not also use them in peacetime to achieve other public goods, including victory over unemployment, poverty, and ill health? Could we not use the power of the state to build a better world for Canadians? There was little doubt then that the post-war era would see Canada catching up to other countries in the development of social programs. We were ahead of some of them in our commitment to full employment. So the agenda of Keynesian economic management on the one hand and the completion and expansion of the social safety net on the other meant that post-war Canadian governments would not be small and quiescent. Canadians, in their search for economic security, jobs, and prosperity would look to the public sector to advance the public good.

Those of you who are Liberals will excuse my suggestion that one of the best symbols of the new post-war consensus in Canada was not the action of any Liberal regime in Ottawa but came during the 1957 election campaign, when the Progressive Conservative leader, John Diefenbaker, attacked the St. Laurent government for increasing the universal old-age pension, which had been born in Canada in 1951, by only a measly six dollars a month. Now, previous Progressive Conservative leaders, such as Arthur Meaghan and George Drew, had been inclined to attack the very idea of state pensions as undermining the individual's or the family's responsibility to save for old age. That was the old left-right debate. But now in the 1950s, where social welfare was concerned, everyone was on the left. Far from debating the principles of social welfare, the major parties began trying to outbid one another to be the most generous champion of social benefits. In 1958 Mr. Diefenbaker promptly raised the old-age pension not by six dollars but by eight dollars per month.

With Keynesianism and the welfare state in place by the mid-1950s, a case could be made for suggesting that it was time to stop looking backward at the Great Depression, especially since post-war economic growth had been so spectacular and sustained. The 1950s in fact proved to be such a good decade that at the end of it another Canadian-born economist, John Kenneth Galbraith, gave our language a new descriptive phrase when he published one of the great economics bestsellers of all time, *The Affluent Society*. North America had broken through into historically unprecedented levels of productivity and private wealth. The state had its policies in place to fight unemployment and poverty on the macro level, and some could argue that happy days were at hand for the foreseeable future. But John Kenneth Galbraith wasn't quite in that camp. *The Affluent Society* contained a powerful critique of what Galbraith called "the social imbalance" economic growth was creating in North America because the satisfaction of private wants, in Galbraith's view, was not being matched by equal attention to public needs, except perhaps in the matter of US defence policy.

Galbraith wrote of "an atmosphere of private opulence and public squalor. By failing to exploit the opportunity to expand public production, we are missing opportunities for enjoyment which otherwise we might have. Presumably, a community can be as well rewarded by buying better schools or better parks as by buying bigger automobiles. It is scarcely sensible that we should satisfy our wants in private goods with reckless abundance, while in the case of public goods we practise extreme self-denial." Galbraith's concept of public goods was based on traditional notions of services that couldn't easily be purchased by the individual, often because they created external benefits for the whole community — access to parks, policing, scientific research, mass transportation, a clean environment. These seemed to be public goods that would have to be provided by government or not at all.

Galbraith's analysis was devoured avidly by Canadians, and especially avidly by Canadian liberals, who have surely provided Galbraith's greatest constituency over the past forty years. Already in Canada we had a tradition of the state providing public goods that the private sector was unwilling or unable to supply. These goods ranged from transcontinental rail service in the 1880s to low-cost electrical power in Ontario in the early 1900s, long-distance telephone service on the prairies, and transcontinental broadcasting and air service in the 1930s. By the 1950s the creation of a national television network had been accepted by Canadian politicians as a public good that fell into their bailiwick. So, with the creation of the Canada Council, did the promotion through subsidy of traditional cultural activities — theatre, ballet, opera, literature. And so did the promotion of higher education seem a government responsibility with the introduction of grants to universities. And by the early 1960s Lester Pearson was beginning to wonder whether in fact society had not entered into what he called "an age of grants."

Of course in the Canadian federation the provision of public goods and services is far from being the exclusive responsibility of the national government. The Constitution assigns primary responsibility for health, education, welfare, labour, highways, municipalities, and many other powers to the provinces. A major element of the wartime and post-war reconstitution of the federal system was aimed at creating a fiscal framework within which the provinces could better fill these traditional but by then rapidly expanding roles. By the end of the 1950s, with the baby-boom generation hitting the school system and private affluence increasing Canadians' expectations for better public services, all the provincial governments were increasing their spending, expanding their activities, and beginning to press Ottawa for yet more breathing space and tax revenue. After 1960, of course,

Quebec would take the lead in pressing for more leeway to provide public goods for its people.

There were always some conservative people who believed that the private marketplace did have the capacity to provide such allegedly public goods as education, hospital services, and culture. But social theorists of the Galbraithian persuasion, some brought up in the thirties, some schooled in agrarian dislike of big business — both of these were true of Galbraith — and others, such as Tom Kent, coming out of the British or European socialist tradition, had a deep suspicion of the private sector — indeed of capitalism itself. These theorists thought that market failure or market oppression was the norm under capitalism, that a free-market system could never generate much in the way of public goods, and that virtually all social or collective goods had to be provided by the state and funded through the tax system. Theirs was an agenda for the constant growth of government, at least as fast as the private sector was growing, in order to right deeply rooted social imbalances. Did social justice involve simply creating safety nets, or did it point towards serious redistribution of wealth, aimed at promoting greater equality of outcomes?

Canadians had always looked to a certain amount of government spending on public works as contributing to the public good because of the employment it created, and that has been especially true in the geographically or politically disadvantaged regions of the country. Westerners and Maritimers had traditionally argued that equalization of employment opportunities across the country was a public good to be promoted by the national government. From the 1920s the concept of Maritime Rights had included the view that there was something wrong when people in any region of Canada did not enjoy equal outcomes with regard to employment and income, and argued that it was a public good in a country like Canada for governments to target unequal or disadvantaged regions, such as Cape Breton and the coal areas of Nova Scotia, for special help.

In the 1950s, these ideas were as appealing to a politician from the depressed province of Saskatchewan as to one from Cape Breton, and again Liberals will generously recognize that the Diefenbaker government pioneered by putting in place the first major programs aimed at stimulating regional development and at equalization. The Pearson government inherited and expanded upon them, and by 1968, Pierre Elliott Trudeau talked about the hope of creating a just society in Canada. Here we are thirty years later, and doesn't it strike you as amazingly optimistic that a government of Canada in 1968 should have believed that it had a crack at creating what philosophers and statesmen and prophets had been contemplating from time immemorial? A just society! What optimism! What confidence! What *hubris*! Should we add, what folly?

Well, if folly it was, we can come to understand it by understanding the roots of optimism in the post-war golden age of active government. I've been playing on the most important overriding factor: a belief in visible hands, a belief in the possibility that the visible hands of planners, civil servants, politicians, and managers could do a better job of solving social problems than the invisible hands of Adam Smith's *Wealth of Nations* in the open marketplace.

In the twentieth century, the old nineteenth-century idea of progress, which had been largely market oriented, had given way to an even more optimistic notion of the possibility of progress through direct human action: taking charge, taking control, planning for the future, managing social change, even engineering social change. Socialists believed in the possibility of planning and reshaping society. So in fact did right-wing corporations. So — even especially — did the very optimistic masters of business administration in the United States, who were taking over control of the largest private organizations the world had ever seen and who claimed that with rational planning and management they could dominate and shape their markets virtually without limit. Remember that the most admired member of the very popular John F. Kennedy administration, next to the president himself, was the Harvard MBA and former president of the Ford Motor Company, Robert S. McNamara. McNamara was the leader of a group of whiz kids who were going to bring the chaos of the Pentagon under proper public control and would soon turn their efforts to calculating how to handle the job of reorganizing a relatively small, backward society on the other side of the Pacific.

Here in staid Canada we hardly thought of civil servants of the Clifford Clark, Mitchell Sharpe, or Michael Pitfield persuasion as whiz kids — better to dignify them as mandarins — and we certainly respected them. Indeed, a few jokes apart, we respected all of our civil servants in those years. In part thanks to the closing down of the private sector during the Depression and the war, the top civil servants really were among our very best and brightest. They did seem to know what they were doing, to have the capacity to plan rationally and accurately for the future, to oversee and regulate the chaotic private marketplace, to do the job of guiding and engineering social change.

If you doubt it, look at the record of achievement by the visible hands in Canada. Look at how successful the war policies of the government of Canada had been, even though they'd included running enormous budget deficits, implementing strict controls on the whole economy, subjecting Canadians to very high levels of taxation. Look at how successful post-war Canadian governments had been at keeping unemployment down, at giving out welfare benefits, at avoiding inflation, and at stimulating industries and the arts through the early subsidy policies. It all seemed to have worked: war-borne optimistic activism, the can-do attitude that came naturally to marines storming beaches and politicians running for public office.

Even if it didn't always work exactly as we'd expected here in Canada — well, there were always bound to be setbacks, glitches, miscalculations. Unlike the British or the Americans or even the Japanese, we had the immense good fortune of having the ultimate social policy safety net, which was the wonderful natural wealth of our country. In a world running short of some natural resources and destined to run short of the rest of them eventually, we had inherited — or somehow obtained from the native peoples — half a continent of minerals, wood, and every form of energy going. The spectacular natural wealth of Canada, so evident during the post-war boom from 1945 to 1973, would surely support any number of government programs aimed at advancing the public good. In a pinch we could always fall back on our latent wealth and the certainty of growth.

Well, how far could we go with optimism, a glowing track record, and the confidence that, no matter what happened, our resource base would never let us down? By the 1960s, we could take the welfare state a very long way, all the way into the state's undertaking to finance all our health care needs; we could go all the way into some of the provinces preparing to cover most of the costs of university education; all the way into talking about the idea of guaranteeing to all Canadians a reasonable annual income. Perhaps we would even abolish poverty once and for all.

As well, in our mood of national confidence, which perhaps peaked in centennial year, 1967, we could take the notion of controlling our future into new realms of protectionism; we could build new barriers to restrict the less wholesome impact of, say, the mighty economy and culture to the south; we could control foreign investment; we could limit cultural penetration; we could perhaps create a distinctively Canadian society, being a different kind of North American — perhaps North Americans who had a stronger sense of the role of the public sector in promoting the public good.

We were after all a people who had never rejected the Crown but had taken control of it and used its powers to promote the common weal. Our Canadian revolution was directed from the top down, not the bottom up. Perhaps that was the essence of what George Grant was writing about in the 1960s. And if you wouldn't buy that kind of rationale, at least in the face of American imperialism, we could probably put up enough cultural tariffs to guarantee our survival.

In every Canadian province in the 1960s, the combination of prosperity, heavy responsibilities, high public expectations, and optimism led to a vast expansion of government activities. In retrospect it's surely no surprise that the government of Quebec — under various administrations, and reflecting the same optimism about the capacities of government and social engineering that was driving the government of Canada — transformed the notion of province-building into one of nation-building. The frictions of the provinces, especially Quebec, with Ottawa are a side issue for my talk today, but we all know how often and how seriously in the past thirty years that alleged sideshow took over centre stage.

Still, even as we continue to argue in Canada about collectivities and their rights, including, of course, the obligations we have to Canada's First Nations, almost all of us have believed that the collective or the public good is primarily a route towards improving the lives of individuals. Why else do we want to become employed, wealthy, healthy, and educated if it is not to have more opportunities, more choices in life? And however much we disagree today about "Distinct Society," Quebec's right of self-determination, and the rest, there is in fact a fundamental comity in Canada to respect two official public languages and to tolerate, even to encourage, a multiplicity of private cultures.

In fact, expanding the sphere of the individual's freedom gradually became an explicit public good in post-war Canada, as we moved from dealing with economic and cultural policies to human rights issues themselves. I'll cite John Diefenbaker one more time — the eccentric old coot who prattled on about a bill of rights for Canadians, who put one through Parliament in 1960, and can fairly claim to have been the godfather of today's Charter of Rights and Freedoms, the most fundamental and popular constitutional innovation in Canada since Confederation. Despite the very deep roots of rights concerns and the obsessions of mavericks like Diefenbaker, most rights issues only began to flourish in the second generation of the post-war age, beginning in the 1960s with American civil-rights issues, quickly expanding to include aboriginal concerns here, the rights of women everywhere, problems of visible minorities, and, by the 1980s, gay rights.

Historians will forever debate the emergence of the Charter in 1981-1982. Did it flow naturally from the evolution of Canadian society, or was it imposed prematurely by another maverick politician riding an intense personal hobbyhorse? Whatever the answer, few Canadians — I suppose I should say outside of Quebec — would dispute the view that the public good in this country has been substantially codified in our charter of fundamental human rights. Most Canadians believe it would be in the public good to strengthen the Charter rather than weaken it.

Surely it is in the Charter rather than in, say, subsidies for cucumber plants in Newfoundland that we really begin to implement the ideal of the just society. And as people in this region of the country know all too well, many of the regional development policies of the last thirty years have had decidedly mixed results at best, and indeed have been failures in the minds of many. And today, of course, we now stand at a distance from the optimism of the golden post-war years, and we're starting to develop a critical sense of the gap between our aspirations and our achievements. If Allan MacEachen decided to begin a new career in Parliament and stand and be elected again, his maiden speech would probably be about unemployment and the problem of the coal industry in his riding, and there might be less optimism in 1996 than there was in 1954.

What went wrong? The post-war golden age ended, I think, with the energy crisis of the early 1970s and the beginnings of stagflation. In macroeconomic policy we found that Keynesianism wasn't the answer, or else we didn't know how to apply it; we found that our welfare state was becoming very expensive, perhaps unaffordable in its full universal dress; and we found that certain of our safety net programs, such as liberal unemployment insurance benefits, seemed to create baffling problems of dependency.

By the 1980s, the whole of government activities aimed at providing public goods was starting to come under scrutiny, not least from economists, who are now scrutinizing the workings of government as carefully and critically as governments had previously examined the private sector. Could it be that politicians and civil servants might be driven by self-interest rather than ideals of selfless service? The programs to subsidize public goods, such as the arts or advocacy groups — could they really have something to do with politicians' establishing patron-client relationships with special-interest groups? Was economic nationalism simply a rationale for a resurgence of old-fashioned protectionism? Did planners and social engineers actually have the capacity even to forecast the future, let alone change it? Did publicly owned companies work as effectively as privately owned companies? Were the visible hands of the bureaucrats and the politicians actually as nimble and responsive and self-correcting as the invisible forces of markets, even in the provision of public goods?

And here is what I think is my most important contribution to this debate. I want to argue that the surge of neo-conservative critiques of big government in the 1980s and the resurgence of interest in market solutions to economic and socio-political problems was partly driven by the profound social changes wrought by our post-war economic and social success. In particular, we're now starting to realize that the thrust to increase individual opportunities and individual freedoms, to create autonomous individuals has been very successful — *and* it's been accompanied by the strengthening of individuals' distrust of most of the organizations that have traditionally claimed roles in helping to organize their lives. The children of the post-war age — affluent, self-assertive, empowerment-seeking — began calling one organization after another into question: churches, corporations, marriage, the family, even political parties and government itself. It seems clear that Canadians of the twenty-first century wish to have control of their lives vested neither in the invisible hands of the marketplace nor in the visible hands of government, but in their own hands. This is having and will have profound implications.

Here in Canada there was another blow to our confidence: the shaking of our faith in the land itself. When natural resources prices collapsed in the 1980s, when the National Energy Program and other mega-projects were tossed into the dustbins of history, when ecologists told us that our northern lands were too fragile to support old-fashioned development, when governments began finding that there wasn't enough growth in the economy to generate the revenue to cover soaring deficits, it began to sink in that our ultimate social safety net, our natural wealth, might also be an illusion. Had we Canadians actually inherited the richest country in the world, a cornucopia of natural wealth, or had we inherited a barren, cold wasteland, its seas empty even of fish? We ask ourselves questions

like this as we drive around these areas of Nova Scotia and Cape
Breton: what is the value of all of this coal?

So now, at the end of the century, as the torch is thrown from
one generation's hands to the next, we're left with fewer illusions, I
think, about the capacity of our visible hands to do a better job than
the marketplace in providing public goods. The post-war golden age,
when we were all social engineers, if not socialists, together is long
gone. We move into the new millennium debating the old issues of
the role of government *vis-à-vis* the private sector all over again. It's
déjà vu all over again. It's *déjà vu* to the 1920s, perhaps to the 1880s.
How best do we promote the public good?

I began by talking about the difficulty of defining the public good,
but maybe that's not really the issue. We know what we want as a
people. We want to have jobs, good and steady incomes; we want
to be free to choose the language we speak, the gods we worship,
the ways of life we cherish. A constant aim of public policy in every
generation is to find the best way of advancing these goods.

After his talk, Michael Bliss took questions from the audience.

QUESTION

Professor Bliss, I certainly would agree with your thesis as to the
origins of the new neo-conservative wave that's sweeping not just
Canada but the world, but it doesn't take away from the fact that
there will always be a tension between an individualistic, let's say
market-based, notion of the public good and a more collectivist,
government-mediated notion. What seems to have changed now, and
it's hard to see how that tension is going to remain symmetric in the
future, is that globalization of the economy has really robbed us of
those collective institutions that can, within a democratic framework,
internalize all the conflicts. Really, the stage is completely global.
And it seems to me that we're driven almost to market definition
exclusively until one can come to a set of international institutions
— and I think they have to go beyond the World Trade Organiza-

tion and the United Nations — that can start to internalize some of those trade-offs. I guess in the absence of any real model of how that's going to happen, one could conclude that we may be in for a very long run of a focus on the individual side of this dialectic tension and that market forces are going to be ruling the world for a long time yet.

MICHAEL BLISS

I think you're right, and it looks to me as though history isn't going to easily repeat itself and that the period I talked about, the half-century after World War II, was a moment in human history when control seemed possible and collectivism had an opportunity. I think the fact of victory in 1945 and the fact that in effect North America ruled the world, economically and in every other way, was the defining factor in the post-war age.

What you say about the future and life in the global world does seem to me to be there. And I believe that we sense very much these days the same sense of helplessness that many people felt in the 1930s — that you were in the grip of global forces that you had lost the possibility of controlling.

QUESTION

What's common through your whole historical talk is that the institution we'd looked to to define the public good or to provide the public good was government, and that people had some sort of faith in government in terms of its ability to provide that public good, I think for a whole lot of reasons that no longer exists. And as one of the new generation, what really terrifies me is that the institution that we've always depended on to provide the public good has lost the credibility to provide that public good. So I worry that we are not going to have a public good in the future, and perhaps you could comment on that.

MICHAEL BLISS

It is important not to succumb to historical pessimism. And when I talk about a sense of the optimism fading, the danger is that we will discount the achievements of the last half-century, and I'm trying to say that in a way we are the victims of our own success. People distrust government because they want to run their own lives, they want power to flow from the people, not from politicians. Surely, in many ways that's healthy, though it's tough if you're a traditional politician.

But in talking about the new world that we've created, isn't it a lot better to be a woman in the 1990s than in the 1950s in Canada? Aren't there many more opportunities open for women? Look at things like the gay pride marches and think of the fact that we have stopped abusing and demeaning homosexuals, that we have in fact had a human rights revolution in Canada. And it's causing us problems because, when Mr. Trudeau said, "The state has no place in the bedrooms of the nation," now people are saying, "The state has no place anywhere in our lives, get out!" But that means that people are taking over their own lives.

Michael Bliss's lecture was broadcast on November 5, 1996, as part of a month-long series on different aspects of the common good.

Debating the Welfare State

WILLIAM KRISTOL
BOB RAE
ABRAHAM ROTSTEIN
JOHN CRISPO

The viability of strong government intervention to alleviate social problems — the welfare state — is an issue of keen interest throughout the western world. In 1996, as part of the Mallon Harding Visitorship at the University of Toronto, Bob Rae, former New Democratic Party Premier of Ontario, and William Kristol, publisher and editor of The Weekly Standard, *a weekly journal of US politics and ideas, squared off over the proposition that the welfare state must be rolled back. Their debate occurred, appropriately enough, the night after President Bill Clinton, in his annual State of the Union Address, declared the era of Big Government to be over.*

WILLIAM KRISTOL

Let me make three very simple arguments as to why the welfare state should be rolled back, prefaced by one statement: the era of Big Government is over.

Bill Clinton said that last night — the Democratic president of the United States, the president, the leader of a party whose reason for existence is to manage Big Government, whose proudest achievement really is creating Big Government in the United States, creating the

145

welfare state. And there is much to be proud of in that achievement of Roosevelt and, to some degree, of Kennedy and Johnson.

Bill Clinton says the era of Big Government is over. Jean Chrétien is rolling back the welfare state, cutting real spending, as I understand it, year to year. Tony Blair, the leader of the socialist party of Britain, has just announced that he's in favour of a stakeholders' society, which in part would replace the traditional welfare state. So I just feel I should group myself with Clinton, Blair and Chrétien, and sit down.

Still, it is actually striking for Bill Clinton to say the era of Big Government is over. It's obviously a shrewd electoral manoeuvre by him, but it does suggest something about the new political era I think we're entering. And I think it is an era that involves rolling back at least part of the welfare state and reforming other parts of it.

Three reasons why the welfare state should be rolled back: economic, social and cultural. I'll divide it that way.

The economic reason's obvious: welfare states tend to go bankrupt — or at least are on a path towards bankruptcy or insolvency. "Tax and tax, spend and spend, elect and elect" — the famous slogan of the New Deal, which served the Democratic Party well for forty or fifty years in the United States — no longer works. What originally were welfare benefits became entitlements, and entitlements became uncontrollable entitlements. What originally were targeted interventions in markets became subsidies for industries, and because of the political dynamics of the welfare state, industries never lost these subsidies, even when they were no longer necessary.

Then you have the obvious situation around the world of budget deficits, mounting debt, unemployment. In the same welfare states that were held up as a model to those of us in the United States as recently as five, ten years ago — places we should model our welfare policies, our unemployment policies, our job-training policies on — now have eleven, twelve per cent unemployment, even in reasonably good economic times. And suddenly Europe looks less attractive as a model. And in all the public policy schools, students are studying Chile's privatization of social security, and when students at the cutting edge of public policy start studying Chile and stop studying Germany or France, something big has happened.

And I think what's happened is that reality hit. We can't afford the welfare state, given the size it is now, given the political dynamics of that welfare state and the difficulty of ever reducing entitlements, cutting spending, weaning interest groups off government welfare. Obviously, politicians are now trying to do that and are encountering great difficulties because of the political dynamics that are built in; more power to those politicians who can. But to some degree, economic reality, first of all, requires rolling back the welfare state.

The second reason, I think, is perhaps more important in a way. Even if the welfare state were economically sustainable, I don't think it would be worth sustaining because it's not accomplishing the fundamental thing it was supposed to accomplish. At the end of the day, the welfare state was supposed to help the poor. That is the moral justification, surely, for Big Government or for the welfare state. And the degree to which welfare policies now help the poor — in the United States at least, the country I know about — at the most is problematic.

In some respects, giving people money does help them, but in other respects, the situation of the poor has not improved at all, despite huge increases in expenditure, in transfer payments, in welfare subsidies and the like. And we have had the disaster of welfare dependency from generation to generation, the huge growth of illegitimacy, family breakup and the like. None of that can exclusively be ascribed to the welfare state per se. But I would argue that the incentives, the spirit, the ethos of the welfare state, as well as the strict incentives of welfare policies, have contributed to a failure to progress in reducing poverty and, in some ways, to worsening the state of those who, unfortunately, find themselves born into poverty because of the socio-economic conditions that now surround them when they're poor.

Welfare policy is at the heart of the welfare state. It's not an accident that the welfare state is called "the welfare state." And welfare policies in the United States, I think here in Canada, and in most of the western world, are generally conceded to have failed. They need to be reformed and, to some degree, I think the attempt to have the state intervene so heavily, not just in the market but in society, and replace the private provision of charity has backfired.

How to unwind the welfare state in this way without hurting the poor is obviously a tricky question. That's something that serious people are grappling with here and down in the United States and elsewhere because, even if it is now doing damage, it's like being on a drug that's hurting your system. It's not necessarily the best thing to simply pull people off the drug cold turkey. You have to think of ways to wean people from the drug and to improve their circumstances and build other institutions that can step in to replace the welfare state when it's rolled back.

But still, it seems to me, insofar as the main justification for the welfare state was that pre-welfare-state capitalism and pre-welfare-state democracy didn't help the poorest among us, it is pretty hard to make the case that current welfare policies are doing good things for poor people or for poor children.

And third and last, in addition to the economic argument and the social argument, the argument about poverty, the third reason to roll back the welfare state, I would say, is a broader argument — harder to quantify, harder to put one's finger on, perhaps — but let's call it a cultural argument. The dynamics of the welfare state, I think, do various things that, over the long run, turn out to be damaging to social harmony, social cohesion, even to the sort of specific character of the society.

You see this — I think in the United States, at least — with the increasing balkanization of society, partly due to government policies, well-intentioned ones to begin with, that count people by race, that allocate positions by race and ethnicity and gender. This is something that was started with good motives and now, I think, contributes to the worsening of inter-group relations in the United States, rather than the bettering of them. And again that is an area where, I think, the welfare state does more harm now than good, and a rollback would be healthy for all concerned.

Similarly, the growth of what you might call the "psychology of victimization" is the ultimate effect, I think, of a welfare state in which people are given lots of incentives and lots of reinforcement for thinking of themselves as the victims of policies beyond their control and not as reasonably self-reliant individuals, families, communities, able, in most circumstances — at least, in normal circumstances, barring a Great Depression or natural catastrophe — to mostly take care of themselves and their neighbours.

And at some level, the whole psychology and sociology of victimization undercuts not just initiative, not just the ability and the willingness of people to rely upon themselves and their own families, but also the ability to help others — neighbours and fellow citizens. And at some level, therefore, I think the culture of the welfare state really undercuts and damages the civic culture of a nation or of a community, and that maybe it's the most intangible damage done by the welfare state, but it's real, I think, nonetheless.

So I would argue, along with President Clinton — when you're abroad, you're never supposed to criticize your own president, so it was very fortunate that last night he decided to become a conservative — I would argue, along with President Clinton, that the era of Big Government is over, the era of the welfare state, in its current size and configuration, is over. It has done some good things, it has done some bad things. But in any case, it now should be rolled back.

BOB RAE

Well, I do differ quite substantially from Mr. Kristol's perspective. Why do we have a welfare state and how did we get it?

It was not the product of Lyndon Johnson or one presidency or one era in our history. It's been something which we have made as societies in the western industrialized world for the better part of two centuries. We made it by extending public education to all children at the elementary age. We made it by ensuring that people had pensions which allowed them to retire. We made it by ensuring that, when there were tremendous dislocations which caused unemployment, people would not be punished as a result.

Poverty is not a moral disorder of the individual. It is not a sign of moral failure. If you read the political economists in the nineteenth century, when they brought in the new Poor Law in 1834, they regarded pauperism as a disease. They regarded destitution as a sign of moral failure. And they argued, just as Mr. Kristol has argued and with precisely the same arguments, that, if you provide help for the poor, you will somehow make them dependent and that that dependency, in and of itself, is an evil. Far better to ensure that we build workhouses and put the poor in workhouses and make sure that the conditions under which they work — one might even describe it as workfare — are less enjoyable than the conditions which would otherwise pertain in the marketplace.

The only problem with Mr. Kristol's theory is that, ultimately, people revolt against it. It may take time. But it is no accident that we have unemployment insurance. It is no accident that we've created health insurance. It's no accident that we have a strong, common, civic desire for accessible education. None of us is self-made. We make our way in the world because of the sustenance of our families, because of the choices that we make ourselves and because of the opportunities that are presented to us by society. The illusion that somehow we can do it all on our own, that we made it here on our own and that there is no sense of obligation holding us together within this capitalist society is a terrible illusion.

Let me deal quickly, if I may, with Mr. Kristol's arguments — not that they can be refuted quickly, because, in fact, one has to recognize that the arguments that he has made and the views and sentiments that he's expressed have a certain currency, just as they did in the England of the early nineteenth century and just as they have, clearly, in the United States today.

The first premise is that we're going bankrupt. Nonsense. That is one of the great fatuous myths which has been spread about in the land.

The second is that it somehow is a sign of our failure if we try to sustain people who are genuinely in need of care, in need of help and who are poor.

And the third is that, culturally, there's something terribly wrong with a civic culture in which we determine that we shall, in fact, express a degree of, a sense of, mutual concern.

We are not bankrupt as a country. We are not bankrupt as a province. We are not bankrupt as a group of countries in the western world. We have the capacity to pay for what needs to be paid for. The question is: do we have the political will? Do we have the willingness to sustain programs? That's a very different question from the notion that there is only one model to be followed.

In the United States, the government is responsible for a little over thirty per cent of the economy. In our own country, it's closer to forty percent. In other countries, in Europe, it's responsible for fifty to sixty percent of the economy. There are many different models, many different ways in which capitalist societies can work.

The argument is not between capitalism and socialism — that's not the argument anymore. The argument is: what kind of capitalism do we want to have, and do we still have a capitalism that is prepared to recognize its limits and prepared to recognize the appropriate place for society and the appropriate place for other social institutions?

This is not to say that the welfare state can't be changed. This is not to say that it can't be reformed. This is not to say that it can't be improved. But pure and simple rolled back, pure and simple cut, pure and simple simply displaced? No, I don't think that's the necessary course, and I don't think it's the right course.

Yes, one can say there are serious disorders in our society. But let me ask Mr. Kristol, and let me ask all of you, is it inevitable that we have inner cities in which people feel unsafe? Is it inevitable that we have in the inner cities of the wealthiest country in the world a rate of childhood death higher than in a great many Third World countries? Is it inevitable that we have a growing gap between rich and poor, such that President Kennedy could say in his time that a rising tide lifts all boats, and we can only say in our time that the rising tide appears to lift only the yachts among us? Is that inevitable? No.

I do not believe that's inevitable. We face a capitalism which, in and of itself, is generating not more equality but more inequality, which is generating greater gaps between rich and poor. Faced with this problem and this challenge, are we completely powerless as a society to say, "The effects of this should be alleviated, we should respond, we should attempt to redistribute again"? I don't think we should be powerless, and I don't think government and the state should accept society as powerless.

Finally I do believe in a political economy of inclusiveness. I do believe in one of efficiency as well. The notion that efficiency and social justice should be permanent enemies is absurd. We should not give to the right, to the conservatives, the entire argument in which they say, "In order to be economically efficient, we have to be socially unjust; in order to be economically efficient, we have to abandon those who are less able among us; we have to cut off social programs, we have to cut health care programs, we have to withdraw support for higher education and put the president in a terrible position of having to constantly ask for more support."

I don't share that view. I believe in a genuine policy of inclusiveness. Yes, this includes a recognition of differences. Yes, this includes the recognition in our own society that we live in a multiracial society. And, yes, it means recognizing that there are aspects of our society which have produced discrimination, which we must strive to end. That's not balkanization, that's inclusiveness. And that's recognizing the challenges which lie ahead.

WILLIAM KRISTOL

Just two simple points: I don't think it's fair to put the contrast as between unfettered faith in markets and some role for government — I don't have an unfettered faith in capitalism, and I'm perfectly happy to have government intervene where appropriate — and I don't think the most powerful criticism of the welfare state is that it reduces economic efficiency or that it curbs economic growth.

The most powerful criticism, I think, is precisely that, whatever its intentions in strengthening civil society and strengthening the bonds of community, it doesn't. I mean, this is an empirical fact. And we can look at the last twenty-five years of western history and ask if these well-intentioned efforts — whether of income redistribution or of forms of affirmative action or lots of other types — really increase the bonds of community among citizens. And if they don't, there's not much point saying, "Well, they should; human beings should be different." They are having counterproductive effects. And I think that is the most serious criticism really of the welfare state.

Though I do believe that problems of debt and deficit and slow economic growth are real problems, the deeper problem is that it turns out not to be good for our society as a society; not to be good, I think, for citizens as citizens to view other citizens as dependants, to view themselves as taxpayers upon whom ever-greater demands are placed for causes that they don't think are justified. There are increases in the resentment of taxpayers and those who receive tax benefits; a certain tendency for everyone to try to become a victim to receive the benefits; a tendency for others to try to pay as little as possible since the demands have gotten so great; and then a tendency, especially when one starts counting people by race or by ethnicity, to resent others, even when they have gotten what they ought to have gotten or what they deserve to have gotten.

One can make fun of the new Poor Law of 1834 — and I'm no expert on this — but, in fact, I believe there is quite a lot of evidence that the new Poor Law of 1834 reduced poverty in England and reduced dependency, which was a terrible problem in the early nineteenth century. And, indeed, the nineteenth century was not that bad a century for an awful lot of people. People were a lot better off at the end of the nineteenth century in England than they were at the beginning. The Victorians must have been doing something right. We can sit here and smirk at them, I suppose, at the end of the twentieth century. The twentieth century hasn't been such a wonderful century for an awful lot of human beings, and we shouldn't be so confident that we have surpassed the wisdom of those foolish Victorians, who built lasting civilizations and managed to avoid some of the traumas of the twentieth century.

But again, I think the point about civic culture — and one can say, "We shouldn't throw people out to the marketplace; they should depend on the sustenance of families as well as on their own efforts and the support of society" — I don't differ with that. But to be able to depend on the sustenance of their families and other families, families need to be able to keep a greater percentage of their income and to have the opportunity to do more for themselves and for their children and for their friends.

One big problem of the welfare state is the increasing tax bite and the increasing demands it takes out of lots of middle-class families. There are not enough rich people to tax to support the welfare state. That's obviously what's happened over the last twenty, thirty years. That's why middle-class Americans and middle classes around the world have rebelled against the tax burden that's put upon them. And it's not that tens of millions of Americans or millions of Ontarians have suddenly become selfish. It's that they think they're not getting their money's worth for their taxes, and not only that, but that the policies that their taxes are supporting are not only not helping the people they're supposed to help, they're actually, in some cases, hurting the people they're supposed to help. And I again think this is, to some degree, an empirical matter. To some degree it's a matter of judgment, about which we'll continue to differ.

But there surely is a lot of evidence that the welfare state has become too big, that the problem isn't anymore that capitalism doesn't recognize its limits. The problem has become that government doesn't recognize its limits. And no public figure in the last twenty-five years in a welfare state has stood up and said, "Yes, there are some problems in the world that government isn't very good at solving," or, "Perhaps there are costs to trying to solve problems that make us have to stand back and say that those problems have to be addressed in other ways: through civil society, through local institutions of government or whatever."

So I think that the fair choice or the fair argument isn't between unfettered belief in markets and a belief that government has an appropriate role. The real issue is, should the welfare state, as it is, be rolled back? And it seems to me, as I say, there's an awful lot of evidence that, whatever the balance of arguments in 1933 or even in 1963 for an expansion of the role of government, the balance now is surely for curbing the size of the welfare state. In the US, we're simply trying to curb the rate of growth of the welfare state. Here, in Canada, at the federal level and the provincial level, you're a step ahead of us, as is so often the case, and are actually cutting the size of the welfare state modestly. And I think it will turn out to be a good thing, not because anyone particularly likes cutting or depriving people of benefits, not simply because of arguments of economic deficiency, not because of the sudden selfishness of lots of Canadians or Americans, but because these policies do more harm than good.

BOB RAE

I think that one of the ways of describing or defining the difference between the arguments that I've been making this evening and that Mr. Kristol has been making is that he ascribes many of the social ills of our time to something he calls "the welfare state," whereas I would ascribe them something called the "nature of our modern economy," against which the welfare state is trying to do something. To blame the welfare state for high rates of crime or to blame the welfare state for high rates of poverty and a high incidence of family breakdown strikes me as an argument but not necessarily true.

I think it's equally plausible and equally sensible to argue that the poverty and dislocation that we see in many parts of our societies have as much to do with the kind of economy that we've created, with a decline in manufacturing, with the increasing gap between rich and poor in the new service economy which has been created, and with the collapse of our ability to provide a sense of hope and opportunity to a large number of people who are unemployed, not because of the welfare state, but because of the economic dislocation which has produced that desire among people.

I think the second major difference between us — and perhaps it's a reflection of what I think is still a continuing difference between the political culture in this country and the political culture in the United States — is that I don't see the welfare state as doing something for somebody else; I see it as doing something for me.

And I think the most dramatic difference between us is in the area of health care, a very important, critical area of social benefit in Canada which we provide differently than they do in the United States. I don't think most Canadians see health care as something that we're doing for other people. I don't think it's an act of generosity on our part that we're helping out others as an act of private charity. No, that's not how it's interpreted or seen by us. It's seen as something that we're doing in a spirit of self-interest. We're doing it for ourselves as much as we're doing it for others, and it's based on a simple principle of insurance that says, "I know that I'm going to get sick, I know that I'm going to get old, and I know that I'm going to rely on health care and need the health care system." And since it is so clearly a fact of life and a fact of nature and something that we share — it happens to rich and poor, to old and young — the principle that everyone should be covered by some kind of insurance is an advance that we feel we've made in Canada, and we don't feel that it's something that we're doing as an act of charity for others. We're doing it for ourselves.

I think the difference between the kind of society which I'm talking about, and the kind of sense of balance between market and society, between market and the state and government that I'm talking about, and the kind of world which Mr. Kristol describes is that he is looking at something which comes in at the edges and doles out some help and some assistance for those who are somehow victimized or hurt by what it is that society has done, whereas I must say I have a much more, if you like — if I can be bold enough to describe it this way — integrated view of the kind of institutions that we have, in fact, built up in public education, in health care and in our society generally.

Finally, I just think the argument that, in the United States for example, somehow government is huge and the economy is tiny, and you have this huge bureaucracy run by these liberal, pointy-headed bureaucrats who are controlling entire levels of American society — the world that was described in such dramatic terms last night by the speech that I saw by Senator Dole — I must say — doesn't conform to any relatively objective view of the American economy and the balance between the American state and the American economy in comparison with virtually any other country in the western world. Yes, there are improvements to be made. Yes, there are efficiencies to be found. But I don't think this should be seen as an excuse for rolling back and for taking away a basic sense of civic and civil obligation, which I think is a very fundamental aspect of the society that we have built up.

But let me just come back to the point that I made at the beginning, and that is, can we afford it? Are our taxes so exorbitantly high that they must, in fact, be reduced in order for us to be able to afford it? To me, that's a judgment call. And I speak to you as a politician who was obviously overwhelmed in a wave of possessive individualism in the last election, and I accept that verdict with equanimity. Well, a little bit of equanimity, anyway.

But I still believe that, in our society, as in American society, we should not see taxes as some kind of enormous, painful burden imposed by others on ourselves but rather, to borrow the words of a great American jurist, Oliver Wendell Holmes, as simply our chance to buy a little bit of civilization.

After the debate, Abe Rotstein and John Crispo, two prominent scholars at the University of Toronto, intervened from the floor.

ABE ROTSTEIN

Well, may I address very briefly this question of the tax revolt? Poor Mr. Rae has a sense that perhaps it was the tax revolt that bounced him out of office. But those of us who have been doing a little economics for several decades remember back to the time, once upon a time, when we looked at the question of who was paying the taxes. And once upon a time — I don't have the precise figures at my fingertips — if you broke it down, you discovered that about three times as much was being paid in taxes by the corporations a long time ago as was being paid by individuals. The ratio was roughly three to one.

Time and tide went their way. We apparently had a welfare state that was going to individuals. Lo and behold, look at the question of today, who is paying the taxes? It's not surprising that there is a tax revolt, and it's not surprising that it expressed itself so virulently in the Ontario election. The taxes today are being paid by individuals in the precisely reverse ratio of approximately three times as much by individuals as by corporations. We've invented delightful terms like "tax expenditures" to cover that whole beehive of exemptions and reserves and all kinds of ways in which taxes are evaded. And, of course, when the burden falls on individuals, there is bound to be some objection and some kind of tax revolt.

I suggest that the resolution before us today might be amended slightly: should the welfare state for corporations be rolled back?

JOHN CRISPO

I'd love to take on Abe. I can't believe this audience still believes that corporation taxes are progressive — corporations pass on their taxes to the consumers. I just can't believe it. Also, when our corporations are competing in a very global village, to tax them when others aren't taxed is absolutely the height of folly.

But I would make this point to our guest from the United States: I wouldn't count — I'm not sure anymore — but I wouldn't count on winning this debate. This guy has more camp followers than Kefauver and Nixon together. I have suffered at the hands of his camp followers on previous engagements.

There are three principles that should apply to the welfare state, and this would embody a rollback because it would lead to a more responsible, sane and sensible welfare state. Number one: nobody in our society should suffer through no fault of his or her own. Both of our societies are wealthy enough to live with that principle. Number two: any able-bodied Canadian citizen who is collecting any form of social assistance should be prepared to undertake retraining or upgrading, or, failing the availability of that, they should be engaging in some community service. You want to call it "workfare"? I'll use the term "workfare."

And, third, there should be a general clawback on all forms of social security depending on what your total income is from all sources. We had fishermen, on the east and west coasts when the fisheries were doing well, earning up to a hundred thousand dollars in very short seasons and collecting unemployment insurance the rest of the year. Those people should have had all of that unemployment insurance rolled back at tax time.

If we took a more intelligent approach to welfare, it would do more good, it would cost less, and people would have more self-esteem and self-respect.

WILLIAM KRISTOL

This is all an elaborate scheme to buck up Mr. Rae before he leaves politics in two weeks. I think the principle of division should be: everyone who agrees that there are too many lawyers and that they are too well paid and have too much influence should divide with me, and everyone who loves lawyers should go with Mr. Rae.

I don't even know how to begin to summarize in a couple of minutes. I would say, just on a couple of points, I do think it would be a failure of conservatives if, twenty years from now, the welfare state for corporations has not been scaled back. That is part of rolling back the welfare state. As was pointed out by the historian, one of the things that happens when you have a welfare state — a government that's indiscriminate so that it's open to all bidders and to all pleas for help — is that, in fact, the strong, unfortunately, do okay. Corporations end up with an awful lot of the welfare, and you have a system of big, swollen government, where the resources are not targeted to those who genuinely need and deserve help. It's no accident that the growth of the welfare state has been accompanied by a growth of corporate welfare. And I'm happy to cut back corporate welfare. I think it would be good for the economy and is the right thing to do.

And it's a fair challenge to issue to conservative governments that tend to be backed by the business community: will they take on some of their own constituencies? In the United States, for example, will they cut agriculture subsidies, welfare for wealthy farmers, as, in fact, the Republicans in Congress are trying to do? Defence spending is down thirty per cent in real dollars over the last decade in the United States. If spending in other areas could go down one-tenth as much, we would have a balanced budget.

One product of the huge growth in the indiscriminate character of the modern welfare state is that it makes it harder precisely to help those who deserve help. It makes it harder to target government efforts and to have a strong but limited government, instead of a swollen and ineffectual government, which is what we have gotten. So, if you care about having an energetic and strong government — and I am for an energetic and strong government; the vision of the framers, the founders of the American Republic was for a limited but strong or strong but limited government — I think one should be interested in rolling back and relimiting the welfare state. It's precisely the growth of entitlements, after all, that is freezing out discretionary spending of government. If I were on the left, the thing I would want to do, more than anything else, is precisely to curb the rate of growth of these entitlements that go to the middle class. At the end of the day, they will prevent government in another ten or twenty years from doing some important things that it probably should do. So, to be an advocate of rolling back the welfare state, I think, ultimately is to be an advocate of a stronger but more limited and more effective government.

BOB RAE

If you listen to some of the arguments you've heard tonight, you would believe that unemployment insurance causes unemployment and that welfare rates cause people to go on welfare. I think that you will find on the margins, no doubt, some people who are there for that reason. But I think we have to confront the fundamental fact that we're going through periods of economic change which are causing high rates of unemployment. And the reason we have a high cost of unemployment insurance is because we have high rates of unemployment. And we're going to go through periods perhaps when there will be even higher rates of unemployment.

Some talk very provocatively about hours of work, and others talk about the way in which inequality has grown in the last fifteen years, despite all these left-wing, wildly spending, crazy social democratic and liberal governments. What do you know — inequality has grown. All our efforts have managed to accomplish is to assuage some of the worse effects of this. And one of the reasons that inequality is growing is that the distribution of working time has changed more dramatically in the last fifteen years than at any time in the last century. Some people are working fifty, fifty-five and sixty hours, and some people are not working at all, and a large number of people are working less than twenty-four hours a week, even though they want to work full time.

We're going through a period of dramatic social change, in which the participation of women and men in the labour force has changed, in which we have created, in this country, a multiracial society in the space of the last fifteen, twenty, twenty-five years, in which we're seeing the same developments transforming American society. And to me, to pull away those instruments of solidarity at just such a moment, just as we're in the midst of this incredible digital revolution, when some will be riding the Internet and others will be swamped by the wave, is a profound mistake.

"Debating the Welfare State" was broadcast on April 2, 1996.

Common Culture, Multiculture

CHARLES TAYLOR
BERNIE FARBER
BOB DAVIS
Moderated by
DAVID CAYLEY

In recent years, multiculturalism has been the rationale for a movement to broaden the educational curriculum and diversify the character of public schools. Supporters of this movement have argued that the existing curriculum is a deposit of racism, colonialism and patriarchy and must be overhauled. Opponents have criticized the movement for creating a culture of complaint and for breaking education up into non-communicating enclaves such as Black Studies, Native Studies, Women's Studies and so on.

Philosopher Charles Taylor argues that multiculturalism, "the politics of recognition," is an inescapable part of contemporary existence. This leads to the question of whether demands for recognition mandate more inclusive common schools or separate schools for separate groups. Bernie Farber makes the case for state funding of private religious schools; Bob Davis introduced courses in Black History at his Scarborough, Ontario, high school.

DAVID CAYLEY

Public education in Canada was founded on the idea of the common school. At the very inception of Upper Canada's school system in the 1840s, its architect, Egerton Ryerson, spoke feelingly of "the children of the rich and the poor imbibing the first elements of knowledge at the same fountain and commencing the race of life upon equal terms." In practice, the well-off rarely attended public schools, but Ryerson's ideal persisted and gradually drew most of the population into a common system of education with a common curriculum. Underlying this system was an assumption that students shared a common culture, a common religious heritage and a common sense of where each fit in the social order. In the writing of Ryerson's I just quoted, for example, he goes on to say that the mutual respect and sympathy he hoped the common school would engender between classes should "in no respect intrude upon the providential arrangements of order and rank in society, but only divest poverty of its meanness and wealth of its arrogance."

Schooling involved socialization into an assumed and, if necessary, imposed consensus. This consensus no longer exists. Canada was declared an officially multicultural society by the Trudeau government in 1971. Various court decisions have since deprived Christianity of any official or privileged position in the public schools. Native people have reclaimed the standing of distinct aboriginal nations with rights of self-government, including control over their own education. Many other groups have also demanded recognition and some sort of special status. Deep and seemingly unbridgeable gulfs have opened between citizens on moral questions like abortion or the right of gays to marry and rear children. In the 1995 *Egan* case, for example, in which a majority of the Supreme Court broadened the definition of family to include homosexual unions, a broad coalition of Sikhs, Hindus, Muslims and Christians, both Catholic and Protestant, told the court that their traditions stood unalterably opposed to the idea. Abortion polarizes opinion in a similarly fundamental way.

This new pluralistic society in which people are defined by their differences is the site of what Charles Taylor calls "the politics of recognition." The implications for education are profound and I'll come to them presently. But first, I want to explore what Taylor means more generally by this expression. He argues, first of all, that the problem is characteristically modern. In pre-modern societies, he says, people conducted most of their significant social relations

within their own enclaves. Relations with outsiders were rigidly pre-
scribed and raised no question of recognition or identity. Signs of a
change in this view began to appear in the eighteenth century with
the writings of French philosopher Jean-Jacques Rousseau.

CHARLES TAYLOR

You see, what this issue of recognition can be understood as is a
new modern twist on the issue of honour and dignity and possible
dishonour and so on. And what you have in Rousseau is a new position on that. Beforehand, you either had people who thought that
honour and dignity were important and they had an ethic where
someone should live up to their honour code, or you had a very
powerful tradition, which you have in Plato, and you have in Au-
gustinian Christianity, which says this honour stuff is pride, it's bad,
negative, you shouldn't think about that. Putting your life into that
is completely the wrong thing. You should scrap it. It's a tremendous
anti-honour polemic.

Now, Rousseau comes along with a new position which is a
kind of marriage of these two views. He very strongly draws on
the critique of the honour ethic in order to say that people who are
concerned with how they look in the eyes of others have completely
missed the boat. The Stoics said this, and he exactly reproduces this
critique of the honour ethic. But just when you think you're on familiar ground, if you're a reader of the Stoics, you think, okay, he's
going to say forget all this, set it aside. Then he suddenly switches
and he proposes a new solution which we would today call mutual
recognition in total equality. What's wrong with honour, it turns out,
is that it is always hierarchically and unequally distributed. What's
wrong with the search for honour is that it is normally seen as a
desire to have everyone to depend on me and to free me from dependence on anyone else.

The way out is to have absolute equality between the honourer
and the honouree, and Rousseau thinks we can only do this socially.
So he develops the very powerful requirements of a just society which
have been haunting us ever since. According to him there is a series
of very important relationships that are crucial to both power and

honour that will have to be reorganized so that there is an identity between the terms on both sides of the relationship. So there can't any longer be a king who's sovereign over people; it's got to be the whole people who are sovereign over the whole people. You can't have any different relationship to power between A and B because that will break with the requirement of equality.

And Rousseau has this same requirement in the display of ourselves to ourselves. In hierarchical societies, the king makes a progress and all attention focuses on him. We all look at a Princess Di, etc. But in Rousseau's view, the great popular festival must be the whole people parading before, or enjoying itself, before the whole people. The spectators and spectated have to be rigorously the same. That's why he's terribly against theatre, because there you have some people on stage and some people in the dark, not expressing themselves but simply looking at the people on the stage. This ideal was taken up by the French revolutionaries. You see it in the design of all those feasts that they tried to put together in the 1790s, desperately trying to create the new political culture in France. They had read Rousseau and they actually picked up on that. Many of the people who designed those festivals said, we're meeting this requirement. So all the revolutionary festivals had the whole public parading before itself, as it were. Everybody was involved in the parade on the feast day.

Now here you have a theory in which what we would call today being recognized, being acknowledged, is not forgotten. You still have, in Rousseau, this tremendous polemic against honour, as in the Stoics, but it's not just in order to say, forget that, just think about your own conscience or think about your own inner self. Instead the question of honour is transposed into an issue of whether it's radically reciprocal, egalitarian, everybody on the same footing, or whether it has this terrible vice of inequality, of dependence of some on others, and that becomes the new issue. And in a sense, that was the birth point, theoretically, of this modern concern.

DAVID CAYLEY

Rousseau's solution to the problem of honour led in time to the unstable politics of recognition that we know today. His intention was to protect the unique, inward identity of each individual from a distorting dependence on the opinions of others. But his proposal moved towards an equality so absolute that it threatened all differences. This was the tendency that was manifest in the Jacobins of the French Revolution and that has continued, Taylor says, to this day.

CHARLES TAYLOR

If we all had the same identity, this problem wouldn't arise. It's only because there are these differences that they can be misrecognized. That's why the Jacobins were, in a way, on to something. Not that it would ever work, but they did see that the nature of modern egalitarian society is such that it would obviously run a lot better if everybody defined themselves, let's say, purely as a citizen of the French Republic, in which they were like everybody else, and if they took anything that differentiated them, like their religion or their region and so on, and put it into a second category of less important stuff. Then the modern problems of recognition wouldn't exist.

That's why there has been this constant temptation — moves are constantly made on the political checkerboard — to get this problem off the table by making everybody the same or getting everybody to agree that, for political purposes, what ought to be important to them in their identity is only X. And that the things that are different ought to be put in a second category, where they don't count and they don't need to impinge on the political scene. So people will say that all you really need as a citizen is that you are a bearer of certain rights. The Canadian Charter, for example, gives you your rights. That's what should matter to you as a citizen. So what's all this business about your wanting to be French or English or whatever? Take that off the table. There are an awful lot of moves of this kind which are part of the whole game and struggle about identity. What these moves amount to is the statement: "I recognize your identity, but don't ask me to recognize your difference. Ask me only to recognize the way in which you're the same as me, and then there'll be no problem." This is a response to the intuition people have that, in a way, it would all go much easier if we could just set our differences aside. Only that's too much to ask of certain people.

DAVID CAYLEY

But there's also an opposite movement, which is the flight into difference — you can't understand me, you can't write from my point
of view, however it's expressed.

CHARLES TAYLOR

Yes, and that's a very tempting move in cases of really tough sledding
with identity recognition, which is for groups to say, "We don't need
this — we need to be recognized by somebody, but we don't need
you to recognize us any more. We're declaring our independence, as
it were, from you as an interlocutor." And we have to be clear that
human beings need certain interlocutors, and not others, in crucial
identity modes. For example, if a kid's growing up in a family where
there are big problems about his or her being accepted, it may, but
it may not, help if some totally unrelated person says, "I understand
you." What that kid may really need is recognition by what Mead
called "significant others" — maybe the parents, or at least some
narrower group. So it's clear that, when we need recognition, very
often we need it from certain people and not from others.

A modern citizen of democracy has the ideology that everybody's
in it together, we're all in it together. So it tends to be the case that
in such a society we need recognition from our compatriots. But
then you get the move you see among, for instance, certain African
Americans of saying about the white citizens, "No, we don't need
it from you," or the move that says, even further, "It's an act of aggression on your part to try to understand us because only we can
understand ourselves, and don't even make the attempt." But, in fact,
a lot of this "you can't understand us" is a move in a continuing game
of getting recognition. So there's something not entirely up front
about it. In other words, it's still an attempt to grab the attention,
to lay guilt on the other that's involved in making these moves. So
it's a profoundly other-referring move even while it pretends to be
a complete other-cutting-off move. That's why I call it bad faith.
There's a real conflict between the actual human meaning of the
move and the overt claim.

DAVID CAYLEY

In Charles Taylor's view, tension between identity and difference is inherent in the very existence of citizen democracies. Citizens share a collective identity, yet remain profoundly and irreducibly different. Taylor sees this as a situation requiring dialogue, accommodation and a willingness to live in a variegated, asymmetrical world that cannot be neatly resolved into universal categories or mapped onto a uniform Cartesian grid. But Canada's case shows how difficult it can be to achieve this kind of accommodation in practice. The attempt to work something out, he says, is always menaced by the desire for logical, clear-cut solutions.

CHARLES TAYLOR

You have various people who don't accept the requirement to work something out. They're uneasy with differences, and the only general solution they will accept is the uniformizing, Jacobin one, really. So they have great trouble with the ad hoc solutions, and there's going to be a certain "ad hockery" in working out just how we can coexist with each other. Can we actually find a terrain where we can feel together on this? It's going to vary from country to country, it's not going to be based on universal principles, it's going to be messy, it's going to be illogical, it's going to be historically conditioned and so on. And there are people who find this extremely hard to take, people whose idea of a properly running society is one in which fundamentally there's this uniformity which dominates. In Canada it comes in two flavours. There's the Quebec separatist one, which is very, very Jacobin in all its fibres. And there's the rest of Canada, refusing Quebec's difference, which is much more hooked into an Anglo-Saxon tradition. And the existence of the country is constantly in peril because when these two forces together get strong enough to strangle the middle, as it were, the existence of the country is always on the edge of the precipice.

DAVID CAYLEY

The spirit of improvisation that Taylor thinks would preserve Canada without destroying its difference should, in his view, also guide the revision of the curriculum of education. The curriculum, he believes, should certainly be broadened to include previously excluded groups and stories. But this should be done only as it becomes possible to do it well, and not according to some mechanical, prefabricated notion of equality.

CHARLES TAYLOR

The desire to apply universal principles of fairness really gets in the way here. If you start to think in terms of what's just and right and decide you've got to tell all the stories or none, that's almost always going to end up pushing you towards a very watered-down curriculum in which a little bit of this and a little bit of that and a little bit of the other gets a look in. But nobody can get really fired up with something in one or other of these great traditions to the point that it really means something to you, that you can take it and read further or write further or whatever. It isn't going to answer this requirement if you have a tiny bit of the *I Ching* and two pages of aboriginal myth and half of a sonnet by Shakespeare and so on, because then nobody has a chance to get fired up by anything at all. And here I would lean very far on one side. In other words, if your resources only allow you to go very deeply into Shakespeare and not very much else, then don't sacrifice going deeply into Shakespeare just because at the moment you can't provide similar coverage of everything. It's very, very important that people really get sufficient exposure to particular subjects.

On the other hand, we now can move in a multicultural direction more effectively. I am familiar with the university level, and we do have people who are really very well versed in some of these other cultural traditions, who are pedagogically very alive, who can get them across in a very powerful way and meet the requirement I'm asking for — that the subject be taught in a lively enough way with enough depth and breadth that there's some hope that people can actually pick up on something. And we can plan in the universities to increase this element steadily, as long as we aren't hamstrung by the idea that unless we do it all, you know, this year, we're somehow not meeting some requirement of justice or fairness.

DAVID CAYLEY

Taylor's idea that new courses of study should be introduced only when they can be taught passionately and in depth reflects his general approach to the politics of recognition. Circumstances modify principles. There is no one right way or single universal answer. Respect for difference demands variation. Common interests demand common institutions. The proper balance between the two has to be discovered on a case-by-case basis. Taylor takes the same approach to the question of whether ethnic or religious schools should receive public funding and support.

CHARLES TAYLOR

Here again we have one of these standing dilemmas. We have to find some place in the middle or some place that maximizes. There is no doubt that, on one hand, there are real advantages to having schools in which everybody's mixed in. You know, it's quite impressive in Montreal now with Bill 101, which has put all these immigrant children into French-speaking schools together with, you know, *pur laine québécois*. This situation has changed all the players — the old-stock Quebecers as well as the others. It's been very important to their forming friendships and achieving understanding. So that's a real example where there's a real advantage to having everybody in the same school. However, it's also important that different groups can feel that their identities are really being listened to, carried over and so on, as they define them, and this is going to mean that for some groups it's going to be very important to have their own schools. And I can't see that one of these principles is pre-eminent over the other and that you can just, in virtue of the nature of democracy or whatever, decide from the beginning that we're going to take one of these (let's say the common school) and that, therefore, any request for a Jewish school or a Catholic school is just not receivable. So we have to find a way of allowing that possibility, even though I think, ideally, we should try to find a way of encouraging as many as possible to be in a common school. But people have to be persuaded to that.

In other words, in a democracy we have to distinguish between goals, even very good goals, to which people have to be persuaded to adhere — and if they can't be, then so be it — and other things like paying your income tax, where no one's going to ask you your opinion, you've just got to do it. Now, I think that when you have things like paying income tax, on which the whole society depends, or even conscription, in certain cases, in war, then you have a case for making this mandatory. But when you have goals that take the form of statements beginning "we'd have in some ways a better society if . . . ," or "it would be good if . . . ," and so on, then you actually defeat your purpose by compulsion, because very often the goodness of those conditions depends on their being voluntarily agreed to. I think you undercut the very point of the operation if you begin to make those things mandatory. So the fact that, in some ways, it would be good if we all were in a common school system is not a good ground to say to people, "No, you cannot have your own school."

DAVID CAYLEY

Charles Taylor argues that the questions raised by multiculturalism demand a dialogue, and a dialogue, by definition, is an encounter whose outcome cannot be predicted. He accepts that recognition is a real need whose absence can inflict real harm, but he doesn't think that any set of universal principles can settle the practical questions that are entailed in trying to address this harm. Sometimes the answer may lie in the direction of more inclusive common institutions and sometimes in the direction of separate institutions for separate groups. Accordingly, in what follows, I want to look at both cases, beginning with the argument for public support for groups that want their own schools.

For nearly fifteen years, the Canadian Jewish Congress has been campaigning for state support for private Jewish schools in Ontario. British Columbia, Alberta, Manitoba and Quebec now grant partial aid to private religious schools, but Ontario, excepting Roman Catholic schools, does not. In the early 1980s, when the government of Bill Davis extended funding for Catholic schools to grade thirteen — it had previously stopped at high school — it put the question of support for other private schools to a commission headed by Bernard Shapiro, now the principal of McGill University. He recommended that such funding be given by granting private schools associate status within public boards. The government shelved the report. The succeeding Liberal government procrastinated. Then the NDP took power in the early nineties. They, at least, were frank in saying that they would never fund private schools. So the Canadian Jewish Congress, along with the Alliance of Christian Schools, went to court to test the constitutionality of a system that gave public support to Roman Catholic schools but to no other denomination or religion. The Supreme Court of Canada, where the case ended, answered equivocally in November 1996. Nothing prevents the Ontario government from funding private schools, the Court said, but current Catholic education rights in Ontario do not constitute unfair discrimination, because they are part of the political deal that created Confederation and not an instance of a universal right.

Bernie Farber is with the Ontario Section of the Canadian Jewish Congress and has been involved in the question of government funding for Jewish schools for many years. He thinks that the Supreme Court took too narrow a view of minority rights within Confederation.

BERNIE FARBER

When the Fathers of Confederation were carving out this wonderful deal that became Canada and they were looking at minority versus majority rights, there were about 150 Jews and very few other minorities in the province of Ontario. The minority was the French-speaking Roman Catholic population. I would like to think that the Fathers of Confederation were far-sighted, as opposed to the government of today. I think what they were looking at was ensuring that minority rights be protected forever in Ontario and in Quebec. So, if one extends their principle, today the protected minorities would have to include Jews and Muslims and other religious groups. And it is for that reason that we believe these rights should have been extended to these groups. However, the bottom line is they were not. The Supreme Court of Canada said that Ontario was correct in its interpretation that it did not have to fund independent schools, based on the fact that they're funding Catholic schools, but — and it's a very important but, because it brings us all the way back to 1984 again — they said that, in fact, it's a political decision, and if the government wishes to, as a political decision, it certainly can fund independent schools. And so here we are, fifteen years later, having to dance the political dance with the present Conservative government. And it's *déjà vu* all over again.

DAVID CAYLEY

The main argument of the Canadian Jewish Congress and its partners in their case to the Supreme Court was fairness or "equal recognition," in the term Charles Taylor used earlier. Jewish schools follow the Ontario curriculum and operate within the province's civic traditions. So how can it be right, Bernie Farber asks, to fund one kind of religious school and not another?

BERNIE FARBER

We live in an area that's relatively multicultural: north Toronto. On either side of me live two Catholic families, and we get along exceedingly well. However, my neighbour on the right side has children who are of school age and go to the Roman Catholic school literally right around the corner. A school bus picks them up and takes them to the Roman Catholic school. They don't pay a cent. And I don't begrudge them that. I think it's marvellous. If we wanted to send our children to a Jewish day school, we would have to arrange for bus transportation, we would have to pay tuition of approximately seven thousand dollars per child. And I look at this and I think to myself, am I any less a citizen than my next-door neighbour? Why is it that my next-door neighbour has this right to educate his children in his faith, paid for by the government, but I — a Canadian citizen, who pays the same taxes as he does, contributes in the same way to society as he does — do not have that right? That's something we tried to impress upon the courts. The courts, in my experience, are not passionate in their approach. They don't look inside people's heads. They don't look inside people's hearts. They're just looking at the strict application and interpretation of the law. But what they're missing is this issue of fairness, of equity. I am as equal a citizen as anybody else and I don't have the same rights. It just comes down to that.

DAVID CAYLEY

Why are parents sending their children to Jewish schools?

BERNIE FARBER

Generally speaking, within the Jewish tradition, there has been this historical understanding of the need for continuity. Continuity within Judaism is something that has been literally inbred into our minds from day one. And there's a history behind it. No other people on the face of this earth historically have been challenged as the Jewish people have. In the past century alone there was an attempt to wipe out Judaism as a living, breathing tradition, and it almost succeeded. And so, as Emile Fackenheim, a very famous modern-day Jewish philosopher, once said, there is an Eleventh Commandment in Judaism. And that is, never to give Hitler a posthumous victory by walking away from your Judaism. And the position that many Jews take is that in order to imbue their children with all that Jewish life is about, they have to be taught the precepts of the Torah and they have to be taught the Hebrew language. There is an atmosphere of Judaism which can be inculcated only in a full school environment. We are, after all, historically the People of the Book. That's what Jews are. And so for those modern Jewish families who sincerely believe in that, of which there are many, the Jewish day school system is the only way to accomplish this end.

There's also another reason, especially for those who are on the Orthodox end of things, the modern-day Orthodox. There are Jewish holy days, for example, which can number up to sixteen in any current school year. There are laws, specific laws, centring around what can be eaten, and it's just not viable for these Orthodox children to be going to a public school which cannot meet their basic religious needs around food and holy days and that kind of thing. So, at the extreme end of things, you have those families. But the vast majority of Jewish families that send their children to Jewish day schools fit into a modern look at Judaism. They have an honest desire to have their children brought up Jewishly.

We have developed what I call myths and assumptions when it comes to the whole issue of the funding of independent schools. It's a myth, for example, that if we separate our children into denominational schools, in fact we're doing them a disservice because we're separating them, and then they don't get to really play a part in the everyday public life of what is Canada. Well, this is nonsense. It's complete nonsense. I know of dozens and dozens of my own contemporaries who went to Jewish day schools who are today doctors and lawyers and engineers and architects who contribute to the public good. My own children and the children they play with on our own street — many of them go to all kinds of different schools, be they Catholic schools, private schools, public schools. But they come home and they play together in the back yard and they go out to the park on a Sunday, and it doesn't matter if they're black or white or Catholic or Jewish or Muslim. They can go to their separate schools, but they come back together and they still have to live within an environment, live within the community.

So this idea just doesn't wash with me. It's one of those arguments that those who are against the funding of independent schools consistently put forward, and it doesn't work. They also put forward the myth of the destruction of the public school system if you fund independent schools. Well, I say, give me the proof. The proof, for me, is in the pudding, and the pudding in Canada is the fact that provinces in this country already fund independent schools. Are the public school systems in Manitoba, Alberta, Saskatchewan, and British Columbia falling apart? Of course not — quite the contrary. In BC there was a report just last year from the public school system praising the funding of independent schools because it says it offers a challenge to the public schools. There hasn't been this dispersion of children from the public schools into the separate or private schools as a result of funding in other provinces. It just has not happened. Why would it happen here in Ontario?

DAVID CAYLEY

Those who oppose public funding of religious schools often argue, as Bernie Farber just noted, that separate schooling undermines citizenship by depriving students of a core of common experiences. Farber believes, on the contrary, that a solid grounding in one's own tradition often augments citizenship rather than diminishing it.

BERNIE FARBER

When you have a better sense of where you've come from, I really believe you have a better sense of where you're going. Isn't believing in what you are what Canada's all about? It's an experiment, and maybe our great-great-great-grandchildren will be able to make an assessment of whether it will work. I believe it will work. In the wonderful multicultural experiment which is this country, one can be Jewish and Canadian, one can be Muslim and Canadian, Italian and Canadian at the same time, not in a melting-pot kind of an atmosphere as we have in the United States, but celebrating both. And it can work.

You know, my father was a very devout Jew, but when he came to this country, he flew the Union Jack in front of our house, you know, every Victoria Day. He was proud to be a citizen of this country. I remember how, as a child, we used to travel by train to the United States, and when we came to the border crossing, my father always had to show what he called his "citizenership" papers, his citizenship papers. And he would pull them out and he would proudly show them to the border people, whoever they were, and then he would sit and he would show them to me again, and every time we went, he would say, "You see, I'm a Canadian." But he wasn't any less Jewish. So this is the wonderful experiment that we're engaged in. And it's quite right that a young child should be brought up within his own religious tradition or ethnic tradition and understand what that's about. I don't want to say this makes a better citizen, but it certainly makes as good a citizen as anyone who goes to a public school.

DAVID CAYLEY

Multiculturalism, as Charles Taylor argued earlier, mandates a stance, a presumption that other cultures are as worthy as our own, but not a definite policy. Those who take this stance generally agree that public education should be more variegated and more attentive to cultural differences, but there is deep disagreement about whether this requirement is best met by expanding public support for separate schools or by making the common schools more diverse. Bernie Farber argued that religious schools, operating within the same academic and civic framework as public schools, deserve public support. There is also, however, an argument for broadening the curriculum in the public schools. The two positions contrast but don't necessarily contradict each other, at least if one heeds Taylor's opinion that multiculturalism is not a question with only one right answer.

Bob Davis is the author of a number of books on education, including *Whatever Happened to High School History?* and *Skills Mania: Snake Oil in Our High Schools.* From 1975 until his retirement a few years ago, he taught history at Stephen Leacock Collegiate, a Scarborough, Ontario, high school. While he was there, the racial composition of the student body changed rapidly, and by the early '90s a school that had once been nearly all white was thirteen per cent black. Davis responded by introducing two courses on black history, one on Africa and the West Indies, one on the black experience in Canada and the United States since slavery. Both were part of the school's top-level academic program. They were open to all — Davis himself is white — but were taken mainly by black students. Opponents of multiculturalism have sometimes argued that diversifying the curriculum promotes separateness and retards integration into Canadian society, but Davis believes that the courses he taught had the opposite effect on his students.

BOB DAVIS

I think it made them more at home in our school, not less at home. They feel, now we have a little corner in our education here for our own history, which has been left out in a serious way. We are more at home here, and we don't have to just be at home on the basketball court. And we don't just have to be at home producing a fashion show or a talent show. We're in the academic program. And it's very important for them that it be academic. I inherited a situation where students felt they were given a kind of bull-session black history. And I've heard of some schools where they talk about sports and rap the whole time. It's a disgusting lowering of sights. It's the same when it's just in the general-level program and not the academic program. These are very serious courses with lots of reading and lots of hard studying. You're expected to be there and be on time. That's another whole story I could tell you.

I got a number of parents' meetings going, and for one of them I went out and knocked on about sixty doors. And so, contrary to the conventional wisdom that blacks won't come to parents' nights, we had a huge meeting, with nearly a hundred people. A discussion about attendance and punctuality came up. I said that, on average, the attendance of your kids and their punctuality are worse than the rest of the students. Why is that? And I told them that the teachers say that when they talk to your kids, they get attitude and they argue. And the parents said, "That's outrageous, we didn't hear about this. Call us up. Are they scared of them? Tell our kids, don't give me that nonsense — get here on time." But the kids say the teachers are afraid of them.

This is one of the good things that happen when there is an advocate, as I was, of doing black history. You get a cross-fertilization, and there is discussion about how blacks are seen by the other teachers. And I think the students were right that this arguing tendency scared a lot of teachers and they gave up reminding them to be there on time. Later, we had a speaker called Akua Benjamin, from Ryerson, who said, if we're going to talk about the relations of black kids with the police, we have to talk about how our kids talk back. And she said, "If we didn't talk back, we'd still be slaves."

So one of the good things that resulted, I felt, was this kind of ferment about who they are and how they are being treated. And I saw this particularly in their student organization. In most schools, it tends to want to organize a fashion show, but in our school there was a huge emphasis on bringing in educational speakers. And they would get quite an attendance of white kids, too. And so I thought, no, people are wrong. It's the opposite. These students now feel more at home. Most of their time is still spent in the melting pot, and that assimilation to Canadian society is essential, but they had that piece of education which offered security and knowledge that they wouldn't have gotten without it.

DAVID CAYLEY

At the end of the second year of black history at Stephen Leacock, students wrote personal or family histories. Bob Davis collected and published their essays, along with photographs and illustrations, in a series of handsomely designed books called *Our Roots*.

BOB DAVIS

I put the stress on their own personal histories. It started to become popular with some teachers to get them to talk to their parents and their relatives. And that's very good, I think. And I would say about half of my students took up that challenge. But, I said, the bottom line is your own story. They had just spent time reading Maya Angelou's *I Know Why the Caged Bird Sings* and Malcolm X's autobiography. So when I pointed this out, they said, "Well, my life's very boring compared to theirs." So at the start the technique was a little bit inhibiting. But in the long run it became inspiring. And it's quite remarkable, I think, what they wrote. In that sense I'm an incurable progressive in that I think self-knowledge is really, really important, and I think the left has often been as bad as the right in ignoring that and concentrating on principles and things outside yourself.

DAVID CAYLEY

Tell me a little bit more what you mean by self-knowledge.

BOB DAVIS

Well, students would say, my life is boring. But then you need to spend some time with them and ask questions. Where have you lived? Then you find that they emigrated from Jamaica when they were thirteen. You say, my God, that doesn't sound boring to me.

How was it? Terrible. It was really terrible. Is that right? After a while, you get to see there's a whole lot in this person's life that is very important, but they have never, to use a Hegelian expression, taken it up into consciousness. They have never reflected on, "Hey, I have had some rough challenges there to deal with, and it wasn't just that we got into terrible clashes at home."

There's a great novel by Cecil Foster about a mother who comes to Toronto ahead of time, ahead of her child, and the child is, as I remember, quite tiny. But by the time she's ready, with the cash that she wanted to get together, to bring her child up, the kid's a teenager. And it's rough. It's very rough. Well, there are quite a lot of kids in that bracket here who have had that history. But not many people try to get them to think of it in connection with education. To put it to a teacher or to put it to yourself in writing seems to me to be a very noble aim of education. There was a British school of elementary education that espoused getting beyond the "My Summer Vacation" and "My Dog Spot" compositions that kids did and going for something deeper. There was a great flood of wonderful writing in the sixties when people caught on to this, teachers caught on to it. But it never seemed to hit the high schools much. It was thought to be a little kid's enterprise, you know, until we got serious in high school and we got specializing, and I just think that's wrong. I think it should be there in high school, too.

DAVID CAYLEY

Bob Davis regards the black history program at Stephen Leacock as proof that education works best when it takes account of who the student is and incorporates that person's self-discovery into its curriculum. But he says that despite the program's having been such a success, the principle of multicultural education is still contested and its future not assured.

BOB DAVIS

We had quite a battle about getting a proper teacher to replace me who could do those courses and was interested in those programs, because there are no specialty requirements in the agreement negotiated by the teachers' union and the board about this as a specialty. It's too small at the moment to have that. And none of the existing history department felt they were qualified to do it. There were a couple of people in English who, I thought, might be able to, but they didn't feel they were qualified. So they started searching. And it got to the point where we had to have another parents' meeting and get really serious. And the principal went out and found somebody, who's carried on the program. It's still very vigorous now. I think the general tendency at the moment is to shrink such programs, but new ones are starting as well, so I don't know whether one can say for sure at this point which way things are going.

DAVID CAYLEY

Davis's supposition that multicultural education may now be shrinking is based, first of all, on the current ascendancy of a reform movement that is more interested in restoring education's common core than expanding its margins and, second, on the success of the recent counterattacks that have been made against multiculturalism. Amongst the most celebrated of these attacks have been Arthur Schlesinger, Jr.'s *The Disuniting of America: Reflections on a Multicultural Society* and, in Canada, Neil Bissoondath's well-reviewed *The Selling of Illusions: The Cult of Multiculturalism in Canada*. Both of these books argue that cultural recognition is a contrived need, that the preservation and celebration of immigrant or minority cultures is a private affair that should not concern public institutions, and, finally, that failure to assimilate everyone to a common culture will produce a petulant and fragmentary society. Davis, obviously, disagrees. He doesn't disparage assimilation or deny that education should foster a common ethos. Rather, he believes that people's real contribution to society comes through an achieved understanding of who they are and where they've come from. Cultural identity and participation in civic life, in this view, are harmonious rather than antagonistic ends. Like Bernie Farber, he upholds the image of Canada as a cultural mosaic, rather than a melting pot, as the United States is said to be. But Davis wonders, finally, whether this idea is now sufficiently appreciated.

BOB DAVIS

What is wrong — except that, I guess, it was never practised — with the mosaic? Now, we used to think it was practised, people like me, right? We thought Canada was a mosaic. And Canada is different in some ways, but those who have been treated badly say, "Hey, that's a big joke. It was a melting pot here, too." But it's the ideal that I'm talking about that underlies my work. I mean, take my students. They were taking one class out of four per day in black history. The other three were totally mainstream, and if you can consider that, over the four years, if they took two years of black history, then it's a very small percentage of their total education that was strictly on black matters. And so I think we have to try to do both. And the idea that you could be a proud African Canadian or a proud Italian Canadian to me is still a very sacred idea. And its sacredness means something if it is supported by our corporate group through our corporate taxes. We're not going to tell people how to celebrate, you know, Italian holidays — that's in their own families. But in something as important as schooling, I don't really think they can learn properly without these things in the curriculum.

"Common Culture, Multiculture" was broadcast on June 28, 1988, in a series called The Education Debates.

The Ethics of Humanitarian Intervention

University of Alberta Visiting Lectureship on Human Rights

JAMES ORBINSKI

One of the great dilemmas of the modern world, in an age plagued with war, strife and oppression, is when and how to intervene to protect basic human rights. When should we use bombs and bullets to stop gross violations of human rights? And how do we interpret what's being called the "New Humanitarianism" — a policy practised by NATO and other international organizations? Some believe that this policy simply uses humanitarian assistance as a smokescreen for military and political manoeuvring and that it does more harm than good.

Dr. James Orbinski is former president of the international aid organization Médecins Sans Frontières/Doctors Without Borders. He has been involved with MSF since 1990 and was a founding member of the Canadian section. He has worked in the midst of civil war, massacres and genocide, in Somalia, Afghanistan, Rwanda and Zaire.

JAMES ORBINSKI

I want to talk about the work and the principles that guide MSF's actions. The reality of MSF today is in our therapeutic feeding centres for children in Ethiopia, in the Congo with women and girls who are victims of rape as a weapon of war, in Cambodia and Guatemala with sex workers and street children pulverized by poverty, in Kosovo, in Sudan, in Timor, in Belgium, in France, and in Italy, and in more than four hundred projects in eighty countries around the world.

In talking about these, I want to talk specifically about humanitarianism in war — or situations of violent conflict — and what humanitarianism is and what it is not. I also want to criticize what has recently been called the "New Humanitarianism," and in arguing against this New Humanitarianism, I want to highlight basic humanitarian principles and responsibilities and to very carefully distinguish these from the other vitally important work that takes place through human rights advocacy.

I also want to talk about some of the other work that we do, which is provide medical assistance to people in need in nonconflict situations — in, for example, situations where people are in crisis because they do not have access to, among other things, basic health care. I'm also speaking here, for example, of people's right to access essential lifesaving medicines and the obscenity that is the AIDS epidemic and the double obscenity of both market and political failure to address this and other epidemics.

MSF works in war zones and situations of violent conflict in many parts of the world. In the fall of '92, I was working in Baidoa, Somalia, a city that then had become known around the world as the City of Death. Baidoa was then the very epicentre of the famine and civil war in Somalia at that time.

One late afternoon, I saw a man who has stayed fixed in my memory since. He was about forty-five years old and had walked 120 kilometres through the Somali desert to a feeding centre we were running in a town named Burakaba. He had walked this distance with his thirteen-year-old boy on his back and made the journey with about four litres of water, all of which he had fed to his son. The boy was his last child and weighed not more than twenty-five kilograms. The boy was dying of starvation and malaria. Every one of this father's other children was dead. His three boys had been mutilated and shot. His wife and two daughters had been raped and their bodies stuffed in their family well for them to drown. This man arrived at the feeding centre that afternoon, joining some five hundred other people who each had a similar story. We were providing medical assistance in that area alone to twenty-two feeding centres, running thirteen clinics and two hospitals, one that we built. I saw the boy that night, and I knew that he would die within hours.

He died early into the night. And what did the father do? He waited at the feeding centre with his dead son for me. What for? To thank me. He waited at the feeding centre with his dead son to thank me for trying to help his last boy, for not walking away from the horror that was Somalia in 1992 and for the fact that MSF was telling the world about the reality of suffering and need in the hell that was his country. He knew this fact and made a particular point of thanking me for it. He has stayed as an irrevocable fixture in my mind since because he was the first person outside of MSF who actually described to me what our work meant to him.

Some days later, outside one of our feeding centres in Baidoa, I watched in a stupefied horror as a warlord's armoured personnel carrier literally drove over the bodies of women and children sitting outside the feeding centre waiting for food. The scream and the terror of those people, macerated and carved up under the wheels of the APC are with me today. But what stays with me most firmly is the vivid, almost technicolour image that not one of the men on top of that APC turned his head to see where the cries were coming from. They didn't even flinch behind their Vuarnet sunglasses. They didn't even aim their Kalashnikov machine guns or squirm in their Mickey Mouse T-shirts. They sat in cold defiance of the terror beneath them. This is brutality. This is inhumanity. And this is criminal.

Months after the UN humanitarian agencies had pulled out of Somalia, the UN would return under the banner of humanitarianism and the US-led Operation Restore Hope. Initially, the US-led enforcement intervention restored law and order and protected the delivery of humanitarian assistance. But months later, as the UN military operation turned to statecraft, thousands of Somali citizens were killed "collaterally" by UN forces, as US Marines attempted to — in their words — "hunt down" Mohamed Farrah Aidid, the clan leader responsible for the earlier death of twenty-seven peacekeepers. And many other civilians would be beaten, brutalized, tortured or killed by individual acts of barbarity and racism by Canadian, Italian, French and other peacekeeping soldiers — all operating under the official guise of humanitarianism.

All this effectively ended on October 6, 1993, when seventeen US Rangers would be killed by Somali militia and when the now-famous image of one US Marine, naked and dead, being dragged through the streets of Mogadishu would de facto end George Bush's New World Order.

For humanitarian NGOs, they too had to effectively pull out of Somalia. Why? Because humanitarian NGOs had inadvertently come to be seen as part of a UN military enforcement operation that had gone badly wrong. Humanitarian NGOs were tarred with the same political and military brush and were seen as accomplices to that failure to establish peace in a viable state.

Humanitarian NGOs have since returned slowly and cautiously to Somalia, having learned a great number of important lessons — among them the necessity of keeping humanitarian objectives and actions specifically decoupled from other sometimes essential and legitimate international political and military objectives in such political crises. These and other lessons are being misconstrued — or simply forgotten — under what Fiona Fox and Joanna McRae at the Overseas Development Institute in Britain have recently called — and I think with a certain sarcasm — a "New Humanitarianism for a New Millennium."

This is a relatively recent phenomenon — the last ten years or so — and it's a goal-oriented humanitarianism that since the late eighties considers long-term sustainable development within the remit of humanitarianism in war. It is human rights based and seeks to use humanitarian assistance to transform violence and to support a peace process. In response to the call for humanitarian assistance to "do no harm," the New Humanitarianism seeks to apportion aid not simply on the basis of the universal right to relief based on need; it will withhold aid if aid could prolong a conflict or undermine human rights. It rejects neutrality as morally repugnant and as unachievable in the complex political emergencies of the post-Cold War world. It can arguably be seen as an NGO response to shifting donor government support away from development assistance and toward humanitarian assistance in the last ten or so years.

And it represents, I think, not a New Humanitarianism, but a deep confusion about the crucial differences between humanitarianism in war, human rights work in peace and the inherently political dimensions of peace work and development. It also represents — and dare I say it? — a pretentious overestimate of what humanitarianism, human rights and development NGOs can accomplish in the face of a growing political vacuum. Here, powerful states now show little political interest or responsibility toward political stability or crises in states peripheral to their direct national interests.

As the reality of Somalia illustrates, humanitarianism in war is no easy task. It is, by definition, a struggle to create that space — humanitarian space — required to provide assistance and to seek protection for civilians in a situation of armed conflict. There are at least four time-tested principles that make this task achievable. The first is universality, that all victims are worthy of assistance and protection wherever they may be. The second is impartiality, that assistance and protection is given to all victims of a conflict, no matter which side they are on, regardless of race, religion, political or other affiliation, and that this is given strictly and proportionately according to need and need alone. The third is independence, that humanitarian actors remain independent of political or other affiliations whose interests may impinge on universality and impartiality. A fourth principle is neutrality, the traditional view that humanitarian actors must stand apart from the political issues at stake in a conflict. MSF departed from this traditional view of neutrality, and, in fact, it was this departure that was the genesis of the MSF movement.

Let me tell you a little about our history. It's instructive in that it tells why we are who we are, why we do what we do, and, in particular, it illuminates our particular stance on neutrality.

We were founded in 1971 by a group of French doctors and journalists. In 1968, some of these same doctors had worked for the Red Cross in Biafra, Nigeria, where civil war and government oppression led to massive famine. On one particular day, the doctors were working in a small Biafran medical clinic. On that day, the clinic was overrun by villagers fleeing Nigerian soldiers. The doctors notified Red Cross headquarters and were ordered to abandon their posts. They refused and, in staying, witnessed wholesale carnage as Nigerian troops slaughtered unarmed men, women and children. The doctors quit the Red Cross, and when they returned to France, they told the world of what they had witnessed.

Three years later, in 1971, MSF was formed by a group of French doctors and journalists who were outraged at the fact that the Red Cross's interpretation then of international humanitarian law prevented them from speaking out against what was effectively a state policy of forced starvation and migration. It was a reaction to the same view of neutrality that led the Red Cross to remain silent in its knowledge of the Nazi extermination camps used in the Holocaust of World War II.

For many, silence has been confused with neutrality and has been presented as a necessary condition for humanitarian action. From our beginning, MSF was created in opposition to this assumption. We refuse to remain silent in such circumstances. We refuse to remain silent in the face of egregious violations of international humanitarian law and in the face of war crimes or crimes against humanity. We do stand apart from the political issues at stake in a conflict and on the political processes or military actions that seek — successfully or unsuccessfully — to resolve these political processes. We continuously assert people's right to humanitarian assistance and protection. And we are vocal in insisting that humanitarian actors have a primary responsibility to continuously assert and demand that all belligerents respect these rights and that all states assume their political responsibility to ensure that these rights are in fact respected. In the last thirty years, Médecins Sans Frontières has been and is irrevocably committed to this ethic of refusal — an ethic that demands we constantly challenge the apparent futility of the way the world is.

Over the years since 1971, MSF has told the world about atrocities that local governments have tried to hide. In 1979, for example, we told the world about thousands of Vietnamese fleeing their country in small fishing boats, many of whom drowned at sea before we could assist them. In 1985, MSF alerted the world to famine in Ethiopia, even though this meant that we would be and, in fact, were expelled from the country. And in 1991, we proved that the Iraqi government was using chemical weapons on Kurdish villagers. We have taken these and many other actions in an ethic of refusal. This ethic affirms MSF's commitment to universal medical ethics, to our understanding that all people, regardless of state borders or existing interpretations of international law — be it humanitarian law, human rights law, law governing trade in intellectual property rights, or any law — that all people have a right to exist as human beings.

We adhere to impartiality and vigorously protect our independence from political or other actors or interests. To this end, seventy-four per cent of our funding comes from private citizen donations from around the world. We set our own operational priorities and make our own operational choices. More than anything else, at the heart of our work is an irreducible respect for human dignity.

Bringing direct medical action to bear and doing so without regard for borders or other artificial barriers: this is the heart of MSF's work. It is, at its root, a commitment that sees human beings not as a means but as an end in themselves. It affirms that how human beings are treated anywhere concerns everyone everywhere. And it demands that this irreducible human dignity be at the centre of any political project. Indeed — and here's an apparent paradox for you — for MSF, humanitarianism is the most apolitical of all acts, but if its actions and morality are taken seriously, it has the most profound of political implications.

What is this "humanitarianism in war," and what is it not? I was MSF's Head of Mission in Kigali during the genocide in Rwanda, when only the International Committee of the Red Cross (ICRC), MSF and the UN Assistance Mission for Rwanda (UNAMIR) remained. One night in Kigali, after many long hours of surgery, from the hospital balcony I watched packs of dogs that were roaming the streets. They were fat, hungry and vicious, and virtually wild with the taste of human flesh. They were fighting with each other over the remains of a corpse that lay in the street and were threatening to attack a man who had ventured outside the hospital fence in search of firewood.

Later that night, among the thousands of people we either treated or gave shelter to at the hospital, a little girl of about nine years old told me through an interpreter how she escaped murder at the hands of the Interahamwe killing squads. She told me — and I quote — "My mother hid me in the latrine. I saw through the hole. I watched them hit her with machetes. I watched my mother's arm fall into my father's blood on the floor, and I cried without noise in the toilet."

During that time, around Rwanda, Tutsis and moderate Hutus were being butchered in a systematic and rational way. People were killed in their homes or after being assembled in churches, schools and hospitals or bused or marched to mass graves, where they were not shot but had their hands and feet cut off — bleeding to death and being unable to climb out of the graves. People often begged — and paid — to have their children shot, rather than to suffer this particular horror. Over a million people died in Rwanda over that twelve-week period.

It's very hard to describe this to you. I rarely talk about this, but you have to know this. This is what happens in a genocide, and this is where our responsibility as citizens lies. We must stop this from happening again. Let me continue.

In early June of '94, I went to an orphanage in Kigali to give medical care to a group of Tutsi children. This was no easy task. The ICRC, MSF and UNAMIR had spent nearly a full day negotiating a temporary ceasefire to allow passage through strongholds and the checkpoints of Interahamwe and soldiers that were committing the genocide. I had been to the orphanage the day before, and there had been about 360 children. The day before, I had tried to persuade the Interahamwe commander to let us take the children across the front line to our hospital, where we had established a temporary orphanage as well. In the course of our conversation, I asked him if he had children. He was a father of four. He also went on to tell me,

"These children here, these are not children, they are *Tutsi inyenzi* — insects." He said, "They're prisoners of war and will be crushed like insects."

When we arrived that next day, inside there were only some 120 children alive. The night before, more than two hundred children had been butchered and now lay covered by a blue plastic tarp, in a heap of limbs and clothes and blood that made a brown-red mud of the soil beneath them. My most stark memory of Rwanda is not of mass graves or of the political theory underlying the International Convention on the Prevention and Punishment of Genocide, but of small, sausage-like fingers — severed fingers — lying in the mud beside that blue plastic tarp.

As doctors, we could not stop a genocide. Genocide is a political crime that, by definition, defies the very essence of humanity and the most basic principles of humanitarianism in war. In genocide, there is no humanitarian space. Stopping genocide is not a humanitarian act. MSF publicly called for armed UN military intervention to stop the genocide, and we insisted on staying with our patients to the extent we could. OXFAM supported this call, and for the first time in their history, the Red Cross, with whom we were working closely inside Rwanda, spoke out, too. Unlike the little girl in the toilet, we had a voice and could not watch in silence. Nor could we turn away in acquiescence, nor could we become complicit by reducing our presence to a simple, silent, technical medical act of Band-Aids for bullet wounds or an offering of sutures to a rationalized savagery. In Rwanda, we demanded a military intervention to stop the genocide.

After World War II, Churchill called the systematic extermination of Jews under the Nazi regime "the crime that has no name." Rwanda's was the first genocide where the international community had the political freedom to act to prevent and stop genocide, and the first demonstration in unequivocal terms of a moral political failure to stop genocide. As the world watched on television, the Security Council equivocated on its responsibility, and outside powers manoeuvered to maintain influence in the African Sub-Saharan region. The genocide was essentially over before the UN Operation Turquoise was launched, and, as we know, acts of revenge in its name, in the name of genocide, followed in Rwanda and in neighbouring Zaire in 1996 and 1997. And they continue today.

Humanitarianism is not a tool to end war, to create peace or to salve the conscience of political indifference. It is a citizen's response to human suffering and to the political failure that creates it or allows it to go unchecked. It is an immediate, short-term act that cannot erase political responsibility for public security at the national or international level. Our responsibility as human beings — and as what Albert Camus called "doctor as witness" — was and is to speak out, to witness authentically to the reality of inhumanity and to speak out against the moral hollowness of political inaction. When confronted with this, there can be no moral neutrality about what is "good." The only crime equal to willful inhumanity is the crime of "indifference, silence and forgetting." This is its own kind of inhumanity. We are not certain, as MSF, that speaking out can always save lives, but we are certain that silence can kill. It kills today and it will kill tomorrow. If there is silence, there can be no justice, and revenge — which is the lowest form of justice, but a form of justice nonetheless — is the only certainty.

This is why we continue to press worldwide for the arrest of the alleged perpetrators, why we press for the ratification of the International Criminal Court, and why we press for investigations into the culpability of the UN and individual governments that avoided their political responsibility in 1994. Nor have we remained neutral on the failure of the UN in Srebrenica in 1995. Seven thousand men and boys were massacred in Srebrenica while UN peacekeepers were present but while de facto humanitarian space was absent.

We and others have demanded accountability from the UN and its member states, and slowly, ever so slowly, we're getting it. Again, no humanitarian can stop genocide. No humanitarian can stop ethnic cleansing. These are political and not humanitarian imperatives. They are crimes — crimes against humanity, war crimes and political crimes that demand responsibility and direct action from the international political community.

Can humanitarianism in war be a part of a peace process or a broader political framework? Is this, according to the principles I have talked about, a task for humanitarian actors? There's a tendency now in Afghanistan and Sierra Leone and elsewhere to make humanitarian action in war part of a broader strategic framework that includes the restoration of peace, respect for human rights and economic reconstruction. This effort groups humanitarian action with peace-keeping, the restoration of democracy and human rights. The word "humanitarianism" then has come to mean all things to all actors. It can be a comforting approach because it obscures the relatively modest impact of humanitarian action in war by integrating it with a grander design of conflict resolution and the restoration of peace and, again, a broader political framework.

Here, humanitarian organizations that witness massive crimes in war need only convey the information to human rights organizations. In doing so, they avoid the difficult choice between denunciation at the risk of expulsion and silence at the risk of complicity. However, this kind of approach blurs the nature of each organization's responsibility. Public statements made by humanitarian NGOs address not only the violations of human rights, but also and more importantly the quality of relief actions in the field and the obstacles placed in their way. This discreet cooperation between humanitarian and human rights organizations is not necessarily synonymous with greater security for aid workers. Indeed, in a context in which human rights are an element of international diplomacy, giving confidential information this way may be seen by belligerents as clandestine and subversive. Moreover and most importantly, it may make humanitarian assistance and protection for the population concerned conditional on a specific diplomatic agenda that links peace to human rights conventions.

Human rights conventions state general or normative principles for the treatment of individuals by governments and are applicable in peace but can be suspended by governments in war. Humanitarian law, on the other hand, is concerned specifically with armed conflict and goes far beyond general normative principles. Specifically, it sets limits on the use of violence in war. It provides minimum rights in conflict that help guarantee the survival of vulnerable populations in situations of conflict. It authorizes and regulates the relief action and gives responsibility for such action to independent organizations. It sets out specific, pragmatic operational definitions and require-ments regarding humanitarian protection and assistance to precise categories of vulnerable people: civilians, the sick, the wounded and those deprived of freedom in situations of armed international or internal conflict. It also defines the rights conferred upon the ICRC and impartial humanitarian organizations to provide assistance in-dependently of governments or warring parties.

This distinction between normative human rights conventions in peace and operational international humanitarian law in war is vitally important. To make humanitarian assistance in times of war contingent on human rights law that applies in peace — a reality that, by definition, does not exist in war — is to make such assistance and protection contingent on hope or faith alone that a peace process or a broader strategic political framework will be successful.

But what happens to the right of humanitarian assistance and protection when a nation is politically isolated, as in Afghanistan, or when a peace process fails or takes a warlike turn, as it has so often in Sierra Leone? For these reasons, independent humanitarian actors cannot link their assistance and protection role or be seen to link these to any peace process or broader strategic framework.

Finally, on the subject of the "New Humanitarianism," let me choose just one issue from the NATO bombing during the Kosovo crisis to illustrate the importance of the principle of independence for humanitarian actors.

Many western NGOs that worked in the Kosovo region during the NATO bombing were heavily funded by western governments — governments that, in fact, as members of NATO, were bombing in the former Yugoslavia. Are such NGOs independent of western foreign policy objectives, when in many cases they would not have been operational there without western government funding? Can they be seen — by all parties to the conflict and by all civilian victims of the conflict, Serb and Kosovar alike — as legitimate, impartial humanitarian actors? How are they seen and how will they be seen if further political crisis and conflict occurs in the region?

These questions become particularly relevant when a war is sold as a "humanitarian war," as it was in Kosovo. Are humanitarians now the New Warriors, or are the warriors now the New Humanitarians? This kind of ambiguity — or, more clearly, doublespeak — is extremely dangerous. There is no such thing as a "humanitarian war" — in Kosovo or elsewhere — no matter how apparently noble or just the cause.

I've talked about Somalia, Rwanda, Srebrenica, Kosovo, Sierra Leone and Afghanistan. And from these, I think we can draw some clear lessons and hopefully return to a more essential understanding of what humanitarianism in war is and what it's not and why the "New Humanitarianism" represents an unwelcome lack of clarity.

It is clear that there are specific responsibilities and specific limits to humanitarianism in war. It must adhere to basic humanitarian principles of independence, universality, impartiality and neutrality — and a neutrality that is neither silent nor morally neutered. Just as no humanitarian can make war, no humanitarian can make peace. Again, these are political, not humanitarian, imperatives. Humanitarian principles and actions cannot be subordinated to political or military goals, however legitimate these goals may be. For if they are, it is potentially — and more often actually is — to the detriment of both. It is, however, conditional on political responsibility that the humanitarian space can exist in situations of conflict. The rights that exist under international humanitarian law are not the same rights that exist under human rights conventions, and the responsibilities of the humanitarian organization are not the same as the responsibilities of the human rights organization. Humanitarian action in war is not development. It is not peace-building. It is not enforcement by military means. Nor can it be a substitute for politics by other means.

Let me repeat: the humanitarian act is the most apolitical of all acts, but if its actions and morality are taken seriously, it has the most profound of political implications. Today those political implications cannot be seriously examined without acknowledging the impact of globalization. And here, before I close, I come to the second domain — for lack of a better word — that we work in: situations of nonviolent crisis where people are not able to exercise their basic human rights, like the right to access health care.

Globalization is not new, nor is it good, nor is it bad. It simply is. A hundred years ago, the pattern of trade, overseas investment and immigration was essentially today's globalization without the telecommunications revolution that cheaper and faster computers and the Internet have brought and without the accelerated speed and scope of trade and travel that cheap airfares and transportation have brought.

Chris Patton recently gave one of the BBC Reith Lectures. In it, he noted that what makes globalization different today is that the triumph of liberal economic ideas has combined with technology to lower the cost and to speed the impact of the movement of goods, money, people and ideas to an unimaginable degree. He argued that, for the majority, it has produced improvements in the standard of living that do not require a sacrifice in the quality of living.

Well, about this last point — and to return to the daily reality of MSF's work in nonconflict situations — I must firmly disagree. More than a billion people are unable to secure food and water, the most basic measure of disease prevention. Two billion people live and survive on less than two dollars a day. Today's new buzzword is "poverty" — either its alleviation or its eradication. Well, let's be clear: ours is a time of unprecedented wealth. As former president Clinton said only a few months ago, there is more wealth today than at any time in human history. And yet politicians and their patrons tell us ceaselessly that we live in an era of limited resources. Reality today, however, is that we live in a social order that excludes, that marginalizes and that literally leaves open to sacrifice the lives of billions of people — men, women and children — in the name of some future economic benefit that will apparently trickle down to the world's poor, given enough time.

Let's also be clear about what some of the problems are. The single most important global health issue today is the right — the human right — to access health care. Here, access to effective treatment for infectious diseases is among the biggest issues. Sixteen million people live with active tuberculosis around the world today. Eight million people are now developing active tuberculosis every year, and two million people now die from tuberculosis every year. Treatable infectious diseases are the leading cause of death worldwide. Seventeen million people die every year in the South, and only — if you can put it that way — 150,000 die every year in the North of treatable infectious diseases.

Some — not all — but some of the reasons that people die from diseases like AIDS, TB, sleeping sickness and other tropical diseases are that essential life-saving medicines are too expensive because of patent protection, that existing drugs are no longer produced, that there is not an adequate return on investment, or that there's virtually no new research and development for priority global diseases.

Since the beginning of the AIDS epidemic, nineteen million people are dead. Thirty-four million people now live with HIV worldwide, and ninety percent of these people are in the South. Let there be no mistake: what happens to adults impacts on children. There are eleven million AIDS orphans today in Africa alone. AIDS is rampant and it is literally out of control: 5.6 million people were infected last year, and India and Asia stand on the brink of a potential HIV explosion. It is not just an epidemic. It is a global catastrophe that is already a rival to the Black Plague of the Middle Ages. And yet, unlike the Black Plague, it is a treatable infectious disease. Yet thirty-two of the thirty-four million HIV-positive people have no access to anti-retroviral therapy, the existing treatment for HIV. Why? Because patent protection makes these drugs unaffordable and therefore inaccessible. The majority of people with this disease do not exist on the balance sheets and profit calculations of the major pharmaceutical producers. And access is essentially denied as spurious arguments over intellectual property rights allow profit to be privileged over the most elemental human right — the right to exist — for millions of human beings. Poor people have need, but with an income of less than two dollars a day, they're not a market. And so they're not dying of HIV but of market and political failure. This is obscene. There's no other word for it.

Language is determinant. How we phrase a problem defines the solutions we seek and the solutions we get. If we define the AIDS epidemic as a "public health issue with trade and IPR overtones," then we will get the same pasteurized and meaningless response from governments and the pharmaceutical industry. Drug donations or price reductions for the few will follow — buying off public pressure by oiling the squeaky wheel of "concern." The AIDS, the TB, the malaria and the sleeping sickness epidemics are not simply global public health concerns. They are obscene and morally repugnant examples of political negligence that cannot go unchallenged.

Unjust use of trade law around intellectual property rights for pharmaceuticals, the political process around their application, the deification of profit over people's rights and the fact that trade has become a barrier to health of literally billions of people — these are no longer acceptable or defensible from any moral, human rights or public health perspective.

The world's poor are not a market. They are people who have need but not enough money. It is that simple. Nor is state- or private-sector charity the answer. States have a duty to protect, to promote and to ensure people's right to access basic health care. This is not an act of privilege, as charity is, but a responsibility, a duty of states that cannot be ignored.

But what is, in fact, under challenge today? Well, yesterday in Pretoria, thirty-nine pharmaceutical companies brought a court challenge to the South African government's legislation that seeks to legalize the importation of generic anti-retrovirals from countries like Brazil, India and Thailand. These generic anti-retrovirals are cheaper by orders of magnitude than patented anti-retrovirals sold in South

Africa. Now this is a landmark case. The South African government has signed the Trade-Related Aspects of Intellectual Property Rights Agreement (WTO TRIPS) , and its legislation is consistent and fully compliant with the TRIPS Agreement, which allows governments to take such measures when it is in the public interest to do so, such as in a public health emergency.

Well, 4.5-million people live with HIV and without access to anti-retrovirals in South Africa, and the government's Medicines Act is trying to remedy this. This case begins a process of determining if, when, where and how governments can act in the public interest under the TRIPS Agreement. It will also determine, on a very pragmatic level, whether the privilege of profit takes priority over the right to life and the right to access health care.

MSF and OXFAM are calling on the Canadian government and all governments to publicly support the South African government in its efforts to meet its obligations to the public interest. We and other NGOs have been campaigning on this issue — and particularly the broader issue of access to essential medicines — for nearly two years now. MSF, Health Action International, ACT UP, OXFAM, Treatment Access Campaign of South Africa, the Access Network of Thailand and many, many others will not give up this fight until it is won. I can guarantee you that.

Some may say that this is simply wishful thinking. Well, to those who do, I challenge you to look at the history of social movements. We know, in looking at these — and particularly, for example, the movement against slavery, the labour rights movement, the women's suffrage movement, the civil rights movement, the human rights movement and, the environmental movement — that each of these began in a confrontation of sources of power, be they political or economic powers, that seek to maintain a particular balance of power and interests.

This confrontation then moved on to interaction with sources of power, to partnership and then to co-optation of the principles and values that gave birth to the movement in the first place. Such co-optation after — and not before — this process is a good and favourable outcome. Why? Because it means that deeply held principled ideas that were initially on the margins of social thinking and values are now the dominant ideas that are codified in law, constitution and everyday social discourse.

But we know that social change is rarely, if ever, a straight linear process nor can its process can be easily located on the rather simplistic continuum I have just painted of confrontation, interaction, partnership and co-optation. We know, too, that rights achieved must be defended and that constant vigilance is required to maintain hard-won gains. And here, the slave trade in Sudan today, the status of African Americans in the United States today and the human rights of women that are not yet won the world over — these are examples where gains must be constantly defended and reasserted and new gains constantly demanded.

The challenge is to insist that those who are responsible be responsible. This vision must not be blurred by short-term gains with either the state or the private sector. The challenge is not to displace the role and responsibility of the state through, for example, charity, or to become charity-based co-managers of misery with the state, or to allow a public relations coup for the private sector to override a long-term commitment to equity and to justice. The challenge is not simply to achieve a technical standard for the few, but to demand that each human being's dignity be at the centre of any political project — a political project that is just, equitable and accountable.

I have talked about humanitarianism in war: what it is and what it's not. I've argued against the "New Humanitarianism," and I've talked about the right — the basic human right — to exist and to access health care around, for example, the AIDS epidemic. And I hope you've found my talk interesting.

Embedded in my talk tonight has been the responsibility — the imperative — to stand against injustice. The economist Amartya Sen has argued that poverty and the injustice that often accompanies it is not simply about economics but, more importantly, about a fundamental lack of freedoms. It's also about the choices of us who are free — or, more simply put, it's also about how we use our liberty. We here are free to use our liberty in whatever way we choose. And I'm particularly delighted that there are so many students here tonight — students of all stripes and disciplines. Why? Because through your action or inaction, through your voice or through your silence, you will shape the world around you.

And I ask you — and particularly again the students — to use your liberty and the skills you have gained and will gain in future training to act and to insist that the basic dignity of the excluded, the marginalized, the unprotected be acknowledged in their full humanity. This is the man who carried his son to a feeding centre in Somalia. These are the women and children crushed under the wheels of the APC. This is the nine-year-old girl who cried without noise in the toilet. These are the millions of people without access to anti-retrovirals. And this is every man, woman and child who may fall prey to disease, infirmity or political oppression or negligence.

Use your liberty to be who you are: free people who can knowingly choose to make life more bearable for the other. For the "other" is not some anonymous object to be ignored with indifference and not, as Jean Paul Sartre put it, "your hell," but the "other" is your brother and your sister who shares in our common humanity. Do not be paralyzed by fear and do not be anaesthetized by false hope, by illusionary dreams. But do live what is possible through courage, choice and an irreducible respect for human dignity.

Fear and false hope are overcome by what we do, which can be in defiance of the apparent futility of reality. It takes courage to face fear, to overcome false hope, to be and to do. And if you look, you will find courage in the most unlikely of places. You will always find it — your own courage or theirs — in the eyes of the "other." In doing this, we can only but acknowledge, grow and enrich our own humanity.

Dr. Orbinski's argument against the "New Humanitarianism" prompted an audience member to ask how human rights law could possibly be enforced in these situations without there also being military force present to back it up.

JAMES ORBINSKI

First of all, my argument was not against intervention. My argument was against what I called a "New Humanitarianism," not a "New Interventionism," but a new form of humanitarianism. And what I tried to pose was that a brand of humanitarianism that tries to be all things to all people — that tries to be political, that tries to support peace processes, that tries to do development, that tries to do capacity building, that tries to do any and all things, conflict resolution — that this is inconsistent with the primary mission and the primary principles that are required to deliver humanitarian assistance and protection in the situation of conflict. That was my argument.

Now, I would not argue against military intervention in some circumstances. There is no question. In fact, MSF called for UN-led military intervention in Rwanda to stop the genocide. There is no question that there are circumstances where that is a necessary option. Whether it's viable is another question. That raises a whole other series of issues around international governance, the international political system, the role and responsibility and so on of the Security Council, the veto power of individual member states among the permanent five and so on, the actual capacity of the peacekeeping office to deliver troops in a timely manner to a particular crisis, and then also — and I think most importantly — the political meaning, if you will, of a particular military intervention.

I'll give you an example. The western world mobilized under NATO to intervene in Kosovo. And I'm not saying that the crisis in Kosovo was not a crisis. There's no question that there was massive ethnic cleansing taking place. There's no question that there was an egregious situation of suffering, and there's no question that there was an overwhelming situation of humanitarian need. There's also no question that there were many other political circumstances around

Kosovo that drove NATO to intervene — and many other legitimate political circumstances.

Before I touch on those, there are many other situations in Africa, for example, or in Afghanistan, where there are far greater humanitarian needs, but there is no interest from the western world and no interest from individual political actors to actually intervene. Now, that flies in the face of the concept of universality. You cannot be geographically selective in the application of humanitarian action or rationale, which is exactly what the western world has done over the last ten years, and I think the many examples I gave in my talk illustrate that quite nicely.

In Kosovo, Richard Holbrooke said in April of 1999, in a lecture, I believe it was at Princeton — and this is not often quoted, and let's remember that the bombing in Kosovo was sold as a humanitarian war — he said that the objectives and the rationale, if you will, for the NATO action in Kosovo are fourfold. The first is to secure the long-term stability — of what? — of NATO. The second is to demonstrate American superiority in terms of military capacity. The third is to secure the greater stability of southeastern Europe. Then the fourth is, if possible, to achieve some — I'm not sure of the exact wording — stability around humanitarian issues in the region.

None of those first three are illegitimate political goals. I have no qualm with any of those things. But the fact is that it was sold as a humanitarian war, and it affected the ability of independent humanitarian actors to actually be seen as neutral and impartial in the situation of war, and that's the issue that I'm trying to get at. If there is to be military intervention, there are many, many dimensions and many, many sub-issues that have to be addressed.

"The Ethics of Humanitarian Intervention" was broadcast on April 19, 2001, in a series called Taking a Stand.

Remembering Rwanda

ROMÉO DALLAIRE
GERALD CAPLAN
Moderated by
MICHAEL ENRIGHT

General Roméo Dallaire was the Canadian in charge of the United Nations peacekeeping mission during the Rwandan genocide in 1994, ostensibly charged with ensuring that Rwanda didn't become the living hell it did. Underequipped, besieged by conflicting demands, ignored by the UN Security Council, General Dallaire and his soldiers watched as the violence escalated to a murderous frenzy. Even years after the massacre, he demonstrated the human toll exacted on those forced by bureaucracy and poor equipment to simply watch as thousands were butchered daily, an experience he and his personal staff officer, Major Brent Beardsley, wrote about in Shake Hands with the Devil: The Failure of Humanity in Rwanda. *In 2000, Michael Enright spoke with General Dallaire about what he saw, how he understands what went wrong and how he copes. In 2004, ten years after the genocide, Enright spoke with Gerald Caplan, author of* Rwanda: The Preventable Genocide, *the report of the International Panel of Eminent Persons appointed by the Organization of African Unity.*

MICHAEL ENRIGHT

We like to tell ourselves that we learn from our mistakes, but sadly that sometimes seems more honoured in the breach than we care to admit. Repeatedly, we ignore what we know and watch. Shame, tragedy and horror occur again and again. The Rwandan genocide wasn't the most grievous of genocides in our history, but the speed — a few short months — and the death toll — almost a million people — left the world stunned. And it left General Roméo Dallaire a broken man.

General Dallaire, I was thinking, your career — almost thirty-six years in the military — you were a highly disciplined professional soldier all that time. Do you think the discipline helps you now in coping?

ROMÉO DALLAIRE

That's a very interesting dimension. The first thing is, I wasn't always self-disciplined. I mean, I had my rough times during military college, and as a lieutenant, captain, and even as a major we had our wild moments. But my behaviour became more self-disciplined, a dimension which is the essence of a commander, a leader able to pursue his role. What I discovered when I finally crashed, which was four years after the event, was that I had no more self-discipline. I would eat junk food. I would work without controlling my schedules and not sleeping, not being able to do any physical training. Couldn't even read more than a page or two. And that lasted for, well, I was at home for over five months.

MICHAEL ENRIGHT

Your attention span had gone?

ROMÉO DALLAIRE

Oh, yeah. I was not not there. First, the whole physical dimension went — nearly collapsed. More than beyond your normal day-to-day energy. I mean, you start sucking into your actual body capability of resiliency. And then emotionally, you spend a lot of time just crying and yelling, you know, and brooding. And it envelops you. And when it gets really bad, without those pills and so on, then its like a cloudy day and you're into this sort of situation. Cloudy days are terrible for me still. You move into this sort of spiral of everything is wrong and wrong and you keep going in that spiral. And at the end of the spiral is, you know, "Let me out of all this pain." But every now and again, someone or something is a spark of light that turns you off.

MICHAEL ENRIGHT

What stayed your hand? When you got to the bottom of that spiral and said, "I want out, I'm getting out, I'm going to do it, I'm going to kill myself," what stopped you?

ROMÉO DALLAIRE

Incompetence, twice. What I planned seemed perfect to do. I'll give you an example. On one occasion, I was simply driving down the 417 back home to Quebec City on a Friday night. It was wintertime, and I, with the fatigue of the week and so on, thought it would be easy to simply jump the median — because there was a snowbank there — just jump over it and hit some bridge pylons. People would think I just fell asleep and so on. Well, I was driving a little Jetta and it has a very low centre of gravity, so when I hit, instead of the wheels jumping over the bank part of it, it banged back, so I ended up just bouncing across the median.

MICHAEL ENRIGHT

But you did turn into the pylons of the bridge.

ROMÉO DALLAIRE

Oh, yeah. And then once you've been pulled out of it, you feel . . . you're just emptied, and so you just keep on going.

MICHAEL ENRIGHT

Did you find any consolation in your religious phase?

ROMÉO DALLAIRE

I found that particularly overseas, because over there I had met — personally — the Devil. I had negotiated with him. I had shaken his hand. I even made or exchanged jokes with him. And so I was convinced that if the Devil existed, because he's here, then God did.

And as a commander, there are often times when you're very much alone — your staff are doing things and operations are launched and things like that, and you're alone.

Here's an example of how I knew there was another force there. First, there was no communication anymore with the outside world; we had lost that. Second, I couldn't speak to my subordinates, as my job was to maintain my morale and sense of humour and help them. And so I was standing by the window in the headquarters complex, and there was a screen and this sudden sound of a light breeze — and to this day I'm not sure whether it was a light breeze coming through the screen that made this sort of spiritual sound or it was the sounds of women and children and men who were being slaughtered at a distance, you know, screaming and so on, and it had been just muted enough to come in as a breeze.

But I had only that option — there was no one else, you know, and so I felt that that option was there.

MICHAEL ENRIGHT

Were you raised a particularly strict Catholic?

ROMÉO DALLAIRE

Yes, Catholic. Oh, yeah.

MICHAEL ENRIGHT

Then, in the faith that you and I were raised in, you know that it is said that the only unforgivable sin is despair. How did you avoid that and stay away from that ultimate sin in the midst of all the carnage?

ROMÉO DALLAIRE

I'll give you the same answer as I did when I was once asked how I kept my troops from falling apart, seeing these horrors. I mean, we were in a country that had thirty percent AIDS before the war, and we didn't have gloves or anything. And so I said I kept them going by working them until they dropped. And that's literally what they did. They worked day and night. And there were always people to save, there were always convoys to do. They were always trying to get resources, negotiating, and stuff like that. And when they were fatigued enough they slept and they slept, and then they got up, sometimes after four or five hours or something, and then they went at it again. And that's the only way. And so I did exactly the same thing.

MICHAEL ENRIGHT

How much sleep would you get a night?

ROMÉO DALLAIRE

Well, in the first five nights, because of all the negotiations and so on, I averaged about an hour or so at my desk. But the rest of the time, it depended on negotiations, if they went into the night. It depended a lot on the operations that were ongoing because, I mean, the war was still moving . . . and I had a few posts that were very, very vulnerable. I had one post of just about ten Tunisian soldiers and eight military observers, unarmed, all from Franco-African countries, and they stood off three successive onslaughts by the extremist government and the Interahamwe, the military, to kill the Tutsis in that hotel complex. And so every night I'd call them, see how things were, and then I'd sit there and say, "Tomorrow morning when I call them up they'll probably all be dead." And so I'd wake up and then do it.

MICHAEL ENRIGHT

After you arrived, the killing reached a level of, unimaginably, about eight thousand a day. What were you thinking at that time? You didn't have reinforcements. You didn't have a place for personnel. You were low on medical supplies, ammunition, food, no intelligence, and you had a rough band of international soldiers, very small, in the middle of all this, and you could see in front of you the hacked-up bodies of eight thousand people a day.

ROMÉO DALLAIRE

I think that we were put in an immoral situation — there are so many parallels with what's going on in Sierra Leone right now it's uncanny. This is six years after Rwanda, and after all kinds of academics and think tanks and military and political discussions, we responded to Sierra Leone exactly the same as we responded to Rwanda. I say "we" — I mean specifically the leadership of the world, and that's the western nations and particularly the Big Five. And it came to the point while I was there that the media were the only reinforcement I had. I had them coming in and we were flying them in and out.

MICHAEL ENRIGHT

And you used them to get the message out.

ROMÉO DALLAIRE

Oh, it became evident. When I was told by [*Newsweek*'s] John Barry early on that the cavalry were not coming and the option of withdrawal was being pushed, the only means I had was to shame the political structures of the world. Not the UN in its Secretariat, the Security Council — a Rwandan was there; I still don't know why they didn't throw him out — but to try to shame the Big Five, particularly the Americans, the Brits and the French, to actually do something. And so we decided early on, decided that I would risk the lives of soldiers to get the story out every day, and I guaranteed everyone who was there, before they were able to bring in their satellite communications, that they would see an event. And that was no problem — we were being surrounded by all this, and they would have something to report that was pertinent. I would protect them, feed them, house them and transport them, but ultimately their story, every night, would go out. And I would send observers, unarmed, you know, with the blue flag, and they'd take the tapes and they'd drive way up to the Ugandan border, where I had another mission. And then from there a helicopter would fly them into Kampala, and if they got the digital feed there in Kampala, fine; if not, it went directly to Nairobi.

MICHAEL ENRIGHT

I remember, in talking to you on the telephone a number of times, the production crew afterwards would say, "We've never heard anyone, any commander, any field commander, force commander, be so candid. He's going to get in trouble." And I wonder if that thought crossed your mind, that you perhaps were saying too much or you were telling too much of the truth?

ROMÉO DALLAIRE

No. In fact, that's quite interesting because that never, ever entered my mind. By then I'd already told the UN that I wasn't withdrawing, so I'd already disobeyed an instruction, I suppose, and I like to say that I convinced them that I shouldn't pull out.

MICHAEL ENRIGHT

But you thought that the alternative might be that you'd die there.

ROMÉO DALLAIRE

Oh, yes. I'd do my rounds at night around the headquarters, because we had in the headquarters some very senior people that we were able to get out, and the extremist battalions were fighting their way towards my headquarters as the rebels were also fighting their way to my headquarters — but I hoped that it was for a different intent, which, ultimately, it was. So there was nothing worse than what was going on, and the whole decision, to stay was a moral decision. It wasn't a pure military decision because militarily it was totally ineffective, but morally, as within the first twenty-four hours of the war my mandate was dead. But we would not have been able to live with the stigma of actually having abandoned [our post]. And even though the world abandoned us, we on the ground could not see these people abandoned, and if there was a chance of a ceasefire to get at the people to protect them, then that was worth whatever came from the outside. I remember your sessions, but while I was talking to you, you were part of my plan.

MICHAEL ENRIGHT

January 11, 1994. Do you remember the day?

ROMÉO DALLAIRE

I remember the night.

MICHAEL ENRIGHT

That's when you sent the telex, the warning, to New York.

ROMÉO DALLAIRE

I had been debriefed at the end of the day by the sector commander, and Brent and I spent — oh, it took us a couple of hours to get it on the computer.

MICHAEL ENRIGHT

You were asking for permission to conduct raids around Kigali, to get the arms away from the people whom you knew were about to embark on a massacre.

ROMÉO DALLAIRE

When we did our reconnaissance in August of '93, we had just signed an agreement, and we prepared our report in September in New York. Brent and I were working on the rules of engagement for that mission, to see if the concept that we had produced was going to be accepted. And we looked at the Cambodia rules of engagement, where the UN took over the whole country to rebuild it and then hand it over. And we also knew that there had been massacres over the last four years in that general area and there had been others in the surrounding countries — Uganda had some massive problems in the eighties. So we knew that there would be massacres — you know, ten thousand, twenty thousand, maybe fifty thousand people. So we took a paragraph out of the Cambodia one and put it in ours, which essentially said that if we are witness to any crimes against humanity then we have the full right to use all force necessary to stop it.

MICHAEL ENRIGHT

That was in the draft.

ROMÉO DALLAIRE
Yes.

MICHAEL ENRIGHT
What response did you want from New York and what response did
you get?

ROMÉO DALLAIRE
Essentially, I was just telling them that I believed this was an operation that was within my terms of reference. I did tell them that it
could be an ambush; however, I felt that if we conducted it the way
we could, using the Belgians and the UN soldiers, we could swoop
in and do the job and come out. Now, this went up to New York
in January. Remember, in October, just a couple of months before,
the Americans had been hit hard in Somalia, and they lost eighteen
Rangers and seventy-odd injured. The Pakistanis had taken a big hit
a couple of months before that in Somalia also. And so there was
this cloud of concern about our being set up the same way.

MICHAEL ENRIGHT
For an ambush.

ROMÉO DALLAIRE
That's right. And so they would get the Belgians they needed. That
would force Belgium to pull out, and then that would force us out,
and that made all kinds of sense because the political process was
stalling, going nowhere. So all I was saying was that I've assessed the
risks and I'm going in in thirty-six hours.

MICHAEL ENRIGHT
And what did New York say?

ROMÉO DALLAIRE
Well, that it wasn't in my mandate and I was going beyond the terms
of a classic peacekeeping operation, that I had to take action with

the leadership of the country to make them aware of that and to tell them to cease and desist.

MICHAEL ENRIGHT

When you received that response, that return message from the UN, knowing what you knew, was it frustration, was it anger? What went on inside your head when you knew what was going to happen in the absence of your taking any action, and you knew that you were being prevented from taking any action?

ROMÉO DALLAIRE

I knew that the capability was there for them to take action. I did not know whether they would do it or not because I didn't have an intelligence capability, apart from what we saw visually. We had very simple Motorola radios. Even the minimum of electronic warfare would have been able to get in there, and I would have been able to hear everything they said. I didn't have that — it's not in the nature of a Chapter Six peacekeeping mission — and so they were concerned about that side. Then there's the whole Somalia side that they were concerned about, and I think the other dimension was that this was not a Chapter Six job.

And I think I made a real fundamental mistake in using the term "offensive operations." I think if I had written, "I'm going to conduct deterrent operations," it would have been better. And this is an interesting point. We in the military work from action verbs — to defend, to attack, to withdraw, to surround. However, in this generation of conflict resolution, where there is war going on, we can't use those terms. It's more to protect, to create an atmosphere of security, to assist. And we have not taken those verbs and conducted a fundamental rewriting of our doctrine of peacekeeping in order to maximize those words. Instead, what we're finding is that we're often minimizing them because of the risk of casualties . . .

MICHAEL ENRIGHT

Or the politics.

ROMÉO DALLAIRE

Oh, absolutely. But I believe that politics — the politicians on the ground, the diplomats, the military on the ground — can create one plan instead of three or four plans as goes on now.

MICHAEL ENRIGHT

When you look at your time there, are there things that you should have done and didn't or are there things that you did do and shouldn't have? I don't know how you sort out in your mind, looking back now, how it could have gone down a different path, how it could have gone a different way.

ROMÉO DALLAIRE

I think I could have done more. I think that I've got colleagues, general officers, who could have gone there and done better. I could have done more, but I didn't because of one overriding factor, and that was the administration structure of the UN and the countries not providing their troops with the capabilities we told them to come in with. And I'm not talking about the whole Secretariat; I'm talking purely about the logistics side of the UN, which is based on a twenty-year program of building a school system. There's no problem with missions that are there for thirty, forty years, like Cyprus, but they did not have the capability to build a mission in the middle of Africa with no port in just a couple of months.

MICHAEL ENRIGHT

Is that because we didn't care, the world did not care?

ROMÉO DALLAIRE

Well, that's a component of it. One, you need an administrative structure that can respond to a crisis. Two, the administration structure was not budgeted to equip the troops that were coming in because their countries were supposed to do that. And three, I wasn't getting the capability in the force that I needed, and that force was not being supported by the big players because there was no interest. I mean, there were sixteen missions going on: they were building up

Yugoslavia, they had Cambodia, they had Somalia fiddling around, Mozambique was launching off, there were still problems in Angola. So I was to be a small success story — classic Chapter Six.

I remember the French military attaché saying, "You don't need five thousand, four thousand five hundred troops, or your other option, which was twenty-six hundred. All you need is five hundred unarmed observers; there's no problem." Ironically, France was the country that was pressing the UN the most to go in. So we were not on the map. The bulk of the civilian people I had with me were at the first mission. They had no experience in the field because people were peacekeeping'd out, and the UN structure was stretched beyond its capability. And so I had to spend seventy per cent of my time fighting, arguing for the most stupid little things to be able to build that force up, and it got to the point where I preferred facing belligerents or ex-belligerents in heated debate and discussion than facing the administrative structure of the UN.

MICHAEL ENRIGHT
When you say that the third-largest genocide in the history of the twentieth century was not even on the map, that's saying something horrific.

ROMÉO DALLAIRE
Well, this is one of the things that I hope to continue to do, if people invite me: to make them aware. In the Holocaust, of course, there were six million over six years plus. It was Europe — they were Europeans, they were white. That tragedy cannot ever be forgotten, and there are enormous efforts not to let that happen. However, it's interesting that when I met with the extremists on occasions to negotiate these things, they rapidly brought up what the white man had been doing in Europe. And, I mean, we gave them excellent lessons in how to do these steps.

So what is terrible is that there were more people killed, injured, refugeed or displaced in less than four months in Rwanda than in all the five or six years of the Yugoslavian war, and we poured tens of thousands of troops in there. And look at the Kosovo effort. And so I came to the conclusion that the world is fundamentally racist and that the powers of the world are totally stuck on their own self-interest and into their own community. However, I also discovered that middle powers with a work ethic, a respect for human rights, masters of technology, have brought a dimension that maybe we could bring the big powers up to, and that dimension is a more global sense of humanity.

MICHAEL ENRIGHT

Do you think, in the final analysis, that, from the beginning, it was going to wind up that you were going to carry the can for this fiasco, for this disaster?

ROMÉO DALLAIRE

Oh, I never had the time to consider that, and it was irrelevant. I was the commander.

MICHAEL ENRIGHT

But that's a theoretical thing, General, isn't it? You can't be responsible for every death. You can't be responsible for every life not saved or the failure of the mission.

ROMÉO DALLAIRE

It is my responsibility. Either I didn't convince, I didn't explain, or I was unable to avoid it.

MICHAEL ENRIGHT

Or the thing was doomed from the beginning. Maybe it was doomed from the minute you got your orders.

ROMÉO DALLAIRE

Well, I must say that we negotiated and did work with the moderates, and the real extremists never were at the table in the early part. Then they came in, of course, in November, far more overtly. And you could look at that and say this was a classic Greek tragedy. I mean, these guys have been set up, right from the start. However, there was a true feeling that if the UN could get there fast enough with enough capability, they would be able to keep the extremists on both sides at bay and actually bring in a transitional government and move towards a democratic process.

I think one of the stupidities was that my mandate was to bring them, in two years, from a peace agreement to a democratic election in a country where the fourteen per cent minority had, for centuries, dominated the eighty-five per cent majority, and it's that majority that, in the late fifties, threw out the Belgians and also threw out the Tutsi minority. And to think we were going to bring them to such a level of confidence and maturity that they would have elections in two years. I often look back and I say it's incredibly pretentious of us, of the West, to try to do that. We in this country have had debates and laws and so on starting from 1759, and it's still front-page today. Who do we think we are to go there and tell these people they have to adapt to our methods? They were under colonial rule, then during the Cold War we paid idiots to keep control, autocrats and so on. And then, when the Cold War ended, we said, "Well, sort yourselves out." Well, that's what they're doing, and that's the conclusion of not assisting, just washing our hands.

MICHAEL ENRIGHT

When are you going to be able to get rid of it? When are you going to be able to be finished with Rwanda?

ROMÉO DALLAIRE

Never. It'll never end.

MICHAEL ENRIGHT

It has to end, General, at some point, does it not?

ROMÉO DALLAIRE

No, it's just like with people who have gone through the Holocaust — it will never end. The best the medical people can do is to give us a prosthesis that will help us live with it and hopefully master it. But they never can erase it because those events have become even clearer than at the time I was living them. Now they're digitally clear. And so how can I live with that?

But there will always be studies, I hope. There will always be people interested in that fiasco. I think Sierra Leone will only enhance that. I mean, there are countries of the western world that could have come out as leaders of the world by pouring their troops for a while into Sierra Leone, and that didn't happen except for the Brits, who, interestingly, were very uninvolved in Rwanda until near the end when it was a humanitarian mission.

MICHAEL ENRIGHT

In thirty-six years in the military, you've served your country in numbers of ways. Others — the Americans, for example — call you a hero. You see yourself as having failed in a major part of your career. Do you walk around with that all the time?

ROMÉO DALLAIRE

Well, it's not in the forefront, although I lived that inside because I wasn't talking to anybody. I'd tell the story, you know, and spoke a lot in public, but I never told *my* story. And then when I crashed physically and emotionally, it came to the forefront. Since then, it's been a subject of my therapist. Many people say, "It's behind you, get a new life," but I can't Pontius Pilate away eight hundred thousand dead. I can't forget people, with all that hope they had — watching them as displaced people, watching them as they were chopped up and trying to save them. And seeing the terror and the horror in the eyes of children.

I saw a woman in the rain. There were at least fifty thousand people on the road, and it was through the mountains, cold for them. She gave birth to a child, alone, beside the road, took care of the placenta, took the child in her arms, got up and started to walk away and then fainted. And we went and did what we could, but I had no medical supplies, I had nothing. I had one Guinean doctor, who was already taking care of a whole battalion that had surrendered to us with all their families, so he was overburdened. You don't just say, "Damn, I did what I could and it's too bad." Not this time. You're not allowed — I don't think I'm allowed morally to do it. Just like I wasn't allowed to leave the prime minister be killed and not try to give her the opportunity to speak to her country. We continued for weeks and weeks and weeks — and I took casualties and risked the lives of my troops and, well, myself at times — to do something to stall it, stop it, control it, save people until mandates came out. And then forces were promised and never appeared.

So, no, I cannot put that away. But I hope to be able to have more energy. I hope to be able to lecture, to discipline my thoughts, to write, to do research in this whole new dimension of conflict resolution. The nineties were terrible; the future is going to be as bad if not worse in regions like Africa. And anyone who comes forward to me and says, "After over a hundred and fifty years of colonial rule, after thirty-odd years of buying the bad guys to be on our side, it's an African problem, let the Africans sort it out" — anyone who says that is immoral.

* * *

MICHAEL ENRIGHT

Gerald Caplan's latest project is Remembering Rwanda, a worldwide coalition dedicated to ensuring that we will not forget and that we will not let it happen again.

Gerry, the history of the twentieth century is almost an unbroken litany of genocides — the slaughter of the Armenians by the Turks, the starvation in Ukraine, the Holocaust, Cambodia. What is particular about Rwanda that demands our attention and our memory?

GERALD CAPLAN

Well, if you want historical symmetry you can go back before Armenia, which was in 1915, to the Herrero. So genocide started in southwest Africa in this century, when the Germans quite deliberately exterminated the Herrero people of what's now Namibia. From that point of view, Rwanda is kind of an appropriate bookend to the whole century, with this difference: in 1904 it was the white Germans killing Africans; this time it was Africans killing other Africans.

MICHAEL ENRIGHT

Is that important for us to understand? Is it different because we're talking about Africa, and perhaps the world doesn't want to talk about Africa?

GERALD CAPLAN

The world never much wants to care about Africa except when there's disasters or crises or proofs of primitivism, but there's another important aspect of the Rwanda genocide. It is true that Africans did it. It's true they did it to each other. The elite of the Hutu deliberately conspired and went out to kill all the Tutsi they could and almost succeeded. The reason it's become historically important and internationally important and now, for many of us, politically important is because we in the West, who had such a major role in the development of the entire history of Rwanda, including their racism and their ethnic hatreds, could easily — I stress easily — have prevented the entire damn thing. And for almost entirely the crassest of political reasons, we stood by with our hands in our pockets and just let it happen. That's why we're responsible, not because of any kind of phony humanitarianism, but because we could have stopped it and didn't.

MICHAEL ENRIGHT

The crassest of political reasons — what reasons are you talking about?

GERALD CAPLAN

The Americans — the Clinton administration — failed to send Roméo Dallaire the troops he wanted, or didn't allow the Security Council to do so, because the Americans had lost their eighteen Rangers in Somalia six months earlier, and the Clinton administration decided they'd be damned if they'd ever lose another vote, another soldier, which would mean another vote, over Africa. And the Republicans in America would have raked him over the coals if he had done so, for their own terrible political reasons. Before the genocide, the French worked hand in glove with the government, many of whose members were busily plotting the conspiracy, the genocide, and they did it because of some lunatic conspiracy theory that the French have about too much Anglo-Saxon support and power, and they were going to be damned if they'd let a group of Tutsi English-speakers who had come into the country from Uganda take over one of their little French votes in the United Nations. And it's almost impossible to believe that that kind of crassness would have allowed maybe a million people to die, but for both the Americans and the French, that's absolutely the case.

MICHAEL ENRIGHT

Leaving aside the Americans and the French, or perhaps including the Americans and the French, we do have something called the United Nations, and one of the supporting foundations of that organization is that it works to stop this kind of thing.

GERALD CAPLAN

Okay, if you insist.

MICHAEL ENRIGHT

But it didn't.

GERALD CAPLAN

It didn't, and it didn't because, as we've seen in the crises in the last year or so, most of the time the Security Council is simply the weapon of those who have the most power. At that time it was the United States, as indeed it still is. And they had the very strong support — it's one of the mysteries of the genocide that few people understand — of the Brits. The United Kingdom stood foursquare with the Americans in refusing to send the reinforcements that Dallaire kept begging and pleading for. We still don't know why, and the United Kingdom, like the United States, has never had a committee to investigate its behaviour independently. And, I want to stress, in both cases it was both political parties: in the United States, the Democrats and the Republicans, and in Britain, the government of John Major but also the Labour opposition, which barely squeaked about it.

MICHAEL ENRIGHT

I want to look at this question of the importance of mass murder and memory. We say that we have to remember these things so they don't happen again, but then they do happen again. What's the utility of memory?

GERALD CAPLAN

Well, let me challenge your premise. There's no memory, there's no remembering. You may know that I founded an international network of volunteers called Remembering Rwanda, and it was precisely because there's no memory of the genocide. I bet you the vast majority of North Americans, the vast majority of westerners, have barely ever heard of Rwanda, barely ever heard of the genocide, and could tell you nothing useful about it. In my mind — I hope it's not melodramatic — I call it the second betrayal. The first was allowing the genocide to happen. The second was, as soon as it was over, forgetting about the whole damn thing. I mean, there's never been an attempt to give them reparations for the destruction that we allowed to happen. Foreign aid has been a little bit more generous but really tawdry from most countries on the whole. And who remembers the genocide? You can check any anniversary of it and you'll find that a database of *The New York Times* or *The Globe* or the CBC has almost nothing to report on anybody commemorating the genocide or remembering it. It's just slipped off into oblivion. So again, I challenge your premise.

MICHAEL ENRIGHT

What does that say, then, about how humankind responds to these awful things? I mean, if we don't incorporate this into a collective memory of some kind, then there really is no hope that this won't happen again.

GERALD CAPLAN

I think this would likely happen again if the circumstances were anything similar. I think there's no evidence that the powers that be are prepared to lose any of their own troops, for example, by sending them into a war zone. Roméo Dallaire has made the point that somehow the function of armies — which ultimately is to battle and, alas for some soldiers, to die — is no longer true. The West will not send its troops into Africa, at least, or hasn't been prepared to, if there was a chance that any of them would get hurt. This is a whole new way of thinking about armies, and I think it's about Africa. I don't think it's about armies.

MICHAEL ENRIGHT

You think it's because of the geography — it's because Africa is full of Africans and the rest of the world just doesn't pay attention.

GERALD CAPLAN

I think there's an unfortunate amount of evidence for that. I mean, even now, with the tenth anniversary coming up and with a number of people of some prominence interested in it, my judgment is that Rwanda continues to be a marginal issue in the consciousness of elites, a peripheral issue in the consciousness of the mass media. Only occasionally do people really take it seriously and give it the attention that I think, in principle, it deserves — the principle being that genocide is a crime against all of us, not just against the people who are murdered. And, to repeat, we were largely responsible for allowing it to happen.

MICHAEL ENRIGHT

The Bush administration says the country went to war to destroy evil in Iraq. Should the world go to war to prevent evil? Should we have gone to war in Rwanda? Should we go to war in future Rwandas?

GERALD CAPLAN

What's worse is we didn't have to. You saw how easy it was, we saw how easy it was when a small number of British troops were sent finally into Sierra Leone and crushed the rebellion in a very short time. We saw how easy it was in Liberia when some American warships hovered off the coast of West Africa. And what happened? I think — did forty American soldiers actually go on land? That's all it took. As many have said before, preventing the genocide in

Rwanda would have been the easiest thing in the world. The *géno-cidaires* there, the murderers, were not well armed. They were a poorly trained, poorly disciplined crew. Many of them were simply young thugs with machetes and guns and hand grenades. They could easily have been disarmed at the time by — well, we actually know the figure — most people agree by about forty-five hundred soldiers. That's all there was. Two days after the plane crash that killed the president and triggered the genocide, western planes started coming into the capital, Kigali, to evacuate their nationals. At one stage, there were close to eight to ten thousand very heavily armed, very heavily trained western troops from Italy, the United States, France, I think Britain — I'm not sure — and Belgium, all of them within miles of Rwanda, and not one of them — not one of them — ever lifted a finger to try to stop the genocide. They evacuated the Belgians, the French, the Brits, the Yanks, whatever Canadians were there, and they left the murderers to do their thing.

MICHAEL ENRIGHT

Knowing that — knowing what you know about Rwanda and the genocide and how it could have been preventable — does that leave you, if not cynical, certainly pessimistic about this not happening again?

GERALD CAPLAN

I don't know how you can look at the world on any given day and not be pessimistic, but, you know, that's my personal stock in trade, and my own job in life is to keep being active and activist, despite the pessimism that the facts seem to bear out, and trying to get the tenth anniversary recognized is not exactly making me any more optimistic. The United Nations finally passed, at the end of December, a pretty mealy-mouthed resolution, but I still don't even know whether Kofi Annan intends to have a commemoration of any kind. He has acknowledged several times his own angst, because he played a role in failing to gear up the United Nations to help General Dallaire, but I don't know what he's going to do this time. There's a move to have something done in the House of Commons. I hope that works, but none of that has become clear yet, either. So everything is waiting for the last minute. Governments aren't very involved yet in this network I've talked about. We have people around the world, literally: Rwandans, friends of Rwandans, just ordinary people who, for one reason or another, have been touched by the genocide, to commemorate in significant ways in April the tenth anniversary. But we remain invisible to the mass media. We remain a matter of indifference to most governments at the moment. I think some of them will jump in at the last minute, but "last minute" reflects where we are on the priority list, I'm afraid.

"Remembering Rwanda," originally titled "Remembering Rwanda: Ten Years After," was broadcast as part of the series The Enright Files *on February 2, 2004.*

The Legitimacy of Violence as a Political Act

HANNAH ARENDT
CONOR CRUISE O'BRIEN
ROBERT LOWELL
NOAM CHOMSKY

Under what conditions can violent action be said to be legitimate? Legitimate, for example, as a tactic for those who oppose an unpopular war? As a form of self-defence or self-assertion by those who see themselves as victims of a system of oppressive violence managed by the constituted authorities themselves? As a way of bringing about social change in those backward countries where the ruling elite is wholly intransigent and repulses all attempts to modernize or reform?

Hannah Arendt (1906-1975) was the author of The Origins of Totalitarianism, Eichmann in Jerusalem, *and* On Revolution, *among other writings dealing with questions of revolution and resistance. Poet Robert Lowell (1917-1977) was a conscientious objector in World War II and took part in protests against the Vietnam War. Noam Chomsky is a professor of linguistics at the Massachusetts Institute of Technology and has written extensively on the responsibility of intellectuals. Conor Cruise O'Brien is, among other things, a historian of the Irish Revolution, the author of a biography of Parnell, a former UN official in the Congo, and Albert Schweitzer Professor at New York University.*

HANNAH ARENDT

I certainly don't believe in simple solutions, and I argue as though the questions were about the distinction between and possibly even the opposition of power and violence. Power and violence are not the same. Power is inherent in all politics, and all government rests on power. Violence in constitutional government is a marginal phenomenon incorporated in the police and the armed forces, whose instruments of violence are legitimate to the extent that they keep the power structure intact, defend the law against crime and the country against an aggressor. They stand outside the walls of the city, as it were, in order to stand guard over them. The danger, of course, is always that they emancipate themselves from the power that established them, that they invade the city or begin to interfere in strictly political affairs, that they lose their instrumental character, in other words. That is, violence is, by nature, instrumental, and power is the essence of political communities.

Even violence in conjunction with power, as a safeguard of power, indicates our idea that it comes into play where power has broken down. The power of the laws or the constitution rests on it, springs from the consent and support of the people. Wherever this power is intact, violence is unnecessary. The criminal who challenges the authority of the law challenges at the same time the power of all those whose agreement supports these laws. The answer is violence, and even here it is a breakdown of power, the impotence of the law, that provokes violence.

Generally speaking, violence always arises out of impotence. It is the hope of those who have no power to find a substitute for it, and this hope, I think, is in vain. Violence can destroy power but it can never replace it. By the same token, it is a dangerous illusion to measure the power of a country by its arsenal of violence. That an abundance of violence is one of the great dangers for the power of a commonwealth, especially for republics, is one of the oldest insights of political science. To maintain that the United States, for instance, is the most powerful on earth because it possesses the largest arsenal of destructive instruments is to fall prey to the common equation of power and violence. What we see now and have known and could have known before if we had paid some attention to guerrilla warfare throughout the century, is the superiority of power of the guerrilla through an enormous and disastrous display of violence. No doubt this violence can destroy the native power, but it cannot replace it. Nothing will be left after destruction but destruction.

The two best-known theoretical justifications of violence rely on two forceful metaphors. Since Marx, violence has been thought inevitable because revolution was likened to the event of birth, which is preceded by labour pain. In Marx, this is almost inevitable because, as you know, the old society is fragmented by the new, and without this simile the very continuity of history would, for Marx, be in jeopardy. History, in Marx, is a natural process resting on man's metabolism with nature and the processes of labour that mediate this metabolism and make it human. The metaphor leads us astray because the rhyme of human affairs, that which goes on between men, is not part of nature, not even part of the natural human sphere. It is not because we also belong to the great cycle of organic life that we are also political beings.

The second justification is best represented by Georges Sorel, who believed that there is a *mission de création* inherent in violence and that, therefore, a philosophy of violence is a proper philosophy of the producers — that is, the working class — as distinguished from the rest of society, which he sees as mere consumers. The model which is behind the very elaborate philosophy of Sorel is the element of violence inherent in all fabrication. We kill a tree in order to gain wood to make a table. We are forced to do violence to something in order to create something else. In the sphere of fabrication, violence is indeed justified and justifiable by the end product. We know the common view by the saying, "You can't make an omelette without breaking eggs." Well, for an action which is not fabrication, it would be much wiser to say that you can break many eggs without ever making an omelette. Anyhow, violence in the sphere of human affairs as an absolute loses its creativity together with its instrumental character because nothing is achieved in the sea of action that could be likened to an end product. The only final, definite end we will ever be able to achieve in history would be the end of mankind, and this, indeed, we could achieve.

Another last justification is in Sartre's introduction to Fanon's book, *The Wretched of the Earth*. In this Sartre speaks of an irresistible violence which is neither found in poetry, nor is a resurrection of savage instincts, nor is even the effect of resentment. It is man recreating himself. Now, violence is the creator of man. That is a remarkable step beyond Marx, who believed up to his end that labour, not God, creates man. This gives us an idea of the general climate in which we live.

None of these justifications can be understood without taking into account something about which the justifiers usually are silent: the enormous attraction of violence and violent action. Not only does the rage which rises out of impotence release feelings and emotions that are well-nigh unbearable, the acting together in violence, more than any other form of action, releases a rather generous kind of ecstasy. But this ecstasy, though it is real enough, has no consequences. It blows over, like everything that is mere emotion, and Fanon himself, who was much less extremist than Sartre, precisely because he knows what he is talking about, tries to extricate himself from the attraction of violence when he mentions an unmixed and total brutality which he calls "entire revolutionary," though he admits that it is astonishingly like the violence that is typical of revolution. How you actually can distinguish them, he never says, but this total violence, if not immediately combatted, invariably leads to the defeat of the movement within a few weeks.

CONOR CRUISE O'BRIEN

I agree with Miss Arendt in sharing a dislike of a certain romantic mystique of violence which has appeared recently, perhaps a little surprisingly, on the Left, in such things as Sartre's introduction to Fanon. I would tend to disagree with her, insofar as I followed her, on the question of what she described as the opposition between power and violence. I think that Sorel, whom she quoted, is on sounder ground here in making a distinction rather than an opposition when he speaks of force being violence when used by the state.

Nor do I see a legitimizing factor in the fact that violence is used by the state.

I would like to begin my own discussion of the general proposition which is put before us by reminding us of certain specifics, such as who we are — we who are considering what is legitimate and what is not legitimate in violence — and where we are. Here on this continent, whether we're Americans or not, if we're here, we exist as beneficiaries of past violence against the original inhabitants. We are also living under political and social conditions made possible by successful violence in the recent past, in the Second World War. We are living in a social framework defined and regulated by conventions upheld by the sanction of violence or, if you prefer the Sorelian term, force. Even the composition of the population is ultimately determined by violence in keeping out the world's poor.

This being so, unless we are to dissociate ourselves from this society in the most radical fashion by refusing to take its money, which I think few of us do, we are hardly in a moral position which entitles us to tell others that violence as a political method is illegitimate. Or even to tell them what kinds of violence are legitimate and what kinds are not. We can, of course, say that we do not choose ourselves to use violence, but that is a different and personal matter. We can say that we reject this rather bogus mystique that has been made to surround violence and that is almost an aesthetic matter. Or we can say that in certain circumstances violence can achieve no useful result. But that is essentially a tactical decision.

In most of the world, political methods involving violence are the only methods which offer a possibility of bringing about those substantial social changes amounting to a social revolution which everyone agrees are necessary in the poorer world. The democratic conventions which make possible certain kinds of non-violent transfers of power have only a very limited extension in the world. In most poor countries, they either never existed or had only a spurious existence or have been abolished. In these countries, governments are changed by *coups d'état*, palace revolution or, much more often, by mass revolution, and not by any other means. And even in those few poor countries where the democratic process still exists and non-violent change is possible, this functions only within definite and predictable limits. If a party in any poor country which looks sufficiently left-wing to cause alarm in Washington looks like winning elections, then democracy will be abolished by the army. This has happened in many Latin American countries and recently in Greece. No one who knows, for example, the attitude of mind of the Indian officer class will doubt that in equivalent conditions the showpiece of democracy in the East will simply be put on the shelf. Those who, for example, tell the Indian masses to use the democratic process and it alone to attain social revolution are, in effect, telling these people to try to win a game, the rules of which will be changed if they ever look like winning.

According to a nineteenth-century Irish agitator, William O'Brien, violence is the best way of securing a hearing for moderation. Obviously this is not always the case, but it sometimes is, as is proved, for example, by the solicitude which the governments of major American cities show for the welfare of the Negro population during the summer months. We probably all agree that it would be desirable for the human race to attain a condition in which conventions for peaceful transitions and adaptations become so solidly established and so respected that violence would be unnecessary and therefore illegitimate. But progress towards such a condition is unlikely to be achieved itself without violence on a considerable scale.

The real problem seems to me to concern not the legitimacy of such violence, which seems to me, if I may say so, a somewhat scholastic problem, but the possibility of containing it by the tacit recognition of one basic, common interest within limits which will not threaten the survival of the human race.

ROBERT LOWELL

The critic V.S. Pritchett said that the Irish have a sheer, unadulterated joy in destruction. He was talking about Joyce, not the Sinn Fein. This subject is much too serious, I think, for a debate. One can only state one's own opinions and make a kind of personal dedication, which may wash for anyone else or may not.

All year — God knows why — at Harvard, I've been teaching a

course called "Selections from the King James Bible" as writing, and I got very familiar with that text — the text that was quite influential in bringing us to the happy state we're in, though now it's receding. And it's fascinating. It's just as awful as life — I mean, the history of the Jews. It's a vile, terrible history, like most national histories. And the pages of the Bible drip with blood. And it finally ends with the New Testament.

Now — and I'm one-eighth Jewish and nine-eighths goy — what you got in the end, I think — and this must be a large part of the meaning; I don't see how anyone can miss it — was a kind of non-violent activism that had nothing to do with wars of the Roman legions or Jewish insurrections. It was a message which was immediately buried by the Christian church and was never put into practice, but I don't see why it's not something one shouldn't attempt. I don't see why it's utopian. We could hardly do worse than the various wars and insurrections we've fought. I'd agree with Hannah Arendt that what we might call the private domestic violence almost always makes things worse than they were before, and even if it didn't, it would be immoral. And I wouldn't make too great a distinction between that kind of violence and the violence of governments. Something like World War I is more horrible than any number of riots and more immoral.

Now, the trouble is that man always has been faced with these things, as far as recorded history, and I think almost all of these wars have been unjustified and hideous and fought with great brutality. They vary, of course. No two are alike. And, alas, they've almost always been inescapable to the individual. And if we know anything about ourselves, we know that we're very inconsistent, that you might do everything to be a pacifist, then suddenly find you're joining some armed force to defend your community. And it would hardly be human if we weren't that inconsistent. But you try to get over that, like a hangover.

And there might be substitute violence, with words and with passions and things that don't hurt anybody. And I think the real thing is we don't have the courage for non-violent, active work. I mean, I don't think I do very often, and yet one should, and I don't see how the world's going to go on without that. It's getting harder and more dangerous all the time.

NOAM CHOMSKY

My general feeling about this kind of question is that it really can't be faced in a meaningful way when it's abstracted from the context of particular historical, concrete circumstances. I would assume that it's obvious that any rational person would agree that violence is not legitimate unless the consequences of this act are to eliminate a still greater evil. In fact, one might even consider a criterion of rationality that one accept at least that.

Now, there are people, of course, who go much further and say that one must oppose violence in general, quite apart from any possible consequences, and I think that such a person is asserting one of two things. Either he's saying, just to deny it, that the resort to violence is illegitimate, even if the consequences are to eliminate a greater evil, or else he's saying that under no conceivable circumstances will the consequences ever be such as to eliminate a greater evil. Well, the second of these is a factual assumption, and it's almost certainly false, and I won't even discuss it. I think one can easily imagine and find circumstances in which violence does eliminate a greater evil.

As to the first, it's a kind of irreducible moral judgment that one should not resort to violence, even if it would have such consequences, and these judgments are very hard to argue. I can only say that, to me, it seems like an immoral judgment.

Now, there is a tendency to assume that a stand that's based on an absolute moral judgment shows high principle in a way that's not shown by a stand taken on what are disparagingly referred to as "tactical grounds." I think this is pretty dubious. If tactics involves a calculation of the human cost of various actions, then tactical considerations are the only considerations that have a moral quality to them. So I can't accept the first of those two interpretations, either. And for this reason, I don't find it possible, for myself at least, to accept this very general and absolute opposition to violence.

The most that I think I can convince myself of is that resort to violence is illegitimate unless the consequences are to eliminate a greater evil, and this is so near to a triviality that it's not interesting to accept it.

With this formulation, I think one moves from the context of abstract discussion to the context of concrete historical circumstances, where there are shades of grey and obscure relations between means and ends, and incalculable consequences of actions, and so on and so forth. And when formulated in these terms, I think that advocates of a qualified commitment to non-violence have a pretty strong case. I think they can claim with very much justice that in almost all real circumstances there is a better way than to resort to violence.

Let me mention a couple of concrete instances that may shed some light on this question. I read in the *New York Times* this morning an interview with Jeannette Rankin, whom nobody has heard of for a long time but who was the one person to vote against the Declaration of War on December 8, 1941, to boos and hisses. Now, the fact of the matter is, if one looks back, the Japanese had very real grievances, and we had quite a significant share of responsibility in those grievances back in 1941. In fact, Japan had a rather valid case, if you look back. On November 6, 1941, just a month before Pearl Harbor, Japan had offered to eliminate the major factor that really led to the Pacific War — namely, the closed-door policy in China. But they did so with one reservation, that they would agree to eliminate the closed door in China, which is what we'd been demanding, only if the same principle were applied throughout the world — that is, if it were also applied in, say, Latin America and the British dominions and so on. Of course, this was considered too absurd even to get a response, and [Secretary of State Cordell] Hull's answer simply requested once again that they open the closed door in China and didn't even deign to mention this ridiculous qualification that they had added. Now, that qualification was, of course, the whole story: it had been fought about for the preceding ten years, and it led directly to the war.

Now, it was conceivable, at least, that, instead of declaring war on December 8, we could have acted to meet the quite legitimate grievances of the Japanese. Of course, it was politically impossible after Pearl Harbor. That we know. It's very difficult to refrain from striking back, even when you know that the guilt is distributed. But we're talking about what is legitimate and what is moral, not what is a natural reflex. And the advocates of non-violence are really saying that we should try to raise ourselves to the cultural or moral level, both as individuals and as a community, to where we'll be able to control this reflex. We should ask what the consequences were of striking back and what our own role was in creating the situation in which the violence took place.

On December 8, we struck back, quite blindly, quite unthinkingly, and I'm not at all sure, in retrospect, that the world is any the better for it. I might mention that, if you look at Asian opinion on the subject, you'll find that it's very divided. For example, it's quite striking to read the dissenting opinion at the Tokyo Tribunal of the one Asian justice who was permitted to take part and who dissented from the entire proceedings, concluding himself that the only act in the Pacific War that in any way corresponded to the Nazi atrocities was the act of dropping the atom bomb. A.J. Muste, at the time, in 1941-1942, predicted that we would adopt the worst features of our adversaries, of the object of our hatred, and that we would replace Japan as a still more ferocious conqueror. And I think it's very difficult to deny the justice of that prediction.

So I think that Jeannette Rankin, for example, had a very strong argument at that time and that, in that particular historical circumstance, even after Pearl Harbor, advocacy of non-violence, though not an absolute moral principle that at least I can accept, was quite justified in those particular historical circumstances.

The second case — which is the one everybody's got on their mind anyway — Vietnam, raises interesting questions in this regard as well, which are not easy. I'm not going to discuss the situation post–February 1965 for the simple reason that I just can't command the words to talk about it. But let me talk about the earlier period.

From 1954 to 1957, there was large-scale terror instituted by the Saigon government, and the reason was pretty simple. It wasn't just blind and wild. The reason was — I'm convinced of this; this is [Arthur] Schlesinger's theory and I think accurate — that any demo-

cratic institutions that would have been created would have been
taken over by the Viet Minh, and therefore it was impossible to allow any sort of democratic expression. It was necessary to resort to
violence and terror. In the period from 1957 to 1965, there were two
sorts of violence, roughly. There was the mass violence conducted by
Saigon and the United States. Bernard Fall estimates something over
a hundred and sixty thousand killed during that period, Malcolm
Browne talks about the slaughter of the population, and so on. And
there was also the selective violence, selective terror, carried out by
the Viet Cong as part of a political program which certainly earned
the adherence of a good part of the population. No question about
that.

Again, during this period — in fact, during both of these periods
— Americans tended to accept and condone the violence that was
conducted by the United States and the Saigon government, and reserved their indignation for the much more limited Viet Cong terror.
There's no question about justifying the American and the Saigon
government terror. What about the much harder question, that of
the terror practised by the National Liberation Front?

The easiest reaction to this situation is to say that all violence is
abhorrent and that both sides are guilty and that I stand apart and
retain my moral purity and condemn them both. This is the easiest
response, and, to be perfectly frank, I think it's also justified in this
case, but for reasons that are pretty complex. There is a real argument in favour of the Viet Cong terror, I think — an argument that
can't be lightly dismissed, although I don't think it's correct. There
are several arguments, in fact.

One argument is that this selective terror tended to save the population from a much more extreme government terror, the continuing
terror that exists when a corrupt official can do the things that are
within his power in the province that he controls. So killing that
official and frightening others did serve to save the population from
kind of a muted terror that's of a continuing nature.

And there's also the second type of argument, the Fanon-type
argument that Miss Arendt quoted, which also can't be abandoned
very lightly. It's a question of whether this act of violence frees the

native from his inferiority complex and permits him to enter into political life. Again, I myself would like to believe that it's not so. I'd like to believe that non-violent reaction could achieve the same consequence. But it's not very easy to argue this except on grounds of faith. And the necessity of releasing the peasant from this role of passivity is hardly in question. We know perfectly well that, in countries such as North Korea and South Vietnam and many others, it was necessary to rouse, to force the peasants to recognize that they were capable of taking over land. It was necessary to break the bonds of passivity that made them totally incapable of political action. And if violence does succeed in breaking these bonds, does succeed in getting the peasantry to the point where it can overcome the sort of permanent bondage that exists in, say, the Philippines, then I think there's a pretty strong argument for it.

I might mention that an interesting sidelight to this issue in the Vietnam situation is a recent Rand Corporation study which demonstrates that the areas in which American control is most firm are the areas in which there has been the least disruption of the old feudal social order, where the peasants are docile, where they don't raise political issues, where they don't cause trouble and then begin to act politically as human beings, which means, in this case, as members of the Viet Cong, apparently.

There's also a third argument, which, on the surface, sounds pretty abhorrent, but again has a case. That is the idea that violence will lead to reprisal and reprisal will win adherents to the Viet Cong. Of course, that's what happens, in fact. In the first year of the massive American bombardment of South Vietnam, the number of recruits for the Viet Cong increased enormously. Now, although this is, in a way, what one might think an abhorrent or a despicable argument, still I think that it's not without grounds. If it is true, again, that a mass movement will destroy this permanent bondage that exists, say, in the Philippines, then methods which lead people to adhere to this mass movement are justified, perhaps by the ends to which they lead. At least this argument has rational justification.

With all these arguments in favour of this type of violence, I still think there are good grounds to reject it. It seems to me, from the little we know about such matters, that a new society arises, obviously, out of the actions that are taken to form it, and that the institutions and the ideology that it develops are not independent of those actions. In fact, they're heavily coloured by it — they're shaped by it in many ways. And I think that one can expect that actions that are cynical and vicious, whatever their intent, will inevitably condition and, in fact, deface the quality of the ends that are achieved.

Now again, in part this is just a matter of faith. I don't know how strong an argument I could give for that, but I think there are a number of cases that illustrate this point. In fact, one case is the Viet Cong itself. The detailed studies of Viet Cong success, like those of Douglas Pike, indicate quite clearly that the basis for the success, which was enormous, was not the selective terror but rather the effective organization which drew people into beneficial organizations, organizations they entered out of self-interest, that they, to a large extent, controlled, that began to interlace and cover the entire countryside.

I think the study of collectivization in China and the Soviet Union illustrates this very same point. There are no pure cases, of course, in these matters, but it's clear that the emphasis and the use of terror and violence in China was considerably less and that the success was considerably greater in achieving a just society. And I think the really convincing example, the most convincing example, the one about which I think not enough is known and to which not enough attention is paid, is the anarchist success in Spain in 1936. As far as I can make out, it involved the very minimal use of violence, although there was some, and was fantastically successful, at least for a year or two, in developing a collective society with mass participation and a very high degree of egalitarianism and even economic success, it appears.

Well, these kinds of examples seem to me to suggest that there is a relationship between absence of terror, a degree of spontaneity on the one hand, and success in achieving a just society. This is not an unfamiliar conception. It's a sort of Luxemburgian and anarchist conception that a just society cannot really be imposed on masses of people but must arise out of their own spontaneous efforts, guided by their own developing insight and so on and so forth, and I think that this is a valid conception which has some support from modern history.

A final case one might talk about is the anti-war movement, where I think the argument for non-violence is so overwhelming that I'm not even going to mention it. A couple of days ago, I was rather despairingly trying to think of something illuminating that I might say about this subject, and I decided to turn back to some of Tolstoy's essays on civil disobedience, thinking he should have had something sensible to say about it. I'm not sure I found anything very deep there, but I was surprised to discover a note of optimism that I hadn't expected. And since that's kind of a rare treasure these days, I'd like to quote a couple of remarks, just to relieve the prevailing gloom.

Tolstoy wrote an interesting essay in 1897 called "The End Is Near," in which he says:

> Until recently men could not imagine a human society without slavery, and now one cannot imagine the life of man without war. A hundred years have gone since the first clear expression of the idea that mankind can live without slavery and there is no longer slavery in Christian nations. And there shall not pass another hundred years after the clear utterance of the idea that mankind can live without war before war will cease to be. Very likely some form of armed violence will remain, just as wage labour remains after the abolition of slavery. But at least wars and armies will be abolished in the outrageous form so repugnant to reason and moral sense in which they now exist. Signs that this time are near are many. These signs are such as the helpless position of governments, which more and more increase their armaments; the multiplication of taxation and the discontent of nations; the extreme degree of efficiency with which deadly weapons are constructed; the activity with congresses and society of peace; but above all, the refusals

of individuals to take military service. In these refusals
is the key to the solution of the question.

We live in the society which is the most aggressive in the world,
and we live under conditions of almost unparalleled freedom. We
therefore have the opportunity to eradicate a good part of the illegitimate violence that plagues our lives and that is destroying the
lives of many who are much less fortunate. I think we have no choice
whatsoever but to take up the challenge that's implicit in this prediction of Tolstoy's. If we do not take up this challenge, we will help to
bring about a very different state of affairs. Einstein was once asked
his opinion about the nature of a Third World War. He said that he
had nothing to say about that matter, but he was quite certain that
the Fourth World War would be fought with clubs and stones.

*"The Legitimacy of Violence as a Political Act," a panel discussion from
the Theatre for Ideas in New York City, was broadcast on January 8,
1968.*

We the People: A Prescription for Ending the Arms Race

The 1984 Jacob Bronowski **Memorial Lecture**	HELEN CALDICOTT Interviewed by SARA WOLCH

Dr. Helen Caldicott is an outspoken critic of nuclear weapons and the arms race. She's a pediatrician, co-founder and president emeritus of Physicians for Social Responsibility, founder of WAND — Women's Action for Nuclear Disarmament, and founding president of the Nuclear Policy Research Center. Dr. Caldicott is the author of Nuclear Madness *and* Missile Envy, *and she was featured in the Academy Award-winning film,* If You Love This Planet. *What follows is Dr. Caldicott's Bronowski lecture, after which she discussed her views of the re-election of Ronald Reagan as president of the United States with* Ideas *producer Sara Wolch.*

HELEN CALDICOTT

In the medieval times, man believed in God and science had not been discovered, and man lived under the authority of God. And there was a cyclical nature to life. Day became night, man was born and died, and we accepted that as natural. Then we discovered the clock. That transferred the cyclical nature of life into a pathway that kept going. And the cycle ceased to be so important. And then we started discovering the natural laws — in other words, science. And

241

our impotence moved to a sense of omnipotence, whereby we in a certain sense thought, as we discovered the natural laws, and we called it science, that we became, in a way, God. And as we evolved in this way, science is God. The trouble is, today the scientists who in our mind are God are telling us that they're sorry, but what they've done is going to blow us up.

I think Albert Einstein put it best when he said, "The splitting of the atom changed everything, save man's mode of thinking." Thus we drift toward unparalleled catastrophe. Somewhere in the nuclear age, America lost its soul and has never regained it, as did the Soviet Union. America has thirty thousand nuclear weapons. There are only two hundred major cities in the Soviet Union with populations greater than a hundred thousand people. Why then do we have thirty thousand bombs? Well, we have to be strong. The Soviet Union has twenty thousand bombs, so together we have a total of fifty thousand nuclear weapons. There are also other countries with nuclear weapons — Britain, France and China. Together with the United States, these four could independently at any time if they so desired destroy the Soviet Union. If we were in a similar position, we would be somewhat paranoid, as indeed are the Russian leaders. Now, you don't handle paranoid patients by threatening them. When paranoid patients are admitted to hospital, you're very gentle with them. You get to understand the way this mind thinks. You don't stick needles in them or hurt them, because if you do, they're likely to behave irrationally. It is therefore quite obvious to me, and I think many other people, that it's medically contraindicated to threaten the Russian leaders, because, in their fear and paranoia, they could press the button, and I tell the American people, that's an unpatriotic thing to do.

I would like now to describe the medical effects of nuclear war and how close we are to such an event occurring, and then I will go on with the prognosis of the planet, or how long I expect the planet to survive and why things are so grim. And I will, during that discussion, describe an interview I had with President Reagan some two years ago in the White House, and I will describe that to you from a clinical perspective.

The computers in the Pentagon which are part of the early warning system keep breaking down. They're antiquated Honeywell computers that badly need to be upgraded, and in an eighteen-month period in fact broke down a hundred and fifty-one times, putting us on red alert — or for those who've seen *War Games*, Defcon One — thinking we were under attack. The most serious error occurred in November 1979, when someone plugged a war games tape into the fail-safe computer. They played war games all day in the Pentagon — it's quite an interesting sport, I believe. And the computer made a mistake and said that we were under attack from submarine-launched ballistic missiles from Soviet subs in the Atlantic. The whole western world went on red alert for six minutes. The men in the missile silos actually put the keys in the locks, ready to turn them, like in *The Day After*, and they would do it, because they're programmed to do it. Three squadrons of B-52s scrambled and took off towards Russia armed with nuclear weapons. At the seventh minute, they had to officially notify the president, but they could not find him. When the mistake was realized, we were thirteen minutes from nuclear war.

Now, that was headlines in your papers, but in the United States, there was a little tiny article near the obituaries in the *New York Times* reporting that particular event. That is called national psychic numbing. "We don't want to see, we don't want to hear, we don't want to know. Just leave us alone to be comfortable." Last year, there were two hundred and fifty-five serious computer errors. The number of errors is increasing, just going like a straight line up the graph. We assume the Soviet computers have an approximately equal number of errors — indeed, we know their computers are less sophisticated than are ours. One of the reasons they shot that jet down was that they didn't know what it was after tracking it for two and a half hours, according to the CIA, because their system is so antiquated. [On September 1, 1983, a Soviet fighter had shot down a commercial Korean Air Lines flight, KAL 007, after it had strayed into Soviet airspace.]

A mathematician in British Columbia, actually a political scientist, has just done a study . . . and let me back up a bit. There are missiles being deployed now that hit their target in six minutes instead of thirty. Like the Pershing IIs in West Germany. They're to be used for decapitation of the Soviet leadership. Decapitation means you kill them before they have a chance to press the button. Are you with me? The Russians have missiles in their subs just off our coast that can be used for decapitation of the Washington leadership, too, in six minutes. Now, because there's no time in six minutes for human decision-making, the Russians and the Americans are going to proceed to a system called "launch on warning," where, when the computer gets the message that they're under attack, it presses the button, with no human intervention. So it is assumed by this political scientist, called Michael Wallace, in British Columbia, that during a time of heightened international tension, because of the risk of decapitation, both sides would move to "launch on warning" or computerized nuclear war. And his analysis shows that if an international crisis like the Cuban missile crisis lasted thirteen days, there would be a fifty per cent chance of self-activation of the system. In other words, a fifty per cent chance of accidental nuclear war.

When that jetliner went down, I guess that there was an international crisis for maybe seven days. The Europeans think that the fifty per cent probability may actually be higher because America has a policy of first use of nuclear weapons. In other words, if Russia invades West Germany with tanks, if NATO is losing, she reserves the option to use nuclear weapons first on invading Russian tanks, on the theory that Russia wouldn't be so crazy as to retaliate with nuclear weapons because that would obviously start a nuclear war. Russia, on the other hand, has a policy that she promises she will not use nuclear weapons first, but should one — but one — be used against her, she will retaliate with the whole arsenal. You can't have a limited nuclear war all by yourself, like you can't have a marriage alone.

Now, because of the first use of nuclear weapons, there's a situation in Europe called the Permissive Action Link, whereby in a time of heightened international tension, the authority to use nuclear weapons moves downwards through the chain of command so that relatively young people and relatively junior people in the American military will be authorized to use tactical nuclear weapons. In fact, they have backpack nuclear weapons in Europe — they carry them around in backpacks. There are six thousand tactical nuclear weapons on the front line between East and West Germany, and the military dictum says if Russia invades West Germany, we have to use them or lose them, which actually indicates automatic nuclear war, first use or no first use.

So you can understand that nuclear war could occur any day by accident or design. We live in a very tenuous position. And let me say just one more thing before I describe the medical effects of nuclear war: war is obsolete. Now that's a very blanket statement, but it also is true. The reason is that America has no conventional forces. All the air wings — in fact, all the airplanes — all the army divisions and eighty per cent of the warships carry nuclear weapons. There are many warships down there in the Caribbean now, many of which will have nuclear weapons on board. Hence, a war in Nicaragua involving America with nuclear weapons down there, and possibly involving the Soviet Union, could in fact blow up the world. And that's what Einstein meant when he said, "The splitting of the atom changed everything, save man's mode of thinking." So we live in a very tenuous position, and you and I are lucky to wake up each morning, and each day that we live is a gift from God.

Let's now describe a bomb dropping on Toronto. I'm going to drop a big one. It's twenty megatons, equivalent to twenty million tons of TNT, or seven times the collective energy of all the bombs dropped in the Second World War, including the two atomic bombs on Japan. You probably won't get a big one. You might get a MIRV-ed footprint, which means multiple small bombs which come in on a single missile, and you can kill more people with many small bombs by the blast effects. The physics is better — it kills more people. But it's more complex to describe, so I'll drop a big bomb for simplicity.

Let's imagine for the sake of argument the button was pressed in Moscow fifteen minutes ago. And I don't know what sort of emergency system you have on your radios, but in the States, you're listening to music — you know, maybe Bach's Brandenburg Concerto

— and the music stops, and the man says, "This is just a test of the emergency broadcasting system." That's the last sound you'll hear before you die. I want you to think about your life and what you value most in your life, who do you love the most, what are you living for . . . how much are you in love with the earth . . . and then I want you to think about that as I talk.

The bomb will come in at twenty times the speed of sound in ten minutes, and explode here in a fraction of a millionth of a second with the heat of the sun, and dig a hole three-quarters of a mile wide and eight hundred feet deep, turning us and the building and the earth below to radioactive fallout molecules injected in a mushroom cloud.

Six miles from here in all directions, every building destroyed. The heat is so intense concrete and steel will melt. Every person killed, most will be vaporized. In Hiroshima, indeed, people disappeared, and they left their shadows behind them on the pavement.

Twenty miles from here in all directions, everyone killed or lethally injured. Winds of five hundred miles an hour literally pick people up and turn them into missiles travelling at one hundred miles an hour. The overpressures enter the orbit and extravasate the eye — so a man was standing clinically shocked in Hiroshima, holding his eye in his hand. The tongue is also extravasated. The windows popcorn, and shards of glass flung at one hundred miles an hour will enter human flesh and produce decapitation. I'm describing Pentagon documents now. Others will be charcoalized — in Hiroshima, a woman was running, holding her baby, and she and her baby had been turned into a charcoal statue. Everyone out to twenty miles grotesquely burnt or will die, some immediately and some over days in the most intense agony, covered with lethal fallout, developing symptoms of acute radiation illness, which is vomiting, liquid diarrhea and hemorrhage.

Twenty-six miles from here, the heat flash travelling at the speed of light is so intense that clothes spontaneously ignite so you just burst into flame. Fifty miles out, a reflex glance at the flash produces instant and permanent retinal blindness, like looking at the sun. And the whole area then could be engulfed in a holocaust of three thousand square miles, so if you got into a fallout shelter, the fire literally sucks the oxygen out of the shelter and you'll be asphyxiated, and the blast and heat turn the fallout shelters into crematoria.

I only dropped one bomb. Last year, the World Health Organization did a study of the medical consequences of nuclear war, and they took only seven thousand bombs out of a total of fifty thousand, because they couldn't find any more legitimate targets to bomb. They bombed every city and significant town in the USA, Canada, China, Russia, Europe, England, India, Vietnam, Korea, Australia, New Zealand, the Philippines, Hawaii, Guam, and then some more.

Now, before I say the next thing, I want you all now to stop again and think of somebody in your life who's died that you've loved. Have you ever lost a baby? Or a child? A parent? A spouse? Brother, sister, or a dear friend? Think of how precious that single life was to you and how you've never really recovered. In the first hour alone in this limited nuclear war, they found that one billion people died of the effects of the blast. I repeat, one billion people. And in the next two weeks, one billion more died of the effects I just described. That's half the world's population. Have you got the message?

Let me go on now and describe to you the meeting I had with President Reagan. I think he's probably one of the most important historical characters in this century, and probably the most significant person at the moment in the history of the earth. I was taken in to see him in the White House by his daughter, Patty, who was worried about his lack of knowledge on this issue, and she thought I could change his mind.

Before I went in, I prayed that I could convince him to be like Nixon, who I think in retrospect was a great statesman. Nixon had the vision and courage to go to China and made friends with Mao Zedong and a billion communist Chinese. So now America has more communists on her side than Russia does on hers. So this issue that we're talking about has nothing, but nothing, to do with communism. Nixon also went and made friends with Brezhnev and established détente and negotiated nine excellent treaties. So I thought I could convince Reagan to be one of the greatest presidents who'd ever lived.

We went into the downstairs library of the White House, and I said, "You probably don't know who I am." And he said, "Yes, you're an Australian. You read *On the Beach* when you were a young girl, and you're scared of nuclear war." I said, "That's right." He said, "I too believe in preventing nuclear war, but our ways to prevent it differ. I believe in building more bombs." Simplistic but true. He told me then that the Russians are totally evil godless communists, so being a good clinician I asked for objective data and said, "Have you ever met one?" He said, "No." When I did psychiatry twenty years ago, that was a sign of paranoia.

Then he didn't want to talk about the medical or ecological consequences of nuclear war, which we've just discussed. He only wanted to talk about numbers of missiles, which is partly why I called my new book *Missile Envy*, à la Freud. He would anecdote on with incorrect data as if he'd learned it by rote from the teleprompter, and then I'd stop him and move in and correct him, not exactly being a wallflower. There was no animosity though. He got a bit tense, but it was fine. But he didn't listen to anything I said. He was not interested, and he had absolutely no background knowledge to debate any point with me at all.

Then he said, "Look, I took some notes before I came down," and he reached into his pocket and pulled out a piece of paper on which he'd written, "People that work for the nuclear weapons freeze are either KGB dupes or Soviet agents." And I said to him, "But that's from the *Reader's Digest*." And he said, "No, it's from my intelligence files." It was verbatim from a John Barron article in the *Reader's Digest* published a couple of months before. And then his daughter was getting very upset at one stage, and she said, "Daddy, I know that what Dr. Caldicott is saying is correct because I have a 1982 Pentagon document to prove it." He looked at her and he said, "That's a forgery." She didn't have it in her hand.

I left the White House in a state of clinical shock. I went back to the hotel, and I felt like Paul Revere running up to people saying,

"Do you know what I've just seen?" So the American people voted this year for the economy. This election was about the economy. That is what I would describe as manic denial. As Ellen Goodman, the columnist, said the other day, "Everybody's driving toward nuclear war in the latest model car." Manic denial.

Now, I'm sure some of you are saying, "Well, what about the Russians?" They were our allies in the Second World War, remember? They helped us to beat Hitler. They lost twenty million people. They lost seventy-two thousand towns and cities, and when I was in Russia in 1979, my young guide Sasha said to me, "We have suffered dreadfully." He said, "My grandmother has seen people eat people twice in her lifetime." The Russian leaders are desperate. They have their backs to the wall. They put a freeze on the table in Geneva two years ago, when eighty percent of the Americans wanted a freeze. It was totally negated. They proposed a freeze in the UN ten months ago. The whole world voted to adopt it, except the US and several of its allies. They have put a unilateral ban on testing of anti-satellite weapons since August, pending negotiations on banning anti-satellite weapons: negated. They're ready to sign — and have been for four years — a complete test ban treaty, and have agreed to on-site inspection: negated. There were fourteen treaties being negotiated with Russia on nuclear weapons when Reagan was elected. He walked out and cancelled all fourteen treaties. They are desperate.

Now, when Brezhnev was dying, his military advisor was called General Milstein. We met him, and he was a very worried man. He said, "We've got our hopes in Russia, too." He said, "If when Brezhnev dies a young man gets in with extended tenure," he said, "we're lost." He said, "You might as well go home and forget about it." He said, "If an older man gets in with limited tenure, we've still got a hope." In other words, the window of opportunity to save the world and prevent the weapons being built that Reagan's doing that make nuclear war a mathematical certainty — in the future, I don't know when — remains open just for a very short time. Yet we're not taking advantage of this at all.

Now, Canada, you're part of it. You are part of NATO, you are part of NORAD, you work hand-in-glove with the American military. The Manhattan Project started in Canada with Chalk River. I think that you should do what the New Zealand people did and create a nuclear-free Canada. Don't test cruise missiles here. Do you know there are war games going on in the north of Canada with the Luftwaffe and with the American B-52s flying terrain, flying in your planes? And you mustn't have any factories here creating parts for nuclear weapons and delivery systems, no testing of cruise missiles, and I think you get out of NATO, because I think — I don't think, I know — that NATO is a mutual suicide pact. You're in the bowling alley, Canada. The weapons go right over you, over the North Pole. You're right in the middle. Do you want to live, or do you want to die?

Okay, this takes stringent action, and that means you've got to change the priorities in your lives. Now, I don't know if you know the studies in the States, but the American Psychiatric Association has studied American children and found that up to seventy-five per cent of primary and high school children know for a fact that they're not going to grow up. There's going to be a nuclear war. Now, you can say, well, they're just kids. I treat children who die of a lethal disease called cystic fibrosis, and little ones, three-year-olds, have said to me, "I'm going to die tonight." I knew they were sick, I didn't know it was tonight. They're right every time. And it was Jesus who said, "Out of the mouths of babes and sucklings comes the faith."

A little five-year-old was at breakfast the other day, and out of the blue she said, "Mummy, if there's a nuclear war, will God make us another world because we've been careless with this one?" A fifteen-year-old pubertal boy came up to me after a talk and shoved a dirty note in my hand — and listen to this, adults, and take it on from a child: "Remember, people should be more afraid of nuclear war than they are to act or speak out against it." I looked at his face and it was trembling, and he burst into tears. He said, "I'm so frightened!" I took him into my arms as he sobbed and held him, and I said, "We'll fix it for you."

Will we? How committed are we to this? Well, we're not committed at all. What does commitment mean? If your child developed leukemia, how much money and time would you commit to your child's life? Everything — every penny and every minute. And if your child died, you would wish you had died instead, and you would never, ever recover. Our children have leukemia equivalent. They know they're not going to grow up, and they feel totally betrayed by us because we lack the courage and conviction and commitment to save their lives.

You and I were conceived and born for one reason, in the history of the earth. We were born to save the planet and the creation. Our lives have no other rationale but that. Everything else we do is displacement activity and manic denial. If you've taken in what I've said tonight, you will enter the stages of grief and you'll feel very uncomfortable. The first stage is shock and disbelief. You're feeling it now: "Well, she's a bit emotional. Some of her facts are a bit wrong." First stage, grief. Second stage is profound and deep depression, so uncomfortable you'd almost wish you were dead. Can't sleep at night. Lose your sexual drive, lose your appetite. Normal. The next state is anger — use it constructively. The final stage is acceptance: yes, the world might die, but I've released an enormous amount of energy that I am using to repress the fear. I'm going to do everything I can to stop it.

How do you do it? You do it through the political process. Why? It's the politicians who represent you, who are as ignorant as you, who make the decisions to build the bombs and create the policies of your country. Every one of you has a local representative in that Parliament. You get in there and you educate them. And you make sure they vote the right way, and you create a tremendous political movement. And you identify every factory in the country that makes nuclear weapons and you stand outside, in your pearls, your high-heeled shoes and your three-piece suits, with signs saying, "This factory makes parts for cruise missiles which end arms control, make nuclear war inevitable." Look nice, then people will say, "They look like me." Canada is one of the most respected nations in the world.

Use it. Get moving. Everything else you do in your life is irrelevant if, in fact, in the next few years we're going to destroy the creation.

I want to end up by reciting a poem to you. I saw *Amadeus* the other day. Is *Amadeus* up here yet? It's the music of Mozart. For me, the music of Mozart represents God. It's the most beautiful music I think I've ever heard. And at the end of the film, I just literally wept from the depths of my soul for about half an hour because I can't imagine the world without Mozart. This poem is by Shakespeare — nor can I imagine the world without Shakespeare.

> Shall I compare thee to a summer's day?
> Thou are more lovely and more temperate:
> Rough winds do shake the darling buds of May,
> And summer's lease hath all too short a date:
> Sometime too hot the eye of heaven shines,
> And often is his gold complexion dimm'd;
> And every fair from fair sometime declines,
> By chance o'er nature's changing course untrimm'd;
> But thy eternal summer shall not fade
> Nor lose possession of that fair thou owest;
> Nor shall Death brag thou wander'st in his shade,
> When in eternal lines to time thou growest:
> So long as men can breathe or eyes can see,
> So long lives this and this gives life to thee.

* * *

In her book, Missile Envy, *Dr. Caldicott wrote: "The 1984 election should be guided and determined by the emotions implicit in the positive feminine principle: nurturing, caring and responsibility toward the life process. The gender gap will loom large, and all good-hearted, moral, patriotic Americans will be obliged to participate." With this in mind,* Ideas *producer Sara Wolch spoke with Dr. Caldicott. The first thing she asked her was, "What's next?"*

HELEN CALDICOTT

Well, I admit things look devastating, but in fact there's another election in 1986 where the whole House and one-third of the Senate are up for election, and we plan to run two hundred women for the Congress in '86 — we're calling it the "200 Club" — and many good men, and hopefully paralyze the administration by taking over the Congress in '86 with people who are well informed on this issue and well intentioned. And then '88 will be sort of the cut-off point, with the next election both for the House and the Senate and the administration. Admittedly, you know, it's pretty late. It's not quite too late yet, and I revised my assumptions because things went so badly and because I sort of hadn't realized that there was another election in two years' time.

SARA WOLCH

In the meantime, Dr. Caldicott, how are you going to get through to the people who voted Republican, who voted for Reagan, including the women?

HELEN CALDICOTT

Well, I think what happened was everyone watched *The Day After*, and they entered the stages of grief. And I think many Americans were very deeply depressed about nuclear war and were practising manic denial. They were denying their fear so much that Reagan reassured them and said, "I'm a nice guy, just vote for me, and anyway I'll make you rich." And they heaved a sigh a relief, a collective sigh of relief, and followed him. But underneath, subliminally, they know that things are in a very precarious, dangerous situation, and we have to mobilize that fear. And I think that forty-one million people who voted for Mondale got a big shock. That's a lot of people, and people are talking about getting out in the streets now and demonstrating, so that there's a more public presence before the television cameras and the radio and the print media. And we will just work terribly hard for the '86 election.

SARA WOLCH

Okay, let's talk a little more specifically about strategy. If one listens to your talks and your interviews and reads your books, it becomes very clear very quickly that if we were to put Helen Caldicott in a room with Ronald Reagan or the guys from the State Department or the guys from the Pentagon, these people will not find a common ground, they will not agree on anything. What do you gain from that?

HELEN CALDICOTT

That's not true. I spoke at the Kennedy School of Government recently to about seventy-five fellows in the Pentagon. They were all deeply moved. Some were still defensive, but they all heard what I said and I got through to all of them. I didn't get through to Reagan, because he's limited. But many of these people are not limited. Many of them are open to hearing the truth and are in fact deeply troubled inside about their children. And also, you're putting the load on me. That's not fair. I'm an educator, and every audience I address, I never know that there may be people with tremendous creative initiative. For instance, we held a symposium in New York, and Jonathan Schell attended, and from that came *The Fate of the Earth*. The symposia we held around the country turned on the bishops in each city; from that came the Bishops' Pastoral Letter. It's not on my shoulders to save the earth. All I can do is educate and plant the seeds and hope to God that there will be people in the audiences who take the baton as I pass it to them and run with it and help to save the earth. So it's really not on my shoulders.

SARA WOLCH

Well, partly, though, it is, because you are regarded as an eloquent spokesperson for the peace movement, and you do have access to people like Ronald Reagan. Lots of people don't have that kind of access.

HELEN CALDICOTT

That doesn't do any good. The only way this thing will turn around is for everybody to take absolute responsibility and make a total commitment of their lives. And that's why I'm really socking it to people now, saying, "Do you want your kids to live or not?" It really freaks them out, and it makes them ponder deeply in their souls what they're here for, and that's what they've got to do. And that's what I'm doing. Turning people on, and then it's up to them.

SARA WOLCH

Is there a way, Dr. Caldicott, that you think we can bridge the gap between the peace movement and, let's say, Reagan?

HELEN CALDICOTT

Absolutely no way. I think that he's incapable of really understanding the gravity of the situation, from my interview with him and from much of the literature. However, you'll notice that he is saying now that he never wants a nuclear war and it can't be fought and won, because of the pressure from the people. Even though they voted for him, he's still aware that the majority of them want a freeze, they want to stop the arms race. So he's moderating his language. But, as Nixon said, "Don't listen to what I say, watch what I do." And it's the same with Reagan. Don't listen to what he says, watch what he does — and he's into putting weapons into space, he's into building all these new weapons, throwing money at the Pentagon and the corporations. And I just don't trust the man at all. I don't think the president has the intellectual capabilities to sit down with the Russians and negotiate a freeze. Maybe his colleagues do, but many of them believe you can fight and win a nuclear war and hate the Russians with a vindictive passion that's unbelievable.

SARA WOLCH

Hearing you talk about Reagan and his colleagues reminds me of Reagan talking about the Soviet Union.

HELEN CALDICOTT

Right. Well, I don't hate Reagan and his colleagues, I'm just worried about them, and I think they're pathological.

SARA WOLCH

Is that helping the peace movement, having you say that?

HELEN CALDICOTT

I don't really care. I'm just speaking the truth as I see it. I mean, I'll speak the truth, and if I'm proven to be wrong, I'll change and say what I think with a new light. But I think that they're a very pathological group of people. The one who's giving me a little hope at the moment is George Shultz, the secretary of state, who seems to have gotten the message that we do have to live with the Russians in the same world and has seemed to have taken power away from the Pentagon and [Defence Secretary Caspar] Weinberger, who I think is in some trouble at the moment, and is speaking with some authority. He looks more relaxed, he looks happier and more at ease than he ever has. He's probably quite deeply concerned, doesn't trust the Russians in the old mode that the Americans have been brought up to believe, but is moving. And I guess I see a little hope in that area. But the only real hope is that the American people rise up and say, "For Christ's sake, stop this!" The people elect a government they deserve, and the people at the moment are practising psychic numbing, and there's a level of ignorance which is quite profound about the weapons systems. So our educational work is one-third complete. They know nuclear war is bad for the health. They don't know about weapons systems or the Reagan policies.

SARA WOLCH

In your book, you talk about the differences between men and women. And if I understand you correctly, what you're getting at is that men — scientists, military people, politicians — are largely to blame for the arms race. This intrigued me, interested me and also confused me somewhat. Since women outnumber men, and women give birth to and raise men, how is it possible that we're in the mess we're in?

HELEN CALDICOTT

Well, because women have been wimps, certainly in the States. They won the vote sixty years ago and have just done nothing with it. Not only do they not vote a lot, but they have not run for Congress. And, in fact, fifty-three per cent of the Congress should be women. At last we had a woman running for vice-president, but it's too little, too late. Women use their creative energies in other ways, and that's giving birth, and it's all-engrossing. You don't have time for anything else when you have a child. We are finding time to do work now, outside the home, but it's tiring. However, we've got to understand, if we want those children to live, we have to commit our lives to the children and get involved politically and really take over the political system.

There's been a fascinating book written called *A Choice of Heroes*, by Mark Gerzon, who says that the United States is run by rich, white, old men — which is true. It's true in the professions, it's true in business, it's true in politics, it's true in every area. And when women join those areas, they become like men, as men. They give up their feminine principle and they become quite tough and join the masculine ethic, which is very damaging because the world is gripped by the negative masculine principle that Jung described — the ego-centric, power-hungry, killing principle. And we've got to get there, using our feminine principle and our power that we've newly discovered, and say to the men, "Stand aside, we're taking over. We're sorry, but you've screwed up. You're about to blow us up." What we're doing is empowering women to feel that they can be as intelligent, as strong as any man, but that we have to change the way the world operates. And so it must operate from the positive feminine principle, which is the nurturing, loving, caring principle that men and women have, but in many men it's atrophied, and many women embody that principle. So we mustn't ever lose sight of that.

SARA WOLCH

Let's turn to men now, Dr. Caldicott. Do you think there's a biological difference between men and women?

HELEN CALDICOTT

Of course there's a biological difference. I mean, the men have got hair all over their faces. We don't have hair on our faces. They have hairy bodies. They have penises and scrotums and testicles, and we have ovaries and vaginas and uteruses and breasts. I mean, how could you not say there's a biological difference?

SARA WOLCH

With regard to their behaviour, does that mean that aggression . . . ?

HELEN CALDICOTT

Yeah, of course. If you give a woman androgens or testosterone because she has breast cancer to try and impede the growth of the cancer, she becomes hairy and she becomes more aggressive psychologically. If you give a man female hormones because he has prostatic carcinoma to slow down the growth of the cancer, he loses his body hair, his testicles atrophy, and he becomes more nurturing psychologically. There have been studies done on children under the age of six, and they found that little boys are more aggressive than little girls. They play more aggressive games. Little girls tend to be more nurturing with their dolls, etc., etc.

SARA WOLCH

Okay, if this is the case, then how can women possibly raise and influence little boys so they won't grow up to be big boys with missile envy?

HELEN CALDICOTT

Well, because men can be taught, or they can learn themselves, how to be nurturing, and you see it happening a lot with men. And the women's movement has given men the impetus to do this. For instance, when I was young and had my babies, when I was twenty-three, you'd never see a man pushing a pram or holding a little baby. In fact, my husband wouldn't do it in Australia. And now, big hairy men come in with little babies into the hospitals, holding them and feeding them and changing their diapers, and it's a very beautiful thing. So you see men getting in touch with their feelings when they didn't do it before. And there are now writings by psychiatrists to show that the only theatre where men can get in touch with their feminine principle is the theatre in a relationship between a man and a woman, where a woman really pushes a man to face himself. And it's tough going, you know, because the men get very upset and petulant, quite bitchy when you push them. And it tends to upset the relationship, but the only way the men can get in touch with their feelings is with a woman helping them. And I don't mean nurturing them, I mean really pushing them.

SARA WOLCH
So we're talking about real changes in behaviour?

HELEN CALDICOTT
Absolutely.

SARA WOLCH
One of your reviewers has said that, by the end of *Missile Envy*, you're really calling for a wholesale transformation of human nature. Changes in the way we live, changes in the way we earn our money, changes in the way we bring up our children. Why do you think that war and violence are separable from the human condition?

HELEN CALDICOTT
Well, because you could say that man is a sexual beast and therefore must always have sex to maintain healthy livelihood, and that's not true. There are many men and women who abstain all their lives. To say that man's aggressive doesn't necessarily mean to say he has to kill. It's very easy to suppress those instincts. And I think one of the reasons men kill is because they don't know how to have normal human relationships with real honesty, and, you know, a good way to let out your aggression is to have a wife whom you love enough to fight and argue with and to be honest with. And if you can let out your aggressions within an intimate relationship, you don't need to go out and spew them all over the world because they're unre-

solved. You resolve them within the intimate relationship. And I don't mean wife-beating, I mean working out your anger and hostility and talking about it, and then taking possession of it and saying, "Yes, I'm anangry man. You provoke my anger, but it occurred in childhood."

SARA WOLCH
Speaking of wives, I'd like to share something with you. This is from a play. The setting is after a war, and the action takes place back home.

> Now countless women, partners in one grief, with soft white hands tearing their veils in two, bedew their folded bosoms with tears like rivers flowing. And new-made brides turn from their silken beds of youth and pleasure and soft luxury, with tender sighs bewailing their young lords taken from them, while anguish eats like hunger at the heart.

Aeschylus wrote this play in 472 BC. He was writing about the Greeks' triumph over the Persians from the Persians' point of view. What has struck me very deeply is that we have something like 2,440 years separating you and Aeschylus. Nothing seems to have changed. How do you suggest we redirect human behaviour?

HELEN CALDICOTT
Well, human behaviour only changes of necessity, and I'm not even sure if we will be able to do it. But it is now a necessity to understand that war is obsolete and that we can no longer fight and kill each other. It was said in the Old Testament, "Thou shalt not kill." Jesus said, "Anyone who has anger against thy neighbour is in danger of a judgment." In other words, it's the anger that's the instinct behind the kill. And we now have to grow up and stop projecting our anger and dark side out on to other people and killing, for if we don't, we'll destroy the planet. So now it becomes a moral imperative.

SARAH WOLCH

You mentioned Jesus. Also, in *Missile Envy*, when you talk about your visit with Reagan, which you also described in the lecture, you say that you told Reagan that you're deeply religious and that you consider what you do a spiritual mission. What do you really mean by that?

HELEN CALDICOTT

Well, I'm trying to save the creation. And for me — I used to be an atheist, or more an agnostic, actually: prove it to me. Now I feel that God is life. It's the DNA molecule, it's everything out there. And a big question I have is, if we destroy life, what happens to God? And I've asked a lot of theologians that question. They look at me blankly, and I don't really know what the answer is, but I'm trying to save God. Now that sounds terribly arrogant, but that's how I feel inside. Maybe I'm wrong, but that's how I feel.

SARA WOLCH

How do you expect people who have not experienced this kind of self-realization to join this kind of spiritual mission?

HELEN CALDICOTT

It's easy, because when they hear under what danger their children are living, and when they really take on the fact that they're not committing themselves to their children's lives, and they're seemingly disinterested in the survival of their children, they get a very big shock. It's a very big personal awakening, and you can see it in their eyes. They just change.

SARA WOLCH

A friend of mine was with me at the lecture last night. She's a mother with a young son, and she left very angry. Rather than feeling empowered, she walked out of there feeling emotionally manipulated and that all her buttons had been pushed and she watched it happening.

HELEN CALDICOTT

That's good. To leave that lecture last night feeling unemotional would be almost mentally sick.

SARA WOLCH

At what point, though, Dr. Caldicott, does manipulating people emotionally prevent them from feeling empowered?

HELEN CALDICOTT

It doesn't ever prevent them. My experience is that when they get frightened, it's as if I've told them they've got cancer. What I did last night was practising medicine. It's what I do with my patients. You have to get a patient to understand the reality of his or her illness and to be able to enter the stages of grief, of shock and disbelief, depression, anger and, finally, adjustment. It's painful. And you would do anything but go through that pain, but it's also reality. People have to be in very severe psychological turmoil at the moment if they're facing the reality of the world practising passive suicide. I think they have to go through the pain and work out themselves what is right for them. I wasn't emotionally manipulating last night. People had their own emotional reactions to what I said. I can't make people feel anything. People decide whether or not to feel good or bad. That's their own business, their own feelings. You own your feelings, you know. I can't make you feel anything. You can't make me feel anything. I decide whether or not I respond to you.

SARA WOLCH

How do you even maintain a drop of hope today?

HELEN CALDICOTT

Because I'm a physician and because we're always optimistic. And if we have a terminally ill patient in the intensive care unit, we're always optimistic until the patient's heart stops or until there's brain death. We turn off the respirator — and sometimes a patient survives. That's my training. I am a physician, period. I'm nothing else. I'm a physician.

SARA WOLCH

But you're also a woman and a mother, and you tell us that.

HELEN CALDICOTT

That's true, but I'm really in the end degree practising preventive medicine. I took the Hippocratic Oath, and I'm practising my profession. That's why I'm an optimist, and I'm also an optimist because I believe in people. I believe in the goodness in the human soul. And your friend who was so upset last night, she'll work it out. It's painful — certainly painful for me.

"We the People: A Prescription for Ending the Arms Race" was broadcast on December 5, 1984.

A Polemicist's Journey

TARIQ ALI

Interviewed by

PAUL KENNEDY

Tariq Ali was a leading light of the New Left in the 1960s. His eloquent denunciations of American imperialism in southeast Asia were to be found in the pages of The New Left Review, *which he helped to found. Since then, he has had an ever-changing career as an activist, essayist, filmmaker, editor, historian and novelist.*

TARIQ ALI

I was born in Lahore in 1943, a long time ago. It was then still British rule in a unified subcontinent, and when I was four years old the city of Lahore, which had been part of India, became part of Pakistan. And I have no real memories of that time. Lots of families suffered, I know, and lots of families moved out. and there were ethnic cleansings on both sides of the border. But fortunately, my family was from that part of the country already and so we didn't move.

My mother described later — she was pregnant with my sister at the time of Partition in 1947, and my mother has not a trace of prejudice in her — but she said there was so much tension that, one day, when she was about eight months pregnant — it must have been March, 1947 — there was a knock on the door, a big, giant

Sikh knocked, and, she said, all the servants of the household were at Friday prayers. And she just saw him and she said the first thought that passed through her head: "This is it. He's just going to kill me." And he smiled and said, "Sorry to disturb you, Madam, but I'm new here. Could you tell me? I'm looking for this street." So she pointed him in that direction and he went away. And she said she felt so ashamed at having even thought that he could do violence to her, but she said that violence was being done. It was in the air. So trust completely disappeared between communities which had lived together for countless centuries.

But that had no impact on me. It was only when I was growing up later, in the fifties, that often I would be sitting in the back of the car, and my parents would be driving to drop me off or see friends, and hear snatches of their conversation. They would talk about streets, houses, point to a house and say, "Remember X used to live there . . . remember Y used to live there." And they were all Hindu or Sikh names. And this city, which was one of the most cosmopolitan cities in the Indian subcontinent, had become a monocultural city.

And even as a young youth growing up, I took all this on board. But you know, we were kids, we were having a good time. It didn't really make an impact on me till much later, and then I realized what had happened to the culture of that particular town as a result of the ethnic cleansings. I mean, you know, people forget now, but this was just two years after the Second World War had ended, and in this giant subcontinent you had nearly two million people killed — Hindus, Sikhs, Muslims killing each other, and the only people who were untouchable were the British, about to leave. And this has always stayed with me, this tragedy.

So that's the atmosphere one grew up in — of a divided subcontinent, of a new country. And yet, one always felt that the leaders of Pakistan, who had virtually no record of having resisted or fought against the colonial ruler, were from the beginning crippled by an inferiority complex in relation to India. [Muhammad Ali] Jinnah, the founder of Pakistan, had died a year after the country started. The leadership which ran the country was so mediocre that it was laughable, and we used to laugh at it. And India had a great political leader, admired all over the world. And we said why is it our bloody luck that they've got Nehru and we've got no one. And then we saw the rapid descent of Pakistan from being, you know, very pro-British into becoming what I would say is virtually an American colony. From the fifties onwards, from '54, when the first pacts were signed with the United States, the American Embassy in Karachi, later Islamabad, became the dominant force in Pakistani politics. And that hasn't changed.

PAUL KENNEDY

Can we talk a bit about your early education in Pakistan? It wasn't quite, I would say, the normal education for a Pakistani boy.

TARIQ ALI

No, it wasn't, you see. I mean, the fact is I came from a very old, crusty, decaying feudal family, and my father was very radical. In fact, both he and my mother were very involved in the struggles against British rule. Both of them became communists. And the choice of schools for upper-class Pakistanis was limited. Either you went to the top private school in the country, which used to be called Chiefs' College because it was designed by the British simply to educate the children of chiefs and princes — later the name was changed to Achison College after some Scotsman who no doubt was a principal. This was where the elite was educated. And there they were largely educated in how to play cricket, how to play polo, how to behave properly, and a bit of education was provided as well. And my father said, you will go to that school over my dead body, and so the only other choices were missionary schools. And I went to a missionary school run by Irish Brothers, which was a strange experience but quite a nice . . . I mean, I never liked school, but that would have been the case, wherever I'd gone.

But what was weird about this school was that, growing up in Pakistan, you had friends from every social layer in society, but I was being educated in a Catholic missionary school by a bunch of priests who were pretty reactionary on every front. And I think the fact that they were so reactionary made me rebel. Because they were so bad that I said, this can't be happening. You know, we had one brother — I still remember his name, Brother Loeb — who used to defend Franco in the Spanish Civil War because Franco defended the Catholic Church. And I remember going home and telling my father this, and my father said, "They can't be that backward." I said, "They are. This is the school you've sent me to," and he said, "Oh well, get on with it, get on with it." So that's where I was brought up.

And the other thing about these priests was that there was a real streak — not in all of them; there were one or two very decent ones — but in quite a lot of them there was a real sadistic streak. For instance, they used to love corporal punishment. Bend down, canes which had been oiled — you know, beating young boys on the buttocks. Put out your hands. When you were hit on your buttocks it was called "benders." When you were hit on your hands it was called "cuts." And, of course, there were some priests who, then as now, would espy a sensitive, good-looking boy and say, do you want twelve benders now with your pants on in front of the class or three after the class in my study? And these poor kids were sexually harassed and, you know, all sorts of horrid things happened. Nothing like this happened to me. I was hit, but in public. But we heard stories from kids, and when we told our parents, I don't know what they did. They said, "The boys must be exaggerating, surely."

So that's what it was like. It was a very strange education. My first political activity was in 1956 when Britain, France and Israel invaded Egypt — the Suez Crisis. And university students were pouring out of the universities, demonstrating on the streets, and they said, "Close the schools down." And our school wouldn't close, and the university students — it's a very strong memory I have — poured into the school, and suddenly the principal — I recalled his name, Reverend Brother Xavier Henderson — who we thought was a total brute, six-foot-two tall, suddenly clambered on top of a truck and said to these university students, "I understand why you're demonstrating. Look at my hands." The fingers of his left hand were bent. There were, of course, lots of crude jokes which the school students used to make: perhaps he played with himself too much, etc., etc. But he now said that this was the result of being tortured by the British in the Black and Tan wars in Ireland in the twenties. So he closed the school down and let us go out, and that was the first indication we had of his own past. And so we developed some respect for him, and afterwards we said, "Why did you never tell us that?" He said, "I don't want to encourage you."

So it was a strange, strange education in that sense, but I learned from it negatively, if you like — what I was interested in, what I wasn't interested in.

PAUL KENNEDY

You've written that you were never religious — in fact, that you were always an atheist. Talk a bit about that.

TARIQ ALI

It's quite strange now, when I look back, and, you know, we are living in times, the beginning of the twenty-first century, when there's so much talk of religion everywhere, both in the Islamic world and in the United States. Even in Britain: we have a prime minister who's quite a hard-core Christian. But it's now very interesting that, when I was growing up, I remember, at a very young age — when I was nine, ten, eleven — not believing in God. Initially for the most vulgar, empirical reasons — you know, how could he exist when there are so many awful things going on in the world, etc., etc. But then I gradually began reading a lot more and later became philosophically engaged reading Bertrand Russell's skeptical essays and so on.

But what is interesting is that none of my friends — close friends, and I had quite a large circle of close friends — were believers. And this was in a country which was predominantly Muslim. We were not believers. It didn't occur to us to be religious. All the religious festivals were observed, like Christmas is in most parts of the world. But, you know, religion never bothered us. In fact, the mullahs used to be mocked constantly as thieves and perverts. And we just grew up in that atmosphere. There were some acquaintances — actually, more than some, quite a few — who were religious, but even their religion was not an in-your-face religion. They believed in it and they went and said their prayers, and we never really discussed it. It was not a subject of discussion, and that's very different from the world in which we live today.

The reason I stress this so strongly is to appeal to young people today growing up in the world of Islam, in the Diaspora, everywhere. It's perfectly possible to appreciate your culture, admire its finer points without being religious at all. Do not get trapped into thinking that the only basis of your identity is a religious one. And I've had lots of correspondence and e-mail with young people from all over the world on these questions.

But it's absolutely true that I had no interest in supernatural beings. I didn't believe in them from a very early age and it never bothered me. People would say, "Well, what do you think will happen when you die?" and I would say, "We will go back to being mud" — you know, that's where we came out from and that's where we will return; there's nothing else.

And some older relations were very perturbed by this, and I remember them telling my parents off — you know, the way you're bringing these kids up. And my parents would say, "We never interfere." But clearly, at one point, my father felt I should at least know the religious mythologies so that I knew what I was not believing in. And I said, "Well, I don't want to," and he said, "No, you have to." So tutors were brought into teach me the Qur'an, and various wooden-headed uncles came in to tell me early stories about Islamic mythology. They were so boring and dull and unbelievable compared to the books I really used to read, which was the mythology surrounding the ancient Greek and Roman gods and all the tricks they could perform, and compared to what we had, it was sort of very dull.

So none of that left a very deep mark on me. Though the one thing I do regret is that I had the chance to learn Arabic as a young person. I could easily have learnt it, but because it was the divine language, I said, "I'm not having anything to do with this," because it was only the language of religion for us. And often people recited the Qur'an without understanding a word of what they were reciting and believed in it, and this blind faith repelled me.

I guess I should have learnt Arabic. I've always regretted it because the culture is so rich — you know, the poetry, the novels, the short stories — and just being able to converse with all my unbelieving Arab friends would have been wonderful. But anyway, I didn't do it.

PAUL KENNEDY

By any measure, it was a long way from a newly independent Pakistan to the ancient ivory towers of Oxford University in England. Tariq Ali began to make headlines not long after his arrival. He was elected president of the Oxford Union and began to publish political essays attacking both the Right and the Old Left. He was in his element. But it should probably also be noted that, in the beginning, it really wasn't where he wanted to be.

TARIQ ALI

Well, the first thing I must insist on is I had no desire to come to Oxford. I was very happy in Pakistan. We had a military dictatorship from October '58 onwards. My first university was in Pakistan, the Punjab University. I went to Government College, Lahore College, with a very rich tradition, had dozens of very close friends, was very active in the struggle against the first military dictatorship. And I remember, you know, those were days when we weren't allowed onto the streets. All political activity was banned — trade unions, political parties. But within the space afforded us by the university, we could speak up, though there were spies, as long as we didn't go on the streets.

And then one day, I think in '61, we got news that the newly independent Congo had lost its leader, Patrice Lumumba, who had been murdered by the United States and the United Nations or a combination of the two. Nothing changes. And we said this was shocking. This is a country with a great leader whom we liked. He was a young, intelligent African intellectual. And I called a meeting at the college and said, we're just going to go demonstrate outside the main buildings against the killing of Patrice Lumumba. And to my amazement, about five or six hundred students followed me and we had the demonstration. And on the way back to the college, just as

we were approaching the precincts of the college, we started chant-
ing anti-military slogans, saying we want democratic rights, death
to the dictatorship, etc. And then ran into the college. Nothing happened — to our amazement. The next day, our example triggered
off a demonstration by twenty-five thousand students.

And then things got nasty and got nastier still, and there were
bigger crowds three days later, and the army opened fire. I saw two
students — I didn't know them, but not far from me — dropping
dead. Massive funerals. At this point, my maternal uncle, who was
a very senior figure, brigadier-general, senior figure in military intelligence, rang my mother up and said could he see her alone? And she
said yes. And he went with my file, which was, you know, pretty big,
and he said, "I'm not showing you this but this is the size of it. And
get him out of the country. He will spend the next ten years in prison
if he carries on like this. We have detailed reports of things he says,
what he does. I can't protect him any longer." And my parents then
called me in and said, "We think it's better for you now if you carry
on your further studies in Oxford." And I said, I don't want to go.
And they never told me the truth, because they knew if they had I
wouldn't have left. You know, why would I leave my friends behind?
What's so special about me? But they didn't say that, and my father
said, "Look, you'll learn much more, and there's a shortage of libraries here. Certain books are banned. In fact, all left-wing literature
is banned. It isn't allowed into the country. Just go for two or three
years and study at Oxford, become a lawyer and then come back,
and then, you know, you can defend yourself if you're under attack
or your friends are being arrested." So that was the plan.

So I left and came to Oxford to study politics and philosophy
and remained active. And, you know, the strange thing is that all
sorts of things were going on in Oxford, and suddenly the Vietnam
War erupted and I just got obsessed with it. I said, our continent is
being attacked yet again. And I felt if I couldn't be there, one had
to do something in Oxford, and we did start getting very active on
this question early, as early as 1964-1965. By that time, the Pakistani
authorities had said that I wasn't allowed back into Pakistan. So I
got stuck here. My passport was later taken away. Then it came back

to me again. So it's been a see-saw, my relations with the Pakistani authorities. They're quite calm now. I go in and out of the country, thank God, but in those early years it was very difficult.

It was when I was still at Oxford, my last year at Oxford, that we had the famous Oxford-versus-Harvard debate. It was the first time a satellite was being used, and the BBC studios in Shepherd's Bush in London and CBS in the United States had set up this debate between Oxford and Harvard on Vietnam. And they said there are two students and a senior student or lecturer — you choose. So we chose Michael Foote, who was a left-wing Labour member of Parliament and he was with us.

And I remember going into the BBC studios where we had our side of the audience, all our friends, and the director-general, Sir Hugh Green, came up to me and said, "It's an evil war. Let them have it." You know, the day when the BBC director-general said that to kids has long gone. But he did say it. And so the debate started, and it was shown live on CBS coast to coast; I got a massive mail-back. But the interesting thing about that debate is that the Harvard side had two students and a senior person called Henry Kissinger, who was an academic at Harvard. None of us had ever heard of him — totally unimpressive. And I promise you we really did slaughter them. We won that debate hands down, and later, when Kissinger became the Svengali he did, I always used to wonder, how did this guy ever make it? This is the guy we hammered in a debate.

But there's a very interesting footnote to that. About three or four weeks after that debate, I was sitting in the Oxford Union and they said, "There's a phone call for you. There's an American woman on the phone." So I went, and she said, "Hi, are you so-and-so?" I said, "Yeah." She said, "Marlon Brando is here. I'm his secretary, and he'd like to have dinner with you because he saw you on the CBS debate." And I said, "Yeah, pull the other one. Look, I know one of my stupid friends has put you up to this, but I'm not falling for it," and put the phone down. She rang up twice and said, "Look, it really is me." And I said, "What's the point of carrying on? I know it's a joke." The third time she said, "Just don't put the phone down," and a familiar twang came on, and he said, "Hi, it's Marlon Brando. It is me, and I heard you really destroy those Harvard idiots on the war in Vietnam. I agree with everything you said and I'm in London and I'd love you to come and have dinner with me." You know, when I told my friends they said, "We can't believe this," but it was true. And so, you know, it's a sort of strange triggering of things which happen once you're politically active, and that happened then.

PAUL KENNEDY

Vietnam politicized you, I suppose, although you were political before. It politicized, really, a complete generation in a way that hasn't happened since.

TARIQ ALI

That's absolutely true. It was a war which was so evil and corrupt and immoral and wrong and unjust that it had to be opposed. And I was then also involved in opposing it. But then we had an amazing set of public intellectuals at that time: Bertrand Russell here, Jean-Paul Sartre, Simone de Beauvoir in France. And Russell and Sartre decided to set up an international war crimes tribunal to try the United States for war crimes when no one was even admitting to any atrocities taking place, because the Cold War meant that the media on both sides were pretty solid. So I went to North Vietnam at the height of the bombing, from December '66, and I was there for three months. And what I saw just shocked me. I mean, the scale of the bombings, the use of chemical weapons, the use of anti-personnel weapons. I mean, the sight still haunts me. And I remember that when I watch what's happening in Fallujah in Iraq — of kids being killed, young kids, their legs blown off — these horrible little anti-personnel devices they used to just drop on the country so — you know, they looked like a guava: you picked it up, it blew in your face. And they called them pineapples and guavas, which they dropped from the sky. So we saw all this. And, you know, how could one not be moved?

I remember meeting the North Vietnamese prime minister, Phan Van Dong, in Hanoi at that time, and I said, "Look, we feel very helpless. Can't we form international brigades to come and fight with you guys?" And he said, the war is so technological that you lot would be a liability. This is not Spain in the thirties. He said we would have to devote so many resources to try and protect you and keep you alive that it would be a diversion, and then we saw how right he was. I mean, hospitals being destroyed. It was quite a horrific experience for me and very formative. And then when we came back, the tribunal finally met in Sweden, where one gave, you know, evidence before it. And the Americans had been asked to send a representative but hadn't done. The entire US media and British media denounced the tribunal, and some months after the tribunal's findings had been denounced, news of the My Lai massacre came into the open, that there had been these massacres.

But no one in those days said, "Hey guys, sorry, you were right and we were wrong," because that wasn't the world in which these things were said. But I think it had a very big impact, and I think the fact that the Vietnamese were winning, couldn't be defeated — that began to radicalize America. And when that movement spread into the American Army, then we knew it wasn't long before they'd have to call a halt. Because once your own army is infected by radical ideas and soldiers don't want to fight because they know they're fighting an unpopular war, then you have to bring it to an end. Kissinger and Nixon delayed it as much as they could and bombed Cambodia into the bargain, but nonetheless it was an important victory.

PAUL KENNEDY

We should talk about your writing, and I think we should maybe begin at the beginning. You've since gone on and you've done all kinds of writing — non-fiction, fiction, film writing — but you began early as a non-fiction writer, almost an essayist.

TARIQ ALI

Yes, I began as an essayist, concentrating on non-fiction. The first complete book I wrote was a book on my own country, Pakistan, which I wrote after the big uprising of '68-'69, an uprising not much referred to in books on '68 which are all over the place again. But the only successful uprising in '68 was in Pakistan. It started in November — November 7, the anniversary of the Russian Revolution. But no one then knew it. It was an accident. And it ended in March, and it escalated each month and the repression couldn't stop it and the dictatorship was toppled. And it was a wonderful sight when I went there in March and the dictator had just said, "I cannot carry on any more." And the demonstrations and, oh, it was joyous, joyous. And yet, people in the West barely knew it was going on.

So I sat down and wrote a book called *Pakistan: Military Rule or People's Power*, which was my first book, in which, unfortunately, I predicted that the situation in Pakistan was so bad between a ruling class based in the West and the majority of the population living in East Pakistan, a thousand miles away, divided by a thousand miles of Indian territory, that this semi-colonial rule by West over East would result in a total disaster and that Pakistan would break up. Now, when I first wrote that, people went crazy. Oh, Tariq, you're mad. This can't happen. Modern states don't break up. I remember so many people on the Left saying that, and, of course, the military was livid, saying this was a treacherous book. It was banned in Pakistan. And when I went to Bengal, East Pakistan, Tarkar, now Bangladesh, I warned the Bengalis, a big student audience. I said, "Have no doubt you are going to go for autonomy or independence in a big way, and that army will crush you. They will kill. Have no doubt about it."

Afterwards, I was called in by two senior leaders of the country, or what became the country, and they said, "You seemed very sure." I said, "I know these guys. They will try and crush you by force." Two years later, it happened: massacres in that country. Lots of my friends in East Pakistan perished as a result of that. And those killings tarnished Pakistan forever and that ruling elite, in my eyes. I could never feel the same about it. I said, "You people have really crossed the line. This is now not just ordinary opposition, when you go and massacre your own people in this way." I felt completely alienated. So I wrote *Pakistan: Military Rule or People's Power* predicting the break-up of Pakistan.

And then the Americans, bless them, imposed another dictatorship on us. General Zia al-Haq, who was the worst dictator Pakistan has ever had, an Islamist dictator, brought the religious groups up. The religious groups who are now dominating parts of the country were his creation, created from the top with total American approval because the enemy was a secular enemy. Communism, nationalism, anything like that had to be crushed. And this guy brutalized the political culture of the country. People were flogged in public. There were public hangings. The country's only elected prime minister at that time, Zulfiqar Ali Bhutto, was executed after a fake trial and fake charges. And the United States watched all this because they needed him to fight the Russians in Afghanistan.

I then wrote my second book, *Can Pakistan Survive?* General Zia, the dictator, did me a big favour by publicly denouncing the book, which helped no end because there were clandestine copies distributed, and in the '90s I would run into retired Pakistani generals at airports and they would say, "You know, I read that book. I didn't agree with everything but a lot of what you said was true." I said, "I'm aware of that, but I'm glad you read it." They said, "No, no. It was read by the entire high command." I said, "Oh, well, that's nice to know."

PAUL KENNEDY

Friends in high places.

TARIQ ALI

No, what amazed me was not that. What amazed me was that they could actually read. I mean, the thought of these guys reading books was quite impressive.

PAUL KENNEDY

For twenty years, beginning in the mid-1960s, Tariq Ali waged polemical warfare as a leading spokesperson for the New Left. He wrote books, he published articles and essays, and he edited *The New Left Review*. But for Tariq Ali, as for so many progressive writers, the entire world changed with the collapse of the Soviet Union.

TARIQ ALI

I didn't retreat totally, but I retreated, if you like, not backwards but sideways. From 1984 to 1998, I did a lot of television work, documentaries, drama, cinema, and in '91 I started writing fiction. And I've got two fiction projects. One is what the late Edward Said dubbed "The Islam Quartet," except it's the Islam Quintet, which is a set of novels exploring the relationship between Islamic and Christian civilizations from the earliest times till now. And the first three of these novels, *Shadows of the Pomegranate Tree*, *The Book of Saladdin*, and *The Stone Woman,* are completed, out, translated, published everywhere. Two more to come on that.

And then the second, parallel series of novels is on the fall of communism. So the first was a satirical novel called *Redemption* — quite savage, quite funny in parts, but basically it was a ferocious attack on sectarianism on the far Left, which I just couldn't stand. And I compared it to religion. And at the end of that satirical novel I have a big conclave of the far Left's Trotskyist groups of the world deciding that they have failed. Communism has collapsed, and the only thing they can now do to have any influence at all is enter the three great religions of the world. So the Jewish Trotskyists enter the synagogues, the Muslim Trotskyists enter Islam, and the Christians enter the Catholic Church, and their leader tells them, "Go forth and multiply. I want cardinals, ayatollahs and rabbis — that's how we'll take the world." And, of course, we all had a good laugh. Some people didn't find it very funny, especially those who'd been lampooned.

But about four years after this novel came out, I ran into an Egyptian friend, a very dear friend and a columnist. He said, "Tariq, you make these jokes which make us laugh, but, you know, sometimes it's not so funny." I said, "Why? Tell me." He said, "Because in Egypt three leading sons of bitches who lead the Islamist groups are all ex-Maoists from the sixties and seventies." Subsequently, I found out this was the case in Algeria, this was the case in Pakistan. Quite a few people from the Left had actually made that turn. I hadn't known about it. If I had, I'd have referred to it in the novel. So this satirical novel's suddenly becoming a reality for people in some parts of the world was strange.

The second novel in that series captured the tragedy of communism, the betrayed hopes, the lost illusions, how the idealism of peoples exploited by the Stalinist system was just destroyed, and the tragedies. That's called *Fear of Mirrors*, and one more is to come in that field, which will be about people on the Left who suddenly move Right — that's also in my head. So I've got three more novels to complete before I sleep. Let's hope that I find the time to do it.

I never thought that I would start writing non-fiction again till 9/11 happened. So I can't write in the same way as I used to in the sixties, seventies, eighties even. It's affected my non-fiction, I think for the better. Lots of people tell me, all over the world, that they're much more convincing. But it's because we live in a different world, too.

PAUL KENNEDY

There is, though, an obvious homogeneity in your writing. It's not as though you, as a fiction writer, put on a completely different hat and write about different topics.

TARIQ ALI

This is absolutely true. I've not changed that much. I mean, I don't believe that sectarian politics and stupid ways of organizing are the way to the future. But I do believe we have to keep a radical presence and dissenting voices alive in this culture, even more than in the sixties, because it's become a very monotone culture and it's constantly under attack. If you look at what went on in the United States and Britain during the Iraq War, which a large chunk of the population in Britain didn't want and a sizable section in the United States didn't want, and how they used the media to tell lies, to repeat the lies endlessly to frighten a skeptical population to go to war. And so, in these times, I think that many of the things we did in the sixties are even more important.

And it's extremely important to keep up a barrage of critical writings, critical talks, and also hope that, in so doing, one encourages

a new generation, which is happening. One of the real joys of travelling around the world, which I do a lot now, is to go to a meeting
and find that eighty per cent of the people sitting in front of you are
kids in their twenties or under. And then you just feel that you are
talking to a new generation and that, in the best sense of the word,
without being patronizing at all, the baton is being handed on to
a new generation and they'll pick it up. And I was so moved that,
when the war on Iraq began and they began to bomb Baghdad, tens
of thousands of kids poured out spontaneously from their schools
all over the world to protest. And it's this new generation which
gives one a lot of hope. And they are the people I really write for.
You know, when you write a book of fiction, essentially you write it
with about twenty, twenty-five people in mind. But when you write
non-fiction like this, you have to have an audience in mind, and my
audience is this young generation which is growing up and which
reads and talks and is very exciting.

PAUL KENNEDY

Now, this generation could be, I suppose, paralleled to your own
generation. They grew out, as you describe it there, of a war, of
protesting an American war, an imperialistic war in another part of
the world. How are they the same and how are they different from
the sixties generation?

TARIQ ALI

The big difference is that the sixties generation grew up in a time of
enormous optimism — people believing that if we got off our back-
sides and did something we could actually change the world. And
what happened in '68 came close to it. It didn't succeed. Students
and workers in Czechoslovakia wanted socialism with a human face.
I mean, can you imagine the impact that would have had if it had
come off? Because the big fight in those days was that socialism may
be fine but it's not democratic. But if we'd had a democratic socialism
in place in Czechoslovakia, showing that you have more freedom of
the press and means of communication in a country like that than
you do in a capitalist one, it would have had a dramatic effect. That's

why, when the Russians crushed it, the response from the United States and the West was very muted, very muted indeed. They didn't mind that being crushed.

Then in France you had a general strike involving ten million workers who occupied their factories, and when the trade union leaders went and said, "We've got you a forty per cent wage rise," they said, "Stuff it." And when the union leaders said, "Well, what do you want?" they said, "We want the whole cake." So that was a very strong feeling. Now you live in a world where these generations have grown up in a period, if you like, of defeats.

But now, with the war, we have a completely new generation involved, and this new generation is thinking, why did this war happen? And I always tell them that the neo-liberal monster always walked on two legs. One was the economic leg and the other was the military leg, and now both are working in tandem in Iraq. So think about it. But still, I mean, they do think and they are radical, but in terms of transforming the world, they're not there. And how can they be when the powers that be are arrayed against them like that?

The other big difference is that in Vietnam, in Czechoslovakia, in other parts of the world, you had people who were good models. You know, you could totally sympathize with them — if they win, it'll be really great. Today you can't really think that. With the Islamist groups in Iraq and elsewhere, there's no alternative social vision which is superior to that of the imperial power. That's the big problem we confront today, and that is what makes even the radicalization very different. But the fact that it's there is important, and I think people will learn. They'll learn in their own way and in their own time. And no generation is ever like the other — never happened like that. I remember when we were out on the streets in the sixties and seventies, sometimes we would have veterans from the Spanish Civil War with their banners from the thirties coming out, and it used to give us a real feeling of joy and we used to hug them. And that's what the kids do to us now.

PAUL KENNEDY

Well, you were the New Left. They must be the post-modern or the post-New Left.

TARIQ ALI

Well, they are the post-New Left, but *The New Left Review* magazine, with which I've been engaged for many years, is now acquiring a new readership. We know that from surveys we are doing. The kids are reading it, buying it. We've transformed the magazine. It's now run largely by young people. The old guard is still on the editorial board, but it's the young people who run it. So that's really encouraging and very nice to see. And lots of ideas are coming forward. You know, one of the main leaders, though she'd hate the word, but one of the main influences is a young Canadian woman, Naomi Klein, who is known the world over, travels the world over, whom I like a great deal. Sometimes people say, "It's great, you're still speaking all over the world, but where are the young?" They are there and, you know, they're making their way and they'll get there.

PAUL KENNEDY

We should focus for a moment on the question of *Clash of Fundamentalisms*. One of the very refreshing things about it, I must say, is the poetry that swims throughout the book. I mean, it's really laced together almost poetically with poetry.

TARIQ ALI

It is because poetry has played a very important, certainly in the non-western world over the twentieth century and particularly in the Arab world. So the poets I quote, both in *Clash of Fundamentalisms* and *Bush in Babylon*, the great poets of the Arab world, are there not because their poetry is great — which it is — but because of the influence they've had and to show people in the West that this does happen — that, you know, the great poets have had some of their best poems sung by some of the greatest singers in that world. And the reason they sing it is because the words are magical. And the magic of the words lies not simply in the fact that they're beautifully crafted but they're saying something. The people love them because they know they speak for us. These are not venal politicians. These are not crooks placed in power in our countries by the United States to grab the oil. These are people who speak from the heart, and what they speak from the heart is the truth. And that truth, when it is sung back to them by their great singers, has an amazing impact. I don't think one should underestimate that at all. I've been aware of this for a long time, but as I was writing this book, some of those poems were coming into my head, and so I laced the whole book with them throughout.

And the same applies to Pakistan. In times of brutal military dictators, when the truth went round in whispers, the whispers of the poets were the most effective whispers because these were learned by heart and people recited them to each other. And that is still going on in Iraq.

PAUL KENNEDY

I want to talk as well about one of the principles underlying analytical ideas in the book, which is, again, consistent with pretty well everything you've always been writing. That is that Islam is different from, certainly, Christianity in that it never went through a reformation, and that that really colours world politics today.

TARIQ ALI

Well, this is true, and I ask myself this constantly: of the three great monotheistic religions, why did Islam not have its reformation? I mean, it had mini-reformations but never a proper one. And I think the reason it didn't is twofold. Where it could have had a reformation is if it had remained a major European religion, which it was from the eighth century to the fourteenth century. Islam was embedded in Europe: Spain and Portugal, the Iberian Peninsula was an Arab Islamic peninsula. Even though there were Jews and Christians, there were no forced conversions like that, but the culture was Arab. And the Catholic Church's decision to reconquer those regions and defeat Islam and, in fact, expel both Muslims and Jews — who worked very closely together in that region — from Spain and Portugal created, I think, what later became the European identity: monocultural Christianity. Christianity, then, was marked by the Reformation. And my argument is that if Islam had stayed there, it, too, would have had a reformation. You would have had a European Islam very different from others but that would have impacted on the homelands and the heartlands of Islam. But it was physically defeated, militarily exterminated and expelled from the region. That's one reason we didn't have it.

The second big opportunity was the Ottoman Empire, which was jostling, shoulder to shoulder, with Europe. Often you had a creative sultan in power who would see what was happening in Europe and say, in the fifteenth century, "Hey, they've got the printing press; why can't we have one?" And the clerics and the religious leaders would say, "Yeah, they've got the printing press, but do you see what's happening? Remember Martin Luther." They were very conscious of not doing anything that might destabilize the system, and that meant it atrophied.

Then I think Islam, as a religion, probably would not have been noticed at all had it not been for a geological, geographical accident that the bulk of the world's cheap oil lay underneath lands inhabited by Muslims. That gave it a boost again, globally, in the twentieth century.

If that hadn't been the case, let's just assume that Buddhists had been running the oil countries or were inhabitants there, the big clash, Sam Huntington would say, would be with Buddhism. These are code words for the struggle for oil. And Buddhism would have been seen as the main enemy, and all these Hollywood Buddhists probably would have been Hollywood Muslims.

So I think that's the third big effect which Islam has had. And the tragedy is that, with the collapse of all other alternatives — secular alternatives, radical socialist alternatives — in that world which the Americans helped the Islamists to wipe clean from Baghdad to Indonesia, the only alternative left, the only people who hadn't been crushed were the Islamist groups. And the reason young kids are attracted to them is not necessarily because these kids are instinctively religious but because they see these people as the only people who are doing something, the only people who are resisting the United States, the only people who are resisting Israel, the only people in many parts of the world, in a neo-liberal world where attacks on state subsidies for health and education have meant real misery for the poor. In large parts of the Islamic world, the only people, political organizations, who attempt to substitute for the lack of a welfare state are the Islamist groups. In many places they supply doctors free, they supply cheap medicines, and they set up religious schools. So the West is paying a price for the system it's imposing on the world, and kids are attracted to that.

Now, *Clash of Fundamentalisms* is an appeal to these kids that says, I understand what you're doing but you're wrong, because down that route only trouble lies. And it's nothing that will ever rise above its own limitations. It can't do it. And in order to defeat the American Empire you have to have a social vision and a view which is superior to that of the American Empire and is seen, even if they never acknowledge it, by the population of the United States to be superior. I said, you will never do it through religion.

"A Polemicist's Journey" was broadcast as "The Ideas of Tariq Ali" on June 30, 2003.

How the World Has Changed

URSULA FRANKLIN
ROBERT FULFORD
JANICE STEIN
Moderated by
PAUL KENNEDY

On Thursday, September 13, 2001, with the world still in shock after the terrorist attacks on New York and Washington, three Massey Lecturers spoke with each other and Paul Kennedy about terrorism, security, war and peace. Ursula Franklin, who gave the 1989 Massey Lectures, is Professor Emerita of Physics at the University of Toronto and a lifelong activist for peace. Robert Fulford, one of Canada's most experienced and best-known journalists, was the 1999 Massey Lecturer. Janice Stein, with more than thirty years of scholarship in international affairs, is Harrowston Chair of Conflict Management and the founding director of the Munk Centre for International Studies, University of Toronto, and an advisor to governments around the world. She gave the 2001 Massey Lectures.

PAUL KENNEDY

We've all been inundated with words and images over the past two days, and one of the most frightening words that's coming over the horizon now is a word that should not, I think, be used lightly. The word is "war." And many people are saying, "We're at war," that the first shot has been fired in the Third World War. Do you think this is true? Where are we?

URSULA FRANKLIN

I'm not so sure whether we are at war, but I'm sure we are not at peace. And I think that would lead me to my thoughts on peace not being the absence of war. I've all my life, as you say, been profoundly committed to peace and have long learned that peace is not the absence of war but the presence of justice. The presence of justice has been missing in the world for very many people, and what we may have to realize is that fact, that the other side of the coin of peace is justice, or access to justice.

Believe me, I'm a veteran of war — I lived through the bombing of Berlin. Part of my family never returned from concentration camps. I know what war, declared and undeclared, is. I can only shudder at the thought of what happened in New York, but I also shudder — and did so — when the bombs fell on Hiroshima. I'm a physicist. And between the end of the last world war and the detonations in New York, the world was full of absence of peace, of presence of violence, and maybe this is the time to think: what does it take, not to avoid war, but to promote peace?

PAUL KENNEDY

It's a difficult position to move towards, though, from the perspective that we are in right now. I don't sense that there is the kind of rational thinking that can look at the world and say, "War is an absence of peace." How does one move towards peace?

URSULA FRANKLIN

How does one move towards justice? Step by bloody small step. I think I would be inclined to take the position that's somewhat opposite yours. If it isn't now, in the face of horror, that one says, "Force, terrorism, more force, more violence doesn't achieve anything," when is it going to come? One of the things that one tends to forget in periods of quietness is how unsuccessful violence is, even for those who have power. Nothing has been resolved by violence over the last fifty years. The rational thinking that force does not work, even for the enforcer, is staring us in the face — this crisis that says, "Look at the means we use, whatever will do it." I think this is the moment to say, "We are on a path of no return if we do not look at the roots of violence, if we do not look at the indivisibility of peace." I learned very early in my life that peace is indivisible, as is justice. If there is peace for your friends, then there's peace and justice for all the people you can't stand. There isn't one without the other. And if this isn't the moment to see that and to move towards it by the choice of means, there's no point in more push, more pull, more destruction. We've seen that. Sure, the United States can drop an atomic bomb on anyone and everybody, if they so wish. What would then be accomplished?

This is the time to think, to stand back and say, "What on earth has got us here?" If you ask me, you start thinking after the Holocaust. You think about the atomic bomb. You think about the fact that the scientists warned Truman and said, "Please, let the Japanese see the destruction before you inflict it." Oh, no, we have the power. With that comes the lesson: some people matter less than others. Then one is surprised if, a generation or two later, that lesson had been learned, and the only question is then: who matters more than others? This is the time to think.

PAUL KENNEDY

But it's a very difficult time to think when the kind of peace and the kind of justice you're talking about seem infinitely far away, and the kind of violence and the kind of terrorism are very close. Where does one find the thoughtful solitude in which to reflect on the kinds of things you're talking about? People feel very threatened right now. One feels as though the war, the violence, the terrorism, the horror is very close to home and can be anywhere, anytime.

URSULA FRANKLIN

Quite. And that's a matter of the human imagination that, when I talk in times of peace about nuclear weapons, in times of tranquility about biological warfare, people go off to the movies. It's only at the time of crisis that you might get people to think, and you have to get the tranquility.

We have supposedly a day of mourning tomorrow. Now, wouldn't it be nice if that would be a day of quiet. It's not the thing to say to the CBC, but what about shutting up for a day? Be quiet. Let people think. Communicate the essential: the weather, okay; the traffic, okay. And then have a day of quiet. I don't think more talk gets us anywhere.

Just imagine how the end of the Roman Empire looked for people during the time of the birth of what we know as Christianity. It was an awful time. People walked around and asked each other, "Who has any clue of what to do?" Not about the Romans but about life. So, number one: shut up the trivia. Number two: look at your re-sources. Ask, maybe, what's life all about? Is it not more important to bring up children than to see that the big machines fly faster and faster? Give it a bit of quiet. Look at history. Who has said that all people matter equally and nobody matters more than others? Most traditions. Most religions. Not drown it out. And then begin, small step by small step, to increase justice and to say, "We will not resort to violence privately, personally, collectively, provincially, nation-ally, globally." There's no other way. You see how costly violence is. When people say to me, "Oh, it's so difficult," look at the cost of violence. There's cost to peace, but something comes out other than more cost.

PAUL KENNEDY

What would you say to the people — apparently not completely rational people — who perpetrated the incidents on Tuesday? These are not people who are interested in peace, obviously. These are people who believe in something, who were willing to put their lives on the line because of those beliefs, and who are not committed to anything like the ideals that you're talking about.

URSULA FRANKLIN

Quite. But they may never have had a chance to be. I think, of course, I would find it difficult to talk to them, but I may not even find it necessary to talk to them because they are the product, they are the messengers. And I think they may be the easiest people to talk to because one can say, "If you wish to give your life, maybe we can think of other ways of service." These are people who may have no other outlet. I think it may well be not correct to think that the people who perpetrated this would have no use for other ways to live in the knowledge that justice and peace were open to them. I think one should not underestimate the motivations of hope. We are a country of immigrants. People go through horrors to come to Canada. Why? Because they hope for peace for their children.

PAUL KENNEDY

I'm not sure how well-connected the kinds of thoughts and hopes that you're expressing are with what's actually happening.

URSULA FRANKLIN

Yes, you are quite right, Paul. They are totally unconnected. I have spent the best part of my life trying to put these thoughts into the stream that makes decisions, and I've been spectacularly unsuccessful. That, I think, is a reflection on my ability in the climate of the time, not on the value of the thoughts. It's unfortunate that not only I, but so many people who worked honestly for peace and justice have been so spectacularly unsuccessful. It, unfortunately, means that there is more suffering before one sees there is no other way, there is no alternative to justice. It's like gravity. When people began to understand that they couldn't fly, it didn't mean that the dream of flying stopped. I sometimes say, "Pigs can't fly," but pigs can be flown. It is the beginning of seeing how we get from here to there. But it cannot be done except by peace and through the means of justice, and maybe this is the time to say, "We have to learn something else."

PAUL KENNEDY

We are being bombarded with rhetoric, with images, with analyses. Many people are saying, "The world has changed. We are in a brave new world. We are in a situation which is utterly different from the situation prior to Tuesday morning." Is that so? And if the world has changed, how has it changed?

URSULA FRANKLIN

Who am I to say that? I think one has to remember that the world is not North America or the people who pontificate.

I think the world changes all the time, and then come these events, like earthquakes and thunderstorms, that wake people up to the changes. People begin to notice the leaderlessness. The intellectuals break down morale, and, in the absence of human leadership — when the leadership goes underground when it gets hot — you become led electronically. When somebody needs a hug, they get a recorded message. That's how the world has changed. We may not change back, but we have to recognize it in catastrophes. Unfortunately, suffering, like the one that we see, is the catalyst, if there is any, for reality recognition and, hopefully, an evolution towards a less toxic and hostile reality.

ROBERT FULFORD

I see Ursula Franklin's comments as being heavy-laden with pessimism. I was particularly struck when she said that, in searching for peace and justice, I — meaning I and people like her — "I have been spectacularly unsuccessful." In the twentieth century, the first half was a time of horror and terrible crimes around the world. In the second half of the twentieth century, there was peace and justice in many places where they'd never had any of it before. Japan was a classic case. From 1945 to this moment, Japan has lived in peace and has had a high measure of social justice. All across western Europe, people who never heard of the possibility of having a good doctor have had one for the last fifty years. And so on. Tremendous improvements have been made across the world, not just in the western world, in providing peace and justice for the people. We're still having terrible wars, terrible troubles and people who are living in poverty. But the idea that you can call what's happened over the last fifty years "spectacularly unsuccessful" seems to me frankly wrongheaded and almost frivolously pessimistic. So that was one response I had.

Another response was that she says maybe the whole world hasn't changed the way that you suggested in a question that it might have.

She says maybe America has. This happened in New York, which is the consciousness centre of America, and America is the consciousness centre of the world. Like it or dislike it, that is the case. More people know about America than know about anywhere else, except for their own place. This was an event that took place right at the centre of modernity. Furthermore, it was an event heavy with symbolism: American culture represented by the skyline of New York, world trade represented by the World Trade Center, and the military power of the West represented by the Pentagon — three strikes against those things. Powerful, powerful symbolism. Anyone in the middle of India who doesn't notice that, anyone in Russia or anyone with access to the news in China who doesn't know about this is simply unconscious. This is a powerful world event. Anyway, those were two of my reactions.

JANICE STEIN

I understand Ursula's despair. I think, watching these last two days — and I know Bob would agree — the images that we've seen have had, I think, a profound effect on North Americans, who haven't experienced this kind of violence and destruction in the lifetime of most of us. In that sense, it will stand as a day that's etched in the memory of everyone.

Where I think Ursula leaves out part of the story is that she is unwilling, given who she is, to recognize that there is evil — that there are those who do not participate in the same moral discourse that most of the world accepts. The people who perpetrated these acts have reasons, and if we enter into their thinking, there is a certain logic within that kind of thinking. But we could argue that Hitler had reasons and that there was a logic, a connect within the thinking — it wasn't disoriented. But, nevertheless, few of us would accept that there was any conscious moral discourse in the language that Hitler spoke.

There is no escape from the fact that a group of people — twenty people, fifty people — consciously decided to kill large numbers of innocent civilians, as well as themselves, in the name of a cause. That is outside what I would call the boundaries of the civilized community, and I think that's the visceral response that we're seeing, not only in New York and not only in Toronto, but around the world. The horror is shared, even in parts of the world that themselves have raged against the very symbols that Bob talked about: the cultural capital, the concentration of economic power and the concentration of military power. In many parts of the world that have a strong sense of grievance against precisely those symbols, they reject utterly the means that were used on Tuesday in the United States. I think that's what creates the dilemma for so many people. In the presence of evil, which I think this was, what is the appropriate and civilized response?

ROBERT FULFORD

I agree with you in your mention of Hitler. We love to say "madman" about people. Incidentally, we also love to say cowards. I was rather dismayed to hear President Bush call these people "cowards." A young man who will set out and spend months training to throw his life away for a cause is not a coward. I could say a lot of other terrible things about him. He's not a coward. I think we like to say that about people. But we like to say, "Hitler was a madman." He was not a madman. He was a man whose life was organized incredibly well in some regard. He was evil.

Now, there's a certain amount of publishing once more, lately, around the term "psychopath." A psychopath is someone who can't feel the pain of someone. Among other things, a psychopath is someone who can't feel the pain he inflicts on another person. That person lacks moral imagination. I don't know whether these are clinically psychopaths. But the action that they carried out and the action that their supervisors, their handlers, their financers directed them to carry out — this is psychopathic action, because it completely eliminates the possibility of feeling for the object of your actions. They suffer from affective deadening. What did that to them? We don't know. I assume it's religion. It's one of those cases where religion has gone crazy, has gone down one of those strange byways that religion occasionally takes, where you burn a lot of Jews in the square in Madrid or you kill people for disagreeing with Christian theology in the

Middle Ages and believe that you're carrying out a religious act. It's not at all uncommon for religion to go that way, and it appears that possibly a sizeable chunk of Islam has gone down that road, sizable enough to become a terrible threat to the world.

PAUL KENNEDY

I'd like to focus, if I could, on the question that I initially posed to Ursula Franklin, and that was basically to try to get some grip on a word that is being thrown around a lot these days, and that word is "war." Are we at war? Is it possible to be at war with a still undefined group of — apparently — individuals? We're not at war with a nation-state, apparently. We are not at war even with a corporation. This is not us versus Apple or us versus Microsoft. This is something completely different, and I would like both of your perceptions of where we are.

JANICE STEIN

Paul, I don't think we're at war, and I'm dismayed by the growing chorus of voices I hear around me, such as Thomas Friedman. It started with President Bush, who said this is an act of war against the United States, this is not simply a criminal act. I think it was a criminal act. But we're not at war. I say this with great deliberation because I sense among the public a growing apprehension that we are on the verge of war, and we are not. We are not because, from a practical point of view, a war requires an enemy that has a face, and this is a faceless enemy, and that makes war problematic. If you want to conduct a war, it requires a target, and even when we can put some faces to this enemy, as we will in time, there still will be no targets. I stress that because when we come to talk about what kind of response is appropriate — Ursula referred to "means" here — in the presence of evil, there is an important debate about what means are justified and what means are not. Evil actions do not necessarily justify evil means and response.

This is a shadowy group of committed fanatics who are, by the way, in my view, a tiny minority in the Islamic world, a tiny minority. We saw universal condemnation by Islamic governments of the acts that these people perpetrated. An act which has no known connection to any state or any government, thrives underground, flourishes in conspiracy and grows through martyrdom — that's not in any way consonant with what we would normally talk about as "war."

Why I'm troubled by the language of war is it arouses public passion. It mobilizes the public in unthinking ways to authorize really what will only be described as acts of revenge. Unless these acts have a specific purpose and can be considered reasoned and appropriate responses which are likely to prevent further acts of evil, I truly see no such military act on the horizon. That doesn't mean that there won't be one. But I see no such reasoned military response which is likely to succeed.

On the contrary, if, as I suspect, the United States and others use military force against targets that did not participate in planning this, in financing this or in supporting it, we deepen the culture of martyrdom, we encourage new recruits, and we make it easier, not harder, for those who are attracted and seduced by this evil to continue to do it. In effect, we create a war. That's where the real danger is, and that's why I am genuinely troubled by these last forty-eight hours, because it becomes a self-fulfilling prophecy. To give you the most concrete example that I can think of, a lot of our discussion about Osama bin Laden is a shadowy discussion. There are times, if I were sitting with my friends from literature, we might actually consider him a construction, because we imbue him with power and authority and omniscience, which I strongly doubt that he has, but because we have no good explanation of many of these events, there is one master figure which is responsible for a great deal of violence and terrorism.

But Osama bin Laden was originally supported and financed by the United States in the struggle against the evil of the Soviet Union. It was after the Soviet invasion of Afghanistan that he got his operational training. So, to defeat an evil, we use means which create an evil, which comes back to haunt us. To me, the big challenge of these next few weeks is, can we have a measured and appropriate response to evil which will require more of us, at home, in the kinds of accommodations we will need to make in our daily lives? Not for a day, not for a week, not for a month. Are we in fact willing to change our lives so that we can better prevent these kinds of acts and restrain the need for revenge, which is human, which is understandable, which these horrible images that we have seen replayed again and again evoke? Can we restrain the need for revenge until we are persuaded that there is a response that is appropriate and will in fact deter or punish those who actually committed this crime?

ROBERT FULFORD

I agree with the statement that we are not at war. You have to have an enemy for a war, and you need another government to be at war with. Margaret Thatcher said one time that a great deal of the trouble in the world is created by people who take metaphors literally. This sounds a lot like George Bush's father's war on drugs. At one point, he declared a war on drugs. It ended up he had to do all sorts of really, really violent and, in some cases, embarrassing things to carry out this war, and at the end of it no one ever found out who won the war and they just stopped talking about it, which must have left many of the people involved pretty sour. The trouble with war as a metaphor is you expect to win or lose. Americans, for the most part, have won their wars, and they would very much like to win this one quickly and, of course, as is their habit today, with no casualties. You could make tremendous mistakes following that metaphor too far.

I think we may differ a little bit in our understanding of the element of Islam that has gone down this road. You say "tiny." Of course, we don't know. Islam is a gigantic, worldwide religion, and even a tiny part of it can be quite large. We do know that many young men in Palestine are willing to give their lives almost promiscuously, almost casually. I don't know how quickly they make up their minds, but a lot of them have made up their minds pretty quickly in the last few months. We know that the men who took part in this event gave up their lives as well. That cannot be a tiny sect. That must be supported. There must be popular support. There must be a fairly wide spread of support for that idea among the population in some parts of Palestine and elsewhere in the Middle East, because people do not just do that and keep on doing it while the rest of the world, all their friends, relatives, neighbours tell them they're crazy. They don't keep doing it. People are encouraging that. How many people? I don't know. But quite a few, enough to make it a valid idea in the minds of many of the killers.

JANICE STEIN

It's quite interesting because in both traditions of Islam — the Sunni tradition and the Shiite tradition, which is represented by Iran — commission of acts of violence is antithetical to Islam. They're going down through the *shari'ah* and the Islamic tradition, and today mullahs speak out very, very strongly against the killing of innocent civilians for political purposes, even to become a martyr. So, in my view, it is in fact a very, very small group, many of whom have been disoriented.

The Afghani war produced many, many of these because they lost their homes, they fought in the mountains, they fought with very few resources. The social structure fractured and broke down. I can make that argument without justifying the act, and I'm very careful to make the distinction that, no matter how unjust the world — and it is unjust, and it is unequal, and some of these inequalities have grown strikingly over the last twenty years. I think, Bob, as well, the inequalities are more visible, and so they enrage more easily than they might have done thirty years ago or forty years ago, when television and film didn't travel as quickly and make these differences so transparent and so keenly felt.

The conflict between Israelis and Palestinians has been going on for fifty years. There was hope for a brief period of time. Hope has faded, and again I think some of this is a response to hopelessness. But the overwhelming majority of Muslims would condemn these kinds of acts, do not engage in these kinds of acts, and it is that that I find hopeful — that we hear voices from Canadian Muslims, from Muslims all over the world condemning these actions. To the extent that it is a tiny group, that makes it possible to engage in concerted global action.

ROBERT FULFORD

I certainly agree that the great majority of Muslims will not support a suicide bombing and killing. On the other hand, I think that it has gone on so long now and has become so much a part of everyday mythology and everyday news reporting from the Middle East that there must be many people cheering it on. I certainly have read many times of a mother saying she was proud that her son did what he did, and I've heard of other mothers saying they would be proud if their son did this, and so on. I have no idea of the numbers. I'm not sure we could ever find out. I'm satisfied that they're small but big enough that they make a big difference in the world, and they certainly made a big difference in our world on Tuesday morning.

PAUL KENNEDY

One thing that almost everybody is trying to come to grips with is something that does seem new, and that is the sort of omnipresence of the terror — that it could happen, that it could happen so close to what we deem to be centres of impregnable power. The Pentagon was hit; two of the biggest buildings in the world collapsed before the eyes of the world.

ROBERT FULFORD

In a sense, America has become a little bit like Israel, in that in Israel there is always the possibility of terror breaking out.

PAUL KENNEDY

Do Americans now have to become Israelis? And that means so inured to the violence that they can go about their everyday lives knowing that a car bomb could explode and kill their wife, their daughter, their children?

ROBERT FULFORD

We can't know that. We can't answer that question because it's possible these people will be hunted down and done away with in no time — the people who planned and financed this program. However, we do know that, first of all, someone out there has much more imagination and timing and coordination and intelligence than we suspected before. As a former police chief of New York said, we've always relied on the relative unsophistication of terrorists. Well, we can't rely on that anymore.

Now, the fact that it happened this one time, that it was done so well — if we can use the words "so well" about such a horrible thing — that it was done so competently suggests it could be done again that competently, and it could be done again, and it could be done again. In that case, America would be like Israel. The Americans would have to say, "I'm going to go on as the Israelis, in my experience, bravely do. I'm going to go on anyway and do it."

JANICE STEIN

I'm struck: for whom is this new? It's not new for Britain, which has been living with IRA bombs in London for twenty years. It's not new for the French, who went through a wave of terror attacks.

PAUL KENNEDY

It is new in North America, though.

JANICE STEIN

That's right. The world hasn't changed. What has changed is the sense in North America that we were a fortress, that the oceans protected us, that our geography protected us.

ROBERT FULFORD

I think your point is excellent. On the other hand, the IRA has never pulled off anything nearly so powerful as this, nor did the Bader-Meinhoff, nor did anyone in France. Nobody went into the middle of Paris and knocked down two of the most famous buildings.

JANICE STEIN

But there was a very near miss. As you know, the plan was to blow up the Eiffel Tower, and that was five years ago. So some of this is luck. In a sense, it's a deep culture shock to North America that it's becoming like the rest of the world. It's not that the world has changed. It's the shock among North Americans. We're so insulated and so insular in the deep sense of it, of adjusting to the rest of the world. What the rest of the world does, though, North Americans have been unwilling to do. Security at American airports is a disgrace in comparison to the rest of the world.

ROBERT FULFORD

Not in comparison to Athens, for example, or a few other places.

JANICE STEIN

No. But Zurich, Hamburg, Frankfurt.

ROBERT FULFORD

And, of course, Tel Aviv.

JANICE STEIN

There is no security. I wasn't shocked, frankly.

ROBERT FULFORD

You weren't shocked that those people could get on the plane at Logan Airport?

JANICE STEIN

No, no.

ROBERT FULFORD

I wasn't shocked either.

JANICE STEIN

We have done study after study in which people walk through with knives, with guns, and are not stopped. Now, that is really inconceivable. That's partly because we have very short attention spans. And we're unwilling to put up with even the most minor inconvenience for a sustained period of time. We'll do it now. But for how long will we do it? Three weeks? A month? Three months? Six months?

ROBERT FULFORD

In defence of the Americans and the Canadians in this regard, we should notice that no one has done anything like this with a passenger aircraft before.

JANICE STEIN

We had Air India.

ROBERT FULFORD

Yes, we had Air India. They blew up over Ireland, and it was terrible. It was a horrible thing.

JANICE STEIN

But it originated from here.

ROBERT FULFORD

But this is nothing like using a passenger aircraft as a bomb or a missile. This is a new thing entirely. So I would assume that you will no longer have minimum-wage employees standing casually beside those machines in the airport. And I would assume that anyone from now on who gets on a plane with the hope of hijacking it may find himself killed by the man sitting in seat 3B, who happens to be from the FBI. I would assume that will be a part of the fear of hijacking in the future.

But the truth is, you're right, if nothing happens for ten years, then we'll have the minimum-wage employees who've only been working there a month — who, by the way, are not security-cleared — we'll have them running those machines again. But I think it will take a long time for us to go back to that.

In America, they're speaking of having that entire system federalized, the whole thing run by, effectively, a branch of the FAA or the Department of Justice, which I'm sure would be a better system than the present one. In some American cities, you have better security than others and so on, which is pretty ridiculous.

JANICE STEIN

Logan is notoriously terrible, just terrible, because it's a very secure part of the United States. But that's an easy one, and I say this with the greatest reluctance: it could happen far, far worse than it was. It could have been in the subway system in New York. It could be in the water system of a major city. So the issue really becomes — and I think this is something that is going to be more difficult for open, democratic societies to deal with — how much restriction are we prepared to live with? How much intrusion are we prepared to countenance? How much listening to our phone conversations? How much monitoring of our mail? We've been there before, in the fifties and sixties, and some of what was done in the name of preventing infiltration were again excesses that were far greater. The solutions were worse than the problem.

ROBERT FULFORD

Not if you thought that a whole city might be destroyed. If there was the possibility of a city being destroyed, then the solutions were not worse than the problem. The question, of course, then arises, was there a possibility of a whole city being destroyed? I don't think there was. Today, we've edged towards that. With this event, I think they moved up four or five levels of sophistication between the Yemen bombing of the boat and this event, which was breathtaking in its organization.

JANICE STEIN

It's quite interesting because it was actually very low tech. It required plastic knives and commitment.

ROBERT FULFORD

And people who could fly jet aircraft. Not that hard to learn.

JANICE STEIN

No. So it was actually quite low tech. What is striking about it is the discipline, the commitment, the coordination. And it's not even the fact that they're expensive.

ROBERT FULFORD

So far as we know, they tried four, and they scored three out of four — amazing!

JANICE STEIN

But, Bob, that's more a commentary on what's wrong at home, in the US, than what is successful without them, and that was the point I was trying to make. If I were looking for an agenda, I would start in the United States. It's not military strikes in mountains, in the country, where it's unclear what the relationship is between the government and the people who perpetrated this act. It's in North America, where the security provisions that we have put in place are woefully inadequate, and it's with educating the public and say-ing to the public — and that is, by the way, what has succeeded in Israel over the years — "This is a long-term struggle which requires patience, commitment, vigilance."

ROBERT FULFORD

That's why we can't say "war." We shouldn't say "war."

JANICE STEIN

No, "war" is the wrong word because wars are not long.

ROBERT FULFORD

Wars have a beginning and an end, and you expect that. But, Janice, what about the counterterrorism programs of the US government, which, it seems to an outsider, have so spectacularly failed in this case? Quite a few people were involved in these events of Tuesday. We don't know how many, but it wasn't just the sixteen or twenty who were on the planes. There were a lot of other people involved. And somehow the US government counterintelligence, which spends billions of dollars, didn't find a hint of it. Is it as bad as it looks?

JANICE STEIN

Yes, it is. It's partly because so much of counterintelligence is directed to hi-tech problems. There has been, as we all know, a program on the agenda, which will cost a hundred billion dollars, for a missile defence system to protect against a single missile fired by a rogue state. And law enforcement has been cut back. The intelligence budgets have been cut back, both in Canada and in the United States, in the last ten years.

ROBERT FULFORD

But not in Canada because of the missile defence, because we've cut back everything.

JANICE STEIN

That's correct. Because we cut back the state, and because the sense of threat has diminished.

In all of the things I've read, what was most striking to me was that one of the groups approached the ticket counter in Logan, bought one-way tickets with cash. It is incomprehensible to me that a ticket agent would sell those tickets and not alert airport security to the fact that a transaction like that had taken place. So it's a whole re-education of the public that's required. That's a red light in any country.

PAUL KENNEDY

In the brief time that's left to us, I'd like to hear from both of you on whether what you're both saying, I think, means that we are now in a different world. We will have to have new kinds of security. We will have to have new kinds of protection from this kind of terror. Does this mean we're in a new world?

JANICE STEIN

You probably won't like what I'm going to say right now, but I think we've joined the world. We've been the fortunate few, insulated, protected against much of what has been happening in the world. So we in North America are joining the world.

ROBERT FULFORD

We're joining Israel and western Europe, not much else. There's nowhere else that they have the real security — maybe Japan.

JANICE STEIN

Yes, Japan, which went through a similar experience with an attempted release of poisonous gas into a subway system.

ROBERT FULFORD

On the other hand, they weren't very big on civil liberties before that. I don't know if cutting down civil liberties would help that sort of thing. But certainly it seems to me that those people who have been complaining — and I'm certainly among them — that we are an overscrutinized society are probably going to find themselves defeated completely in the next little while. Some of us are annoyed. Some things annoy me, and some things don't. I'm not annoyed by video cameras following me everywhere, but I am annoyed by the idea of someone opening my mail and so on. Everybody has their sticking point. The truth is that it may be that that kind of civil liberties talk, the civil liberties point of view and occasional civil liberties victory may be pushed back. We may lose on that front, may lose some of our liberties, just as, in many crises in the past, the best democracies, for the time being, have given up some of their rights. In England during the war — it was a war, mind you, and not like this — people were told where to work. They were told what they had to do with their lives for those years.

JANICE STEIN

I think the most difficult issue we're going to face is, how do we treat newcomers to our society? Because that will go to the heart, in many ways, of who we are, of our concept of civic communities and our respect for different cultures.

ROBERT FULFORD
And it will be full of conflict and emotion and a powerful, powerful thing for us to deal with.

JANICE STEIN
Yes.

"How the World Has Changed" was broadcast on September 13, 2001.

The American Stake in Europe and the European Stake in the United States

The 2001 Nexus Lecture | RICHARD HOLBROOKE

Richard Holbrooke is a career diplomat. Under the Clinton administration, he was US ambassador to Germany and assistant secretary of state for European and Canadian Affairs. Most notably, he was the chief negotiator for the 1995 Dayton Accords that ended the war in Bosnia, and he was the US special envoy in Kosovo before the NATO bombings. Ambassador Holbrooke spoke at the Nexus Institute, Amsterdam, Holland, exactly a month after the terrorist attacks on the World Trade Center and the Pentagon.

RICHARD HOLBROOKE

When I agreed to make this speech several months ago, I obviously did so under entirely different circumstances. I had planned a different speech. But the circumstances have changed since September 11 in many ways. Nonetheless, the theme of my speech as I originally designed it, "The American Stake in Europe and the European Stake in the United States," seems to be more relevant than ever tonight. September 11 marked the start of a new era in world politics, one that at this difficult moment appears more threatening but that also presents new opportunities, new challenges, new possibilities which we must take advantage of. The date will surely be remembered as a date in world history to stand with June 28, 1914; September 1, 1939; December 7, 1941. Long threatened by terrorism, the United States received far more than a wake-up call. But this wasn't just an attack on the United States, it was an attack on all of us. The rubble that remains on the southern tip of Manhattan is not of the American Trade Center or the New York Trade Center, it was the World Trade Center.

Since September 11, our nation has moved from shock and numbness to anger to a new resolve to pride in our new national unity. We are now being tested to show resolve to fight the new threats that confront us, a resolve to wage a sustained struggle with all our resources, a resolve to fight this battle together with our European friends, to recognize who our enemies are and who our enemies are not. But we understand we cannot fight this battle alone. Victory is only possible if we act together. September 11 shows us that, more than ever, Europe needs the United States and the United States needs Europe.

Prior to September 11, there was a tremendous debate in Washington and throughout Europe about the future of US foreign policy and the fears that, in the coming years, on issues from global warming to missile defence to peacekeeping to the fight against global disease, the US might try to go it alone. This debate is not worth rehashing, particularly at this delicate time, but it is worth pointing out that, after September 11, I believe we have seen the retreat of the unilateralist impulse in the United States, at least for the time being. Coalition-building is in. I want to stress this. Unilateralism is not an option for the United States in this new era. In my view, it never was and should never be. The transatlantic alliance will be at the heart of the set of overlapping alliances and coalitions needed to fight terrorism. Indeed, the threat we face collectively illustrates how our partnership is indispensable and why now, more than ever, the US and Europe need to be together and why the process of enlarging NATO should be accelerated and broadened immediately.

September 11 reinvigorated our sense of common mission. We have experienced such turning points before. The grand alliance that defeated the Nazis turned that resolve into fighting the long, twilight Cold War against Soviet tyranny. Ten years ago this winter, on December 25, 1991, the end of the Cold War came with the lowering of the Soviet hammer-and-sickle flag from above the Kremlin. But history did not stop there, of course. Threat of local conflicts and extreme, virulent nationalism, stoked by cynical leaders like Slobodan Milosevic and Radovan Karadzic replaced the menace of Soviet expansionism as the greatest threat to stability in building a Europe whole and free.

But even as we faced these new threats, we also enjoyed unprecedented opportunities. The past ten years were years of global prosperity and, by and large, the spread of democracy and freedom. Today, Europe is stable and free for the first time in its history, and there's no major threat to Europe from inside Europe. But in many ways, I believe historians will see September 11 as the end of the post-Cold War era. In fact, we might call the years 1991 to 2001 the second interwar period — the first, of course, being the 1930s, when the world stood by and America disengaged as the threat developed from Nazi Germany.

Today, we must put all our energy into creating the transatlantic community's third great alliance, built around NATO, like the ones we established to fight World War II and the Cold War. In an earlier era, the Cold War, we built the institutional architecture of a new era, designed to promote democracy and defend freedom. This architecture remains the foundation for this new coalition. Throughout the 1990s, the interwar period — which I believe we will look back on as a finite, defined, ten-year period in history — we struggled to meet challenges together. We did so by rebuilding central and eastern Europe, stabilizing Russia, revitalizing and enlarging NATO, attempting to promote peace and stability in other parts of the world, enhancing free trade, forming the World Trade Organization, combatting global warming and, most importantly in terms of stability in Europe, ending the conflict in the Balkans, the last major conflict inside the European space, whose ending was essential for political stability in Europe.

The greatest security threats to the US and Europe today stem from problems that defy borders: the proliferation of weapons of mass destruction, pandemics like HIV-AIDS, international crime and, of course, most urgently, terrorism. The challenges, like out-of-area peacekeeping, come in a way that has rarely been part of our security dialogue, and they emanate from places that for the most part the transatlantic alliance has ignored or called out of area: south and central Asia, the Middle East and Africa. In its own horrific way, September 11 illustrates the new imperative for co-operation. We stand together because we must. As horrible as the attacks on the World Trade Center and the Pentagon were, they were just a taste of what the forces of extremism and terror would like to do if they could.

In the US, numerous blue-ribbon commissions, like the Hart-Rudman Commission, warned of these dangers. They offered bold recommendations for what was needed, but until September 11 they were largely ignored, especially by an American media obsessed by celebrity and scandal. Almost five thousand lives were lost this time, but next time it could be fifty thousand or five hundred thousand. It could be in the United States or here in Europe. The threat from weapons of mass destruction that are chemical, biological or even nuclear is real. Does anyone doubt that the annihilistic murderers of September 11, with their indifference to human costs, would use such weapons if they could get hold of them? I have no doubt whatsoever. Indeed, Osama bin Laden said this quite clearly in an interview in 1998 with *Time* magazine, where he said that it would be the duty of every good Muslim — his words — to seek to achieve control of nuclear weapons if it would help in the fight against Islam's enemies. Again, I stress, as he defines them.

So we must be alert to this. The task ahead might prove even more difficult than our fight against communism because this is not a war against ideology and party apparatchiks. This is a war against sincere fanatics — sincere, extreme, nihilistic fanatics who have convinced themselves or have been brainwashed into believing that, in killing themselves and innocent people, they are serving God. It's almost impossible for those of us who are committed to the dialogue about civilization to get into the minds of these terrorists or understand their motivations.

But the danger is that, in fighting this enemy, we allow it to become a war between the West and Islam. This is what Osama bin Laden wants more than anything else — our Crusade versus his *jihad* — one that ends, if it ever ends, with destruction or paralysis of the modern world. So we need to say it loudly and repeatedly: this is not a war on Islam. This is not a clash of civilizations. Islam is one of the world's great religions, but there are those who would use or, to be more precise, abuse Islam, not to spread hope, but to foment hatred for their own murderous ends.

This is not a war on any one country or bloc of countries, although President Bush has been entirely correct to design a campaign not only against terrorists but those who harbour them. These attacks were not micro-managed by someone on a cell phone in a cave in Afghanistan. Culpable as Osama bin Laden is — and there's no doubt that he and his group lie at the core of this attack — he did not personally enroll the terrorists in US flight schools or make their airline reservations. While these operations were inspired by Osama bin Laden and al-Qaeda, they were conducted through cells in the US and Europe, from places like Hamburg, Jersey City, New Jersey, London, and Arlington, Virginia. These enemies of freedom used our freedoms against us. Now, as we fight them, we must also preserve, not sacrifice, what we hold most dear. One overriding fact is that once we have taken care of bin Laden and al-Qaeda, once the Taliban are removed from power in Kabul, the war on terrorism will not be over.

This will be only the beginning. These invisible networks exist all throughout the United States and Europe. For us, we must seize this moment to create institutions, lasting institutions, to address terrorism. Until the current crisis, quite frankly, our efforts to combat terrorism have been paltry and inadequate. Not that the issue has failed from lack of rhetoric or clarion calls. In March 1996, after Israel suffered four suicide bombings within two weeks, twenty-six chiefs of state and heads of government met in Sharm el-Sheikh,

Egypt, to promote international co-operation against terrorism. They agreed on a range of proposals to fight terrorism, but the results, especially implementation, were modest and inadequate.

Three years ago, President Clinton used his annual appearance before the UN General Assembly to speak on terrorism and said it should be at the top of the world's agenda because nobody is immune. Since 1963, the United Nations has negotiated twelve conventions against terrorism. Twelve. But we still don't have an adequate or comprehensive international legal framework, nor do we have adequate mechanisms for information-sharing, law enforcement, interdiction or disaster response. Success will require a new architecture as visionary and ambitious as that designed by our predecessors following the Second World War. Like the international architecture built after that war, this new architecture will need to address a wide range of issues, come in various forms and have mechanisms to ensure compliance.

Let's take the first logical step: hammering out an agreement on the new norms that will govern the new era. As I said, the United Nations has produced twelve conventions over the last thirty-eight years. The Security Council passed a significant anti-terror resolution under binding Chapter Seven authority in the last three weeks. But as Kofi Annan has made clear, we lack an overarching framework. Such an instrument could tie together previous conventions, fill in gaps in the patchwork of previous agreements and create new mechanisms to ensure compliance with key provisions regarding the financing of terrorism, law enforcement co-operation, information and intelligence-sharing. It will also cost money, and I believe the US should be prepared to take the lead. Now is the time to act with a newly invigorated transatlantic alliance and key Islamic allies.

The second institutional gap that needs to be addressed is highlighted by the ongoing humanitarian catastrophe in Afghanistan. So far, with daily air drops, we're trying to ease the burden on the Afghan people. And after the Taliban are removed from power in Kabul, an international effort under the UN, like the ones in Kosovo and East Timor, will be necessary for some time to come and it won't be cheap, but it will be essential.

A third area dramatically in need of new architecture is in the area of law enforcement. There will be a huge debate about whether September 11 represents a law enforcement failure or an intelligence failure or both. I don't know exactly whether it was an intelligence failure or not, but I sure know that it was a law enforcement failure of the most massive kind.

The extent of the challenge is evident simply by examining the al-Qaeda cell responsible for perpetrating these attacks a month ago. The cell was recruited in the Middle East, organized and probably trained in Afghanistan, managed from Germany, and entered the US from Europe by going to at least three different immigration checkpoints. Let's look at one of the men in particular: Khalid al-Midhar, one of the September 11 hijackers on the plane that crashed into the Pentagon. And this will illustrate the failure and the need to correct. When Khalid al-Midhar came to the US first, he was already being watched because in January of last year he had met in Kuala Lumpur, Malaysia, with one of bin Laden's top aides and some of the suspects behind the bombing of the USS *Cole*. After this meeting, he entered the US, and the FBI picked up his trail in San Diego. He enrolled in flight school there, expressing a desire to learn how to fly Boeing jumbo jets, and then left the US six months later. He did not resurface until last July, when he was allowed to re-enter the US from Saudi Arabia, even though the CIA suspected him because of his connections with the USS *Cole* bombers. The CIA turned his name over to the FBI and said, he's in the US, it's your problem. After learning from immigration authorities that al-Midhar was in the US, the FBI began looking for him, but they never shared his name with any other law enforcement agencies or the airlines. He checked himself onto an American Airlines plane on September 11 under his own name.

Clearly, if someone who's already on a watch list and known to the authorities can re-enter the US, hastily attend flight school, disappear for a year, re-enter the US and finally check onto a plane under his own name with no one questioning his intentions, something is desperately wrong. Another hijacker, the suspected ringleader, Mohammed Atta, who spent his formative years in Hamburg at the Hamburg Technical

Institute, was allowed to enter and re-enter the US, even though he had been implicated in a 1986 bus bombing in Israel.

The links between the world's law enforcement agencies need to be dramatically changed. Interpol, the legendary name, is really little more than a shadow operation with an annual budget of only thirty million dollars. Imagine that. It's weak and in effectual.

A fourth key area in need of serious attention is that of building up a more effective system for choking off the money — the lifeblood of terrorist networks. I read in today's *Herald-Tribune* that Mohammed Atta at one point about three or four months ago received a hundred thousand dollars wired to him in the United States from the Gulf. There must be a system to trigger some degree of curiosity when a poor student suddenly receives a rather large amount of money. With more than a trillion dollars a day, however, flowing through the international financial markets, this is tough to do, but it isn't impossible. We're going to need more aggressive international efforts. While we must work together to tighten our own financial system's holes, we must also engage our many partners in the Islamic world. Finding ways to monitor the *halawa* banking system — the traditional but illegal system that is so important to immigrants in Europe and the United States — is going to be particularly difficult.

Still, let us not let such matters interfere with the unfinished business of the transatlantic relationship. If anything, this tragedy increases the urgency and eases the difficulty of the next phase of NATO enlargement. We should move forward rapidly to bring into NATO at least Latvia, Lithuania, Estonia, Slovenia, Slovakia and Romania no later than the Prague Summit a year from now, and indicate our intention to do so immediately. September 11 should make clear to Moscow that NATO enlargement is not aimed at them, something we've been saying for the last eight years, but it's about increasing the zone of stability in Europe. This will benefit Russia just as much as it will benefit all the existing NATO members — indeed, given some of Russia's problems in its southern tier, perhaps more.

Similarly, we should not use this crisis to reduce our commitments in the Balkans. In military terms, our presence in Kosovo and Bosnia is very small, but in terms of its importance to the common effort and to the security of south, central, southeastern Europe, it is indispensable. We must redouble our combined efforts from the unfinished business in Bosnia and Kosovo to the new challenges in Macedonia. Likewise, we must strengthen the mechanisms of the UN and regional peacekeeping in Africa, and avoiding forgetting about Africa as we focus on Afghanistan is going to be very important.

What about the rest of our issues on our massive global agenda, vitally yet not necessarily related to the war on terrorism? How do we avoid letting them become the root causes for calamities a decade or two decades out? I'm thinking, of course, of such issues as the spread of AIDS, the proliferation of weapons technology and small arms, the spectre of global warming and, as I just mentioned, Africa. Angola, Nigeria, Sierra Leone, the Congo, Sudan, Somalia are all potential explosion points which, if ignored, as Afghanistan was after 1989, could come back to haunt us.

In conclusion, let me say that these ongoing challenges, alongside the new war on terrorism, will require total commitment, engagement and partnership from both Europe and the United States. It's time to turn our strong historic bonds into action that will alter the course of history again. I have no doubt we will succeed. Just as we built a new international framework from the ruins and rubble of Europe following the Second World War by working together, so, too, we must now strive to rise from the ruins in New York and Washington to put the world back on a path to security, freedom and prosperity for our citizens and, indeed, for all people. I am profoundly convinced that in our unity with Europeans we will succeed again, as we have so often in the past.

QUESTION

Ambassador Holbrooke, you mentioned the ridiculous claims made in parts of the Arab world as to the cause of the September 11 events. The phenomenon is perhaps not entirely limited to certain parts of the Arab world, as a remarkable number of commentators were quick to blame United States foreign policy for what happened in New York and Washington. Most of these comments followed the line that the attacks, of course, had to be condemned, but that they should be seen in the light of the deep frustrations caused by American policies *vis à vis* the Palestinians, Iraq or even the Third World in general. And some commentators went as far as to imply that the United States had had this coming to it. Were you surprised by these reactions?

RICHARD HOLBROOKE

Yes, of course, I've seen some of the criticism. There's an astonishing article by Simon Jenkins in today's *Daily Telegraph* in effect calling Tony Blair a lap dog of the Americans who's humiliating himself. That's democracy. Let Simon Jenkins write what he wants. In terms of the theory itself, that the Americans had it coming to them or to explain things, there's a French saying, *Pour tout comprendre ne veux pas dire tout promettre*: to understand a thing is not to accept it or condone it. And even if one can understand the anger of certain people towards the United States or other wealthy countries, it does not mean that they can possibly justify this action. If people cannot understand what was behind this, what Michael Ignatieff has called "apocalyptic nihilism," if people cannot understand what's behind this, they're only jeopardizing themselves. And again, I stress that the original target three or four years ago was the Eiffel Tower. So how anyone can say that the Americans had it coming is very, very peculiar to me.

QUESTION

I read in the paper that the Palestinians train their youth to kill Jews. And once in every three weeks they also learn, or they make a statement and have to repeat it, "Kill the Americans." Are you aware of this type of thing and what do you think about it?

RICHARD HOLBROOKE

You allude to a very critical issue, which is the connection, if any, between this and the Middle East. And it needs to be stated, first of all, that these events are unrelated to the intifada and to the crisis in the Middle East. They were planning these attacks for years. When they attacked the World Trade Center in 1993, the stated intent of Ramzi Youssef, who led that attack, was to bring the building down. They put a huge bomb in the garage, but they misplaced it and the pillars were too strong. And he said to the federal authorities, as he was being flown to prison and they flew by the World Trade Center, "We're going to get that building next time." So they were always aiming for that building because of its symbolism, and it had nothing to do with the Middle East.

Secondly, let's be very clear: if Osama bin Laden could get rid of Yasser Arafat and the ruling family in Saudi Arabia and President Mubarak, he'd do it tomorrow. His top two lieutenants are both veterans of the plot that killed Sadat. If you look at the profiles of these terrorists and hijackers, every one of them began his career as an opponent of the local domestic regime of his own country and then left and ended up, through various processes, either in Afghanistan or Hamburg or some cell somewhere else. So these people are not the same as the eighteen-year-old or twenty-year-old suicide bombers who are recruited by Hezbollah and Hamas. If you look at the profile of the people who did this, they were not the impoverished, uneducated, disenfranchised children of the camps in Gaza or in Peshawar. They were educated. Mohammed Atta graduated with honours from the Hamburg Technical Institute. He got high honours on his thesis. Osama bin Laden is from one of the richest families in the world. His Number Two is a doctor. This is a different group of people. They never talk about poverty, disease. What they talk about is their insane version of Islam. What they talk about is the apocalyptic vision of bringing their idea of the kingdom of heaven to earth. It's crazy. Two documents were found in Mohammed Atta's suitcase in Boston. Whether his bag didn't make the plane or he left it there because he wanted to be immortalized, I don't know — but they're very revealing and they're very, very chilling. His instructions for his burial, how he doesn't want any women to be present at his funeral. He doesn't want women to look at him. And the instructions for the last night, how the people have to shave their bodies, have to say a certain prayer as they get on the plane. And then the most extraordinary phrases: "kill the animals swiftly," "be merciful to the animals" — the animals, of course, being the passengers.

There is no connection between what they think they're doing and the desperately poor, needy people of Africa, the Middle East, central Asia, Afghanistan. They're in another world. But one thing I'm sure of, they're not doing it because there are a lot of poor people in the Arab world and it's somehow the West's fault. It's something else. And to understand it is the essence of our task. We, the West, the US and Europe, must understand what we're dealing with here. Forty years ago, when we got into Vietnam, Americans didn't understand the Viet Cong at all, and they stumbled into a war without understanding it. Ten years ago, the Europeans and the Americans did not understand what was happening in Yugoslavia as they stumbled into it. And they didn't understand what lay behind Tito's façade. But our lack of knowledge in these areas was insignificant compared to the level of ignorance we now have about these people.

QUESTION

Are we not overestimating what happened on that Tuesday? In a historical view, there are much more fundamental problems in our civilization, so do we have to start with a world war? Do we have to start with, let's say, the radical movement in Japan, or where do we have to start? Don't we overestimate this particular date?

RICHARD HOLBROOKE

Well, it is important to note that there are other terrorist groups in the world besides al-Qaeda. And we have our own individual situations — two or three people acting in a conspiracy in the United states blew up a building in Oklahoma City and killed a hundred and seventy people. That was homegrown, domestic terrorism, and I have no doubt that those people would have been happy to do something bigger.

So, do we overestimate September 11? No. I take your point. It's intellectually coherent. But five thousand people died, the most on American soil in history, almost triple Pearl Harbor. They were civilians. The nature of the attack was unique.

I've worked my whole life on these issues, and I don't need to be told that more people die in other places than died in New York and Washington on September 11. I'm here to suggest that you will underestimate the anger of the American people or the political and psychological consequences if you get too rational about it. This was an attack, and it never happened before in the United States, and there's a certain feeling among some people that, good, the Americans finally know what it's like. I think that's an unfortunate approach. This was a tragedy of colossal dimensions, and I cannot stress too highly again that, as Blair and Chirac have said, the target was as much European culture and civilization as it was American

QUESTION

Do you think that the United States now will have the heart and wisdom to finally acknowledge the International Criminal Court, which they now do not want to acknowledge?

RICHARD HOLBROOKE

No. I can't speak for the administration, but I can predict this one with a hundred-per-cent degree of certainty: not a chance. And I don't mean to be sarcastic, but let me be clear on this. Remember that President Clinton did accept the ICC on December 30 of last year, so the Executive Branch formally signed it. It would require an act of Congress to accept it. Two-thirds of the Senate would have to vote for it. There is no chance that's going to happen. Nothing that happened on September 11 is going to change this. Furthermore, the current administration would not submit it.

So I understand the question. It's been asked many times of me in the last month by people who think that, since everything has changed, this too would change. But in reality it's not going to happen. So, at a minimum, you do specific courts. When the International War Crimes Tribunal for the former Yugoslavia (ICTY) and then for Rwanda were formed in The Hague, many people in the

United States and in Europe thought it was a public relations stunt, a gimmick. One of the things that I found when I worked on the issue was that the ICTY was enormously valuable as a way of putting pressure on Milosevic and his people. If it hadn't been for the ICTY, we would have had to have Karadzic and Mladic in Dayton because Milosevic wanted to bring them. I told Milosevic, if he brings them we'd be delighted — we'll meet them at the airport and arrest them the minute they land because they were indicted. At that time, Milosevic had not been indicted.

And so I am a very strong supporter of these special courts. But the general International Criminal Court has got so many problems with it from an American constitutional point of view that it just isn't going to happen in its present form. So it will be formed without us, and I'm very sorry to see that happen. It's not something that is going to change because of September 11. However, I hope the new administration will support special tribunals, because the ones I've talked about, Rwanda and Yugoslavia, and the mixed tribunal in Sierra Leone, have all been very valuable.

QUESTION
You talked about getting states like Lithuania into NATO. But why shouldn't we get the Russians into NATO?

RICHARD HOLBROOKE
As a matter of fact, Putin actually raised this question, and the Russians have from the beginning said they want to be considered for NATO membership. And the United States, under both Clinton and Bush, has said, and all of the NATO members have said — I'm using words very precisely now — "We don't preclude the possibility." Which is a diplomatic way of saying, it's pretty hard to imagine, but let's not close the door. Before September 11, it would have seemed inconceivable to talk about Russian membership in NATO, and as long as we have other issues going on between NATO and Russia — a missile defence issue, which is also a problem between the US and our European allies, Chechnya, other issues — it's difficult to see it working. But let's not close the doors here. Things are chang-

ing very rapidly, and Putin is making very dramatic adjustments in his foreign policy.

QUESTION

You mentioned the link between terrorism and drugs. You also said that, when everything is done with, there might be positive developments out of all this. Do you think it would be a positive development if the United States thought through this problem of terrorism and drugs to the extent where they ask themselves whether it is not drug prohibition as such that creates the illegal markets, from which enormous resources become available for all sorts of criminal activities? I think this is an important issue because, if you spoke about Europe and the United States drifting apart before September 11, that was certainly true for drug policy. Europe is drifting away from American prohibitionism, and so is Mexico and so is Canada. So my question is, do you think the Americans, who so quickly adapt to new circumstances and even pay their arrears to the United Nations, would get away from that totally unwinnable war on drugs and prohibition?

RICHARD HOLBROOKE

Well, this is one of a number of social issues on which many Europeans and Americans seem to be divided. The death penalty is another, obviously. But in fact, if you look beyond treating countries as though they're a single voice, there are divisions on these issues within societies on both sides of the Atlantic. Many Europeans actually favour the death penalty; many Americans vehemently oppose it, and every time there's an execution there are candlelight vigils at the prison. The same thing is true on the drug issue. It's a very bitterly divided issue. But if you're asking me to predict how the American public and the political system will go — again, just as with the International Criminal Court, I don't think the issue will be changed in the US.

If you're trying to understand what September 11 did to the US, it's important to distinguish — and I'm going to say this analytically — simply between our attitudes towards foreign policy and domestic issues. On international relations now, all Americans are supporting President Bush. For the time being, he has ninety per cent support. But don't misunderstand that to mean that the great social divides on issues like this one and the death penalty are going to be shifted, because it's very unlikely. It's not the way societies work. So I don't think you're going to see a major change in this.

Now, on your comment about the drug trade and terrorism connection, we don't know a lot about this, but there does appear to be a connection between the warlords in Colombia, and, of course, ninety per cent of the heroin in the world comes from Afghanistan. As you know, it's shifted. It used to be in the Golden Triangle and then it shifted, when the programs were somewhat successful, towards Afghanistan. And so a lot of illegal money came out. Leaving aside whether the US should or shouldn't change its positions on its own laws, I do not believe that even if the US changed its laws, it would change the connection between the drug lords and the terrorists. There's too much money floating in illegal systems here, and even if, in some utopian world — at least what some people would consider utopian — these drugs were legalized, I don't believe that it would dry up the illegal criminal structures that are involved in these things.

"The American Stake in Europe and the European Stake in the United States" was broadcast on January 17, 2002.

What Has Changed: The Impact of 9/11 on the Middle East

The 2003 Barbara Frum Lecture

BERNARD LEWIS

Professor Bernard Lewis, one of the most sought-after and controversial experts on the Middle East, began his academic career as a student at the University of London. In 1949, he was appointed to the newly created Chair of the History of the Near and Middle East at the University of London. In 1974, he was appointed Cleveland E. Dodge Professor of Near Eastern Studies at Princeton University and became emeritus on his retirement in 1986. Among his works are his important 2002 study What Went Wrong? Western Impact and Middle Eastern Response, *and in 2003,* The Crisis of Islam: Holy War and Unholy Terror. *As he delivered the eighth annual Barbara Frum Lecture in the Macmillan Theatre of the University of Toronto Faculty of Music, American bombs rained down on the city of Baghdad.*

BERNARD LEWIS

In the western world and, more particularly, in the transatlantic western world, the attitude to history is well expressed in the phrase "that's history," meaning it's over and finished and done with and of no possible relevance to present concerns. You may recall the scene in the movie where the heavy, the villain, says to his cast-off mistress, "You're history." In spite of an immense investment in history, battalions of tenured historians in the universities turning out hundredweights of historical writings, the knowledge of history is poor, the awareness of history even poorer in the western world.

The Islamic world presents a total contrast with that. If you look at the war propaganda conducted by Iran and Iraq, two Middle Eastern Muslim countries, between 1980 and 1988, their war propaganda is full of allusions — and I mean allusions, not statements or descriptions, but rapid, incomplete, passing allusions — to events of the seventh century, which they could make in the sure knowledge that these allusions would be picked up and understood by their target audiences, even including the not insignificant part of those audiences that is illiterate. An even more dramatic and certainly more immediately relevant example may be found in the writings of Osama bin Laden, who refers very frequently to history, and not only to recent history but often to very early history. His allusions, again we may be sure, are picked up and understood. When, in one of his statements not long ago, he spoke of "the humiliation and shame which we Muslims have suffered for more than eighty years," this sent the Middle East experts in the western world and others scurrying to find out what he meant — the older ones to reference libraries, the younger ones to their laptops — in the hope of finding some explanation. Again, all kinds of explanations were offered, most of them totally inaccurate.

I have no doubt at all that his target audience in the Muslim lands had no doubt at all as to what he meant. He was referring to the year 1918, the end of World War I and the final defeat of the Ottoman Empire, the last, the most enduring and, in many ways, the greatest of the Muslim states and empires — a defeat which ended, for the Ottomans, with their capital occupied, their rulers arrested and detained and most of their territories partitioned between the victorious allies. For Osama bin Laden and those who thought like him, this was the low point, the nadir, the final defeat, so it seemed at the time, in the long, ongoing struggle between the two world religions. It was indeed, in his perspective, a moment of humiliation, of bitterness, of defeat.

And it is, in a very real sense, the turning point, the beginning of a new era. The struggle between Islam and Christendom had been going on for considerably more than a millennium. You can trace it through its various stages of crusade and *jihad*, attack and counter-attack, conquest and re-conquest through the centuries but ending in what seemed in 1918 to be the final and total defeat of Islam.

This sense of history, this awareness of the larger historical perspective is essential for the understanding of what he and his like say and how those to whom they say it respond.

Let me turn now to the starting point, by common agreement, of this phase: Osama bin Laden and his consecutive appeals to the Muslim world. And the question which I think one must ask first is: what is his appeal? Why is it that this man evoked so tremendous a response all over the Muslim world and beyond? I think one may give three answers to this, all of which are relevant.

The first is his eloquence. Eloquence has always been a quality greatly admired in traditional Arab culture. If you look at the Arabic classics of the Middle Ages and even of the early modern period, there are many stories told about great orators, about the depth and breadth and force of their eloquence, how they could move crowds and change history by speeches. This is part of the tradition, a quality much appreciated, greatly admired, but in recent history rarely practised. The form of government prevailing in most Arab countries at the present time relies on force, not persuasion, to secure loyalty and obedience, and therefore the need for eloquence has, shall we say, lapsed. There is also the fact that most of the rulers now come from the military, a profession of many merits, of which eloquence is not normally one. Osama bin Laden's eloquence is truly remarkable. His command of the Arabic language, which he uses very forcefully and very effectively, has won him admiration from all those who are able to appreciate it.

The second — how shall I describe it? — is his lifestyle. In the modern Middle Eastern world, the normal pattern is rags to riches, usually by the exercise of force, with the riches then being shared with other members of one's family, one's entourage, one's solidarity group. There is corruption in every society, in every civilization, but corruption takes different forms. In western society, more particularly in North American society, corruption takes this form: you make your money in the marketplace, through economic activity, and then you use that money to buy power or, at least, to buy access or influence. The Middle Eastern pattern is the exact opposite: you seize power, and you use the power to make money. Morally, I can see no difference between them. This makes the case of Osama bin Laden even more dramatic. Here is a man who was born to riches and comfort and chose a life of hardship and danger. One cannot, I think, fail to see the appeal that this would have in a society accustomed to the opposite.

Third, and perhaps most important of all, is the message that he brings, and it is that message which will constitute my main theme. Both the emphases and the omissions of what he says are important. And let me try to review the aspects of his message, one by one.

The first I would describe as rejection. He is rejecting not so much western power, though it is often presented that way. As far as power is concerned — real domination — that has receded, not advanced, in recent years. The great empires have gone. The British, the French and the Dutch empires all fell apart in the aftermath of World War II. The Russian empire, renamed the Soviet Union, lasted somewhat longer, but then that, too, collapsed, and the former Russian dependencies with Muslim populations became independent, the so-called *stans* — a half-dozen states with Muslim majority populations in central Asia and Transcaucasia.

No, it is not so much against power as, rather, against influence: western ways, western ideas, western notions, western practices which have become dominant. Interestingly, western influence was far greater in the independent states than in those that were under colonial or imperial rule. The most radical changes and reforms in the nineteenth and twentieth centuries were made by independent Muslim rulers like Atatürk in Turkey and Reza Pahlavi in Iran and then many others in many other countries. And it is, therefore, against the "westernizers," rather than against the westerners, that the main anger was directed. He is against the whole notion of westernization, which he sees as a form of apostasy, an abandonment of authentic Islam in favour of adopting alien and infidel ways. And for him and those who agree with him, most of the rulers of the Muslim world are no longer Muslims, though they pretend to be. They are renegades or apostates.

The second important element is empowerment, the feeling that the tide has turned, that the West has become weak, the West is in retreat, and that it is now their great opportunity to reassert themselves and win victory. This comes in stages. At one time, it was fashionable to refer to the 1973 war and the withholding of oil, which, for the first time, gave a sense of power deriving from the possession of oil and the ability to increase or reduce the supply and also to control the price. But what is far more important, as far as Osama bin Laden and his followers are concerned, is a much greater event: the defeat and the collapse of the Soviet Union.

Now, we in the West tend to think of this as a victory for the free world over the Soviet Union, ending the Cold War. That is not how he sees it. In his perception, this was a victory of Muslims over infidels. They argue — no, they don't argue, they assert — that it was the guerrilla struggle, the Muslim fighters in Afghanistan, that drove the Red Army in defeat out of Afghanistan, back home to defeat and collapse. And if one considers the sequence of events, one must agree that this explanation is certainly not lacking in plausibility. This was certainly the immediate cause, at the very least. This gave them a sense of achievement, which is, again, reflected in their various statements. The argument went something like this: "There were two great infidel superpowers. We have defeated one — the more difficult, the more dangerous, the more deadly, the more vicious. Dealing with the other will be comparatively easy."

This is related to a certain perception of the western world in general and of the United States in particular which is constantly reiterated and expressed in a number of different ways. It usually comes something like this: the Americans are degenerate, their society has become degenerate, they are soft and pampered, they can't take it; hit them and they will run. And then, always repeating the same litany: Vietnam, the Marines in Beirut, Somalia and many more, added during the 1990s when, again and again, some act of violence was committed against Americans or American institutions, and the only response was some harsh words and misdirected missiles to remote places. These can only have strengthened the perception that they were dealing with a soft, pampered, defeated enemy, incapable of anything serious by way of response. This perception was also strengthened by visitors to the United States who went back and wrote accounts of what they saw as a corrupt, debauched and degenerate society. These themes, again, come out very clearly in the writings and pronouncements.

This was not, by any means, the unanimous response in the Muslim world to the defeat of the Soviet Union. There were others, particularly those for whom the Soviet Union had been their great patron, whose response was very different. As you know, for the last two hundred years or so, the main theme of modern Middle Eastern history has been the rivalry of the outside powers. They were no longer able to operate as an independent power against the West, as they had done in the days of Islamic greatness, but they had been able to profit from the rivalries of the western empires: first, the British and the French, then the British and the French against the Germans, and, in the final phase, the United States and the Soviet Union.

And then suddenly it came to an end: the era in history that was inaugurated by Bonaparte and Nelson was ended by Bush and Gorbachev. Both the superpowers removed themselves from the conflict and ceased to play the imperial role, the Russians because they couldn't, the Americans because they wouldn't — they simply had no appetite for this kind of politics or policy. And if you look at the accusations against the United States over the last ten years and, more particularly, the charges of American imperialism, if you look into the details, you will see that what they are complaining about is not American imperialism but the *lack* of American imperialism. They are complaining that the United States is failing to fulfill its imperial duties as the greatest power of the world, with a duty to solve disputes, adjudicate between rival peoples and so on and so on. That is asking for imperialism, not complaining of imperialism. And they're not getting it.

The changes that I've described also brought about what you might call a restructuring of ideologies within the Muslim world. For a long time, the dominant ideologies had been of European origin — even nationalism was an idea that came from Europe. Nationality in the sense of ethnic identity existed, of course, in the Middle East, but this was not the primary basis of identity and loyalty. That was determined, first and foremost, by religion, and then by allegiance to this or that state. Nationalism was a European idea which was used to fight against Europe. Nationalism was supposed to bring them freedom. It didn't. It was an unfortunate misunderstanding: it brought them independence. There was a widespread belief — no, not exactly a belief; an impression, shall we say? — that freedom and independence were two different words for the same thing. In recent years they have discovered painfully that they are not two different words for the same thing. They are two different things, so different that they have often proved to be mutually exclusive. The ending of imperial domination and the establishment of independent national regimes all too often meant the replacement of foreign overlords by domestic tyrants, more adept and more intimate and less constrained in their tyranny.

During the last year or two, since Islam has become a popular topic in the western world, an incredible amount of nonsense has been talked. It varies between two extremes. On the one hand, we have those who depict Islam as a bloodthirsty, barbarian religion seeking conquest and destruction and nothing else. At the opposite extreme we have those who tell us that Islam is a religion of peace and love, rather like the Quakers, but without their aggressiveness. The truth, of course, is in its usual place: somewhere between the two.

And I would ask you to remember that when you say "Islam," you are using the word in two different senses. You are using it as the equivalent of Christianity, meaning a religion in the strict sense, a system of belief and worship, and you are also using it as the equivalent of Christendom, meaning a whole civilization which grew up under the aegis of that religion but which contains much that is not part of that religion — much, even, that is opposed to that religion. Hitler and the Nazis are certainly a product of Christendom; they are certainly not a product of Christianity. I make this point, I think, as important to understanding some of the terms that are used, the tactics that are advocated and practised.

Now, what does *jihad* mean? *Jihad* is an Arabic word which literally means "striving." It occurs most frequently in the context "striving in the path of God." It is used in more than one sense: it is used in a moral sense, meaning "striving to overcome one's evil instincts." It is also used unequivocally in a military sense, meaning what is usually translated as "holy war." Since it is *jihad* in the path of God, if it is divinely approved, that makes it holy, of course, so that the translation "holy war," though it doesn't occur in that particular form in Arabic, is, I think, a reasonable one: a divinely ordained war against the enemies of God — that is to say, the enemies of Islam. *Jihad* is a matter of law, and the holy law of Islam regulates it most meticulously, laying down the rules of warfare and forbidding most of the things which are being done now by terrorists in the name of Islam, but contrary to the express dictates of the holy law of Islam.

Let me look at some specifically. First of all, against whom is it legitimate to wage *jihad*? According to Islamic law, it is legitimate to wage war against four types of enemies: infidels, apostates, rebels and bandits. Only the first two count as *jihad*. The third and fourth, rebels and bandits, are assumed to be Muslim and therefore this is not *jihad* — it's justifiable, legitimate warfare, but not *jihad*. The first two are the important ones: infidels and apostates. Apostates, of course, are renegade Muslims — Muslims who have abandoned Islam in favour of some other faith. This is a capital offense. This particular argument is invoked very frequently nowadays in the *jihad*, not against the outsider, the infidel, the foreigner, but against their own rulers, whom they see as renegades, as apostate Muslims who have abandoned authentic Islam and have introduced the ways of the infidel.

Terror and suicide. Terror is, of course, largely a matter of definition. It has been pointed out frequently that one man's terrorist is another man's freedom fighter. Nevertheless, one can, I think, make certain rules and, indeed, medieval Muslim law does lay down certain rules about the conduct of warfare, giving stress in particular to the treatment of noncombatants. They even discuss the use of chemical and missile warfare in early medieval texts — this may surprise you — missile warfare meaning catapults and mangonels and the like, and chemical warfare meaning poison-tipped arrows and poisoning the enemy water supply. There is an intensive debate among the jurists as to whether this is permitted. Some reject it outright; some permit it, subject to severe restrictions; some permit it against infidel enemies. The killing of uninvolved civilians is forbidden by any of these. So I think one may say without hesitation that those who perpetrated the terrorist acts of 9/11 and others like them, there and elsewhere, are in clear violation of Islamic law.

What about suicide? Here again, the law is very clear: Islamic law forbids suicide. It is what in our language we would call a mortal sin. It is a sin which merits eternal damnation. It is even stated that even if one has a blameless record and has merited paradise, by the act of suicide he forfeits paradise and earns eternal hellfire.

So, you say, well, what about all this, then? Well, there is a debate which begins quite early: if a man throws himself to a certain death against an overwhelmingly stronger enemy, does that count as suicide, or is it an act of self-sacrifice in a holy war? Differences of opinion. The second one prevailed. But even there, he does not die by his own hand. He dies at the hand of an overwhelmingly stronger enemy. The traditions of the Prophet laid down that the punishment for suicide in the afterlife is the eternal repetition of the act of suicide. So, if he threw himself off a cliff, he falls eternally towards damnation. If he stabbed himself, he stabs himself for eternity. If he drank poison, he spends his time in hell drinking poison and suffering the pain. One would assume from this that the suicide bombers also face an eternity of exploding bombs. But here again, what was a relatively unimportant minority view within the Islamic world has gained considerable support.

But what is the struggle about? The struggle is against bad government, usually called *zulm*, a word we might translate as "tyranny."

Now, in western languages, the opposite terms are "tyranny" and "freedom." The absence of tyranny is freedom; the absence of freedom is tyranny. These are the two opposite poles by which we define and evaluate good government and bad government. "Freedom," in this sense, is comparatively new in the Middle East. The word is, of course, old, but it had a legal and social, not a political, significance. There's a very interesting passage in one of the most revealing books I know on this topic, written by an Azhari sheikh from Egypt who went to Paris in 1826 to accompany and look after the first Egyptian student mission sent to the West. He stayed in Paris from 1826 to 1831 and wrote a truly fascinating book about the western world which he was seeing — or any of his people were seeing — for the first time. And he makes this very interesting observation. He says the French keep talking about freedom, *liberté*. They devote a great deal of time and attention to talking about this. And he, like his readers, is puzzled because freedom in their usage is a purely legal and social term, not a political term. And then he explains it. He says, "When the French talk about freedom, what they mean is the same as what we mean when we talk about justice."

And that is absolutely right. I think it's an illuminating comment by him. *Adl* — justice — is the ideal of good government. The converse of *zulm,* tyranny, is *adl* — just, good government. This raises, of course, the question, what does one mean precisely by justice? For a Muslim, of course, justice is defined by Islam. Justice means that the holy law revealed by God is applied and enforced — the *shari'ah* law. Freedom, in the western sense, is a temptation. It is licence, debauchery and very dangerous. We have some vivid descriptions of western sinfulness from visitors who went to the western world, particularly but not exclusively to America. This, by the way, is what Khomeini meant when he called America "the Great Satan": the seductive temptation of western debauchery and western immorality, which are seen as constituting a real threat to the good Muslim life. And here again, one must concede that there is, to say the least, some plausibility in this argument, if you share their assumptions.

To blame the Saddam Hussein type of government on the Islamic and Arab tradition is totally false. Let me quote what I think is a very revealing remark. A French ambassador, the Count de Choi-seul-Gouffier, writing from Istanbul in 1786, three years before the French Revolution, tried to explain to his government why he wasn't doing his job as quickly as they wanted. And he says, "Things here are not as in France, where the king is sole master; here it is necessary to persuade the *ulema*, the men of law, the holders of high offices, and those who no longer hold them." And this was profoundly true. This was not a democratic society in the sense of having elected bodies, no. But it was a system of limited government, of responsible government, limited by the holy law, which was not a theoretical but a genuine, serious limitation. Limited also in a more practical sense by the existence of powerful, entrenched groups in society — the urban bourgeoisie, the rural gentry, the military and religious establishments — who acted as a limitation and constraint on the power of authority. You also have the basic Islamic conception of sovereignty, which is both contractual and consensual. The idea of despotism, of absolute rule, is totally alien to Islamic law and tradition and to Islamic practice until, sad to say, modernization made it possible.

This was a system, as I said, of limited government under law. Now, what the process of modernization did was to change it for the worse in two different ways: by strengthening the sovereign power, creating at the disposal of the sovereign power the whole modern apparatus of control and repression, and by weakening or eliminating the intermediate powers which had previously limited the power of the state. We have some very vivid descriptions of this from nineteenth-century observers, both in the region and a few of the more perceptive ones among those who came from outside. I like to quote a certain British naval officer called Slade, who draws a contrast between what he calls the Old Nobility and the New Nobility — the Old Nobility being the old-style nobility of the old order, the New Nobility those created by the reforms and operating at the centre. The Old Nobility, he says, "lived on their estates." For the New Nobility, "the state is their estate," and this remains very much true at the present time.

There is, therefore, in these countries, a tradition of limited, responsible government. Not democratic in the western sense of that much misused word, but nevertheless sharing many features of democratic government and proving, as I believe, a good basis for the development of democratic institutions there, as has happened in some, even in many other — some indeed wildly improbable — parts of the world. And that is why, in spite of many difficulties and many obstacles, I still remain cautiously optimistic about the future.

QUESTION

Professor Lewis, how central do you see the Arab-Israeli conflict as being? I noted that recently Palestinian suicide bombers were saying that they had been giving a gift to the suffering people of Iraq. And I couldn't understand the logic between killing people in Israel and American aggression in Iraq.

BERNARD LEWIS

I know that there is a view according to which this is *the* issue, and if you solve that everything else will go away. I can only describe this politely as nonsense. Don't misunderstand me — I don't mean to suggest that the issue is an unimportant one. Certainly it is very important. But I think we may trust the judgment of Osama bin Laden on the importance he gives to it. If you look at his most important document, his Declaration of War published in February of 1998, he lists three major points, his grievances against the United States. Number one: the presence of American troops in Arabia. Remember that for Muslims Arabia is the Holy Land. That is where the Prophet Mohammed was born and lived and died. That is where the Qur'an was promulgated, where Islam began. The presence of infidel forces in Arabia was indeed seen as an extreme provocation. So it's very understandable that Osama bin Laden gives first place to Arabia — something, by the way, which the British Empire always avoided. The British Empire, at its height, nibbled at the edges of Arabia — Kuwait, Aden — but never landed forces on the Arabian mainland. That's perhaps why the British Empire lasted rather longer.

His second point is: using the base in Arabia for an attack on Iraq. Iraq is in no sense a holy land for Muslims, but it was the seat of the caliphate for half a millennium in the greatest age of Muslim power and glory.

His third point, which occupies just two and a half lines, is: helping what he derisively calls "the mini-state of the Jews." And, he says, while the Americans' main purposes are religious and economic — an interesting combination — they have also helped the mini-state — the term he uses in Arabic is *duwayla*, a kind of dismissive, diminutive form of *dwala*, state — the "statelet," you might say — of the Jews. If you look again at his most recent statement, the letter to the Americans in which he sets forth the grievances, it doesn't occur until the fourth item — not just the third, but this time the fourth item. And there it is one of a list. It is the first of a list — Palestine, Chechnya, Kashmir, Mindanao, Timor and all the rest — a long list of all the points where Islam and non-Islam clash.

So in his view, obviously, it is secondary, and I think this is the general view among the fundamentalists. It is an aspect, a manifestation of a larger evil, in their view. And it has been given exaggerated importance for several reasons. One of them is the obvious one: that Israel is an open society in which journalists are therefore free to report and misreport as they wish without serious danger. This is not possible in any of the other places listed. Second, of course, the Jews are involved, and you know the old saying, "Jews are news." And there are many people in the western world who take a strong position either for or against Jews or anything in which Jews are involved. So that adds to the appeal of the Palestine issue. It is also by now the authorized, licensed grievance which enables people to let off steam, to express resentments which would otherwise be dangerously directed against their own rulers.

Now, again, I stress I do not mean to suggest that the conflict is unimportant or that it will simply go away. But I think it is the larger conflict which makes the Palestine conflict insoluble, rather than the other way round.

QUESTION

Professor Lewis, I was trying to understand how Bin Laden sees the Qur'an as sort of encompassing the people of the Book, and you're saying that essentially he sees it as a struggle between these two religions. I'm trying to reconcile those two viewpoints.

BERNARD LEWIS

As expressed in the Qur'an and, more generally, in Muslim writings, Islam is the final stage in a sequence of revelations. God has revealed the truth through revealed books at earlier stages, of which there are a number. The surviving ones that matter are the Jews, the Christians and then, of course, the Muslims. Now, there are many biblical stories in the Qur'an, and very often the account in the Qur'an differs quite considerably from the account in the Bible. Now, the Muslim explanation of this is that the Jews and the Christians proved unworthy custodians of the revelations that had been given to them, and those revelations were therefore superseded and replaced by the final and perfect revelation of Islam which is contained in the Qur'an. So from a Muslim point of view, Judaism and Christianity are not false religions. They are superseded, to some extent corrupted, religions, but not inherently false. Therefore, the holy law not just permits but requires that a certain measure of tolerance be accorded to Jews and to Christians to practise their own religions.

Now, there is a very important difference between Jews and Christians. There are two kinds of religion in the world, which are sometimes referred to as relativist religions and triumphalist religions. The relativist position would be something like this: the human race has invented a number of different languages to talk to each other; in the same way, they've invented a number of different religions to talk to God. You have your religion, I have my religion, and God understands all of them. That is a fairly general view among religions, including Judaism and all the great religions of Asia. It is not the view of Christians or Muslims, and their view has been described as triumphalist. It means, in effect, we are the fortunate recipients of God's final message to humanity, which it's our duty not to keep selfishly for ourselves but to share with the rest of humanity for their enlightenment. If you accept that message, you will be saved. If you don't, you will be damned, at least in some measure. This is the triumphalist approach, which is shared by Christianity and Islam, and it is this resemblance, rather more than the differences, that has brought them into conflict.

If you visit Jerusalem you will certainly see the Dome of the Rock, the oldest surviving Muslim religious structure outside Arabia. The site is interesting: the Temple Mount, where the ancient Jewish temple was sited. The architecture is interesting, in the style of the earliest Christian monuments — the Church of the Ascension, the Church of the Holy Sepulchre. The texts on the wall, inside the Dome, are quotations from the Qur'an, like this: "He is God, He is One, He has no companion, He does not beget, He is not begotten." This is clearly a polemical statement against a central dogma of the Christian religion. And this was, in effect, the new religion and its new ruler, the caliph, saying to the Christian world, headed by the emperor in Constantinople: "Your turn has passed, you are superseded, we are the bearers of God's final message. Move over."

This was the beginning of this ongoing struggle, which went on for more than a millennium, sometimes the Muslims advancing, sometimes the Christians advancing. And Osama bin Laden and his like, with their very strong sense of history, certainly see things that way.

QUESTION

Professor Lewis, you've diagnosed the situation very clearly, and I hesitate to ask this question because it seems like a hard one to answer. I'm wondering how, then, do we resolve the situation? How does resolution come about? If that's too difficult a question to answer, I'm wondering: is there a role model, either a country or a movement, in that region that perhaps offers an answer to resolution?

BERNARD LEWIS

How does one resolve the problem of this confrontation between the Islamic world and the outside world — more particularly, the Christian or, as people nowadays call it, the post-Christian world? It's not easy, but obviously there has to be change on both sides. I think on the western side we need to have a better understanding and a better appreciation of who they are and what they are, and try and forget the long list of preposterous wrong notions that we have about them. But more importantly, since the attack of the present time comes from the other side, there is need for a change there.

Now, this change is not going to be easy and it will not come overnight. Democracies are not born, like Aphrodite, from the sea foam. Our own democracy took many centuries to develop and was punctuated by civil wars and revolutions and various other minor adjustments. If you look at the struggle to establish democracy even in the last half-century, post-World War II, you will see it has gone through many vicissitudes and suffered many setbacks. But the general record is one of success and of advancement. We see democracy being established in unlikely places. After the defeat of Germany and Japan, the victorious Allies did not establish democracies, but they prepared the way to allow the people of those countries to create and establish and develop democratic regimes. We have cases where democracy seems to have been introduced by victorious enemies, like Germany and Japan, or bequeathed by departing imperialists, like India. The Islamic countries will develop their own ways of doing it.

And there are already promising beginnings of that. There are, as I tried to suggest before, certain elements inherent in Islam which tend in that direction: the contractual and consensual nature of sovereignty, the idea of limited government. This is very fundamental. We are told that in the old Ottoman Empire, when a new sultan succeeded to the throne, he was greeted by the crowds, who cheered him and shouted, "Sultan, don't be proud. God is greater than you," an interesting greeting for a newly enthroned ruler. This element, I think, can be promising, but I'm not pretending that it would be easy, nor can anyone do it but the Muslims themselves. What we can do is to refrain from imposing obstacles and, where necessary, help in removing obstacles.

"What Has Changed: The Impact of 9/11 on the Middle East" was broadcast on April 7, 2003.

The Next Ideology

TONY JUDT
MARGARET MacMILLAN
GEORGE MONBIOT
Moderated by
ANTHONY GERMAIN

In The End of History and the Last Man, *political thinker Francis Fukuyama suggested that the world had reached the end of the ideological line with the fall of the Berlin Wall and the collapse of Soviet communism. The liberal capitalist idea had triumphed and there would be no new ideological challengers. Today that notion seems quaint and perhaps even a bit naive as new forces emerge to shape the political landscape. Discussing the next ideology are Tony Judt, professor of history, Director of the Remarque Institute at New York University, and frequent contributor to* The New York Review of Books; *Margaret MacMillan, Provost of Trinity College at the University of Toronto and author of the best-seller* Paris 1919; *and George Monbiot, author of* The Age of Consent: A Manifesto for the New World Order *and a regular columnist for* The Guardian *newspaper.*

TONY JUDT

I don't think we're going to see anything dramatically unheralded, something we haven't thought of. More likely, and certainly in the foreseeable future, we're going to see two things, both of which would have been quite familiar a few years ago but seem to have disappeared for a while. One of them is the return of an attention to the state. I know that sounds paradoxical, considering all the fuss about globalization and the end of nation-states and so forth. In fact, one of the consequences of the changes of the past ten or fifteen years has been a renewed attention to and concern for the kinds of protections, both physical and social, that a state can provide and that no other legitimate entity can provide, and also the state as the only legitimate user of arms in a world where the right to bear private arms, including private nuclear arms, is going to become an increasing concern. I think the state is going to become a major player once again. And with that, we're going to get a recovery of what disappeared progressively after the seventies, which was the legitimacy of state-centred politics — the notion that welfare states are not doomed, demographically and ideologically, but, on the contrary, may be the only possible prospect for the future. And sitting here in New York, in the country where this seems the least likely prospect, I'm nonetheless struck by the dead end that the anti-state, minimal-state ideologies of the last fifteen years seem to have reached.

MARGARET MacMILLAN

I think we're going to see a revival of left-wing approaches to organizing human societies, and I agree completely with Tony Judt that the state seems more necessary now than ever. I mean, it's quite clear that when states fail the consequences are terrible, and if you don't have organized states NGOs simply can't do it. But I think we tended to assume that socialism was dead because Marxism, which was, of course, only one variant of socialism, came to a crashing end at the end of the 1980s. And what it had produced seemed so appalling that I think nobody wanted to go down that particular road.

But the human desire for a fairer and a more equal sort of society hasn't gone away, and I think we will see a revival of social democracy — I think we're already seeing it in Europe. I think in Canada, certainly, you see people, much more than in the United States, worrying about social inequalities and worrying about the capacity of the state to do something about it. So I think socialism, which we might have thought was one of those ideologies that was relegated to the dustbin of history, won't be. It will revive in some form or another, I would think, in the next decade.

ANTHONY GERMAIN

Do you think more on the Scandinavian model, as in countries like Norway or Sweden?

MARGARET MacMILLAN

Well, they seem to work a lot better. I mean, except for a few die-hards, I think most of us would agree that what was tried in the Soviet Union and eastern Europe and, indeed, in China and else-where didn't work and produced great misery and a concentration of power in a very few hands. But the idea of a social democracy, where you combine democratic politics with some belief that society should care for its less fortunate, that there should be a redistribution of wealth — I think that will continue to be very important.

GEORGE MONBIOT

Any predictions we make now are likely to be overtaken by a number of new material realities. One of those is the global supply of oil peaking and demand outstripping supply massively, which basically means in the long run the end of industrial civilization, because we won't be able to sustain the levels of growth necessary to meet the demands of our debt-based financial system. The second one, which would appear to be cancelled out by that, but unfortunately isn't, is climate change and the massive impacts that'll have, especially on the world's ability to feed itself, and the world's quite likely to go into net food deficit within the next twenty years or so. And allied to that, shortage of fresh water, shortage of various other resources.

Now, this could throw up, of course, all sorts of ideological mon-sters, and we've seen, in similar circumstances before, it throwing up a lot of what I would consider hopeful revolutions. If we look, for instance, at how the 1788 famine cleared the ground for the French Revolution, then we have what I would consider an optimistic model emerging out of scarcity politics, but it could also clear the ground for some very, very dangerous politics indeed, and all sorts of fascist or post-fascist reaction.

There is a trend which might emerge, irrespective of these factors and which relates to what Tony was talking about in particular. And while I think he's quite right to say that the state will have to reassert its presence, at the same time I think we will continue to see a shift of focus to the global level on a whole range of issues, and there seems to be a very basic historical trend here. We've gone from the family to the clan to the tribe to the barony to the nation-state. We're now already looking at the superstate: the European Union, free trade with the Americas and the rest of it. I think, before long, on many crucial issues, we will start to see the planet becoming the fundamental political unit.

TONY JUDT

I agree, in general terms, but I have two observations of detail. One is that what seems to have happened in the last couple of decades is that the limits within which people feel comfortable as part of some sort of community of persons whose identity they can share doesn't seem to reach to the globe. If anything, there's a tendency, even within the — as it were — European superstate, for people to feel more comfortable identifying with regions or with parts of their former states within this larger European confederal vision than thinking of themselves as simply part of one single, large agglomerated community. And I think the fallacy of globalization is that, because the economy is now worldwide, somehow society must and will follow that.

But what I wanted to say were two other things. One, briefly, about the Scandinavian welfare state model: I think that Margaret's absolutely right on that, and one of the reasons is that the Scandinavians under social democracy never entailed large-scale state ownership. This sort of fallacy about this assumption — that social democracy entails the state owning the means of production as well as distributing their product more equally — that never happened in countries like Sweden, and it may be worth bearing in mind that that form of the state-centred model was therefore de-legitimized by the disastrous economic consequences of state ownership in eastern Europe or the Soviet Union.

I think that there's a form, however — to come back to George's point — of international politics that may, at least in the medium term, matter quite a lot, and that is what you might call, in short-hand, anti-Americanism. The rhetoric of anti-capitalism, the notion that the world was divided into two grand narratives, the narrative of capitalist modernity and the narrative of anti-capitalists, the socialist alternative — that division has now sort of recast itself quite rationally, I think, into a sense which may transcend the Bush administration, that America is, symbolically as well as actually, the problem facing the world, and that one of the easy ways to feel that you are part of a radical alternative is to be, rhetorically and politically, anti-America. I'm struck, travelling from Indonesia to Norway, that something fundamental has become available to people everywhere, which is a sense of what is wrong with current international arrangements, even if they don't have any idea about what they ought to be instead. And that, I think, is quite new.

ANTHONY GERMAIN

Let's focus on this anti-Americanism notion for a moment. It's often a popular topic in Canada. Margaret MacMillan, if we take a look at the longer view in the past, when you consider the United States in 1945 and the advent of the Marshall Plan, there was an ethos at that time that the United States was actually the force of good in the world, by many, many people. What happened?

MARGARET MacMILLAN

Well, the United States was seen for so long as a very generous state, and the Marshall Plan, for whatever motives the Americans did it, was seen as something generous. And I think the United States increasingly has been seen as a greedy, consuming society in which Americans use the resources of the world, often in a very heedless and thoughtless way. I mean, just to go back to George Monbiot's point about oil, the way in which the American public, and I think also the Canadian public, continue to expect cheap gasoline as they drive their very inefficient SUVs about is absolutely absurd. And I think there is a perception in the rest of the world that here is this great big greedy power whose citizens enjoy an incredible lifestyle, a wantonly extravagant lifestyle.

I think also, though, that a lot of anti-Americanism is exactly what happened to or is very similar to what happened to the British Empire in the nineteenth century. It's a reaction to what's happening in the world, the changes that are happening in the world. The United States is the most technologically advanced country in the world, and so those who don't like the changes that modernization or modernity are bringing are going to focus on the United States as well. I mean, it's not just a power. It's also a symbol of many things that people in certain parts of the world don't like about the modern world.

ANTHONY GERMAIN

But is being against something or a critic of something, particularly a state, does that an ideology make?

GEORGE MONBIOT

Well, those of us who are opposed to what I would call US imperialism — and let's just go back a little bit here first. We're looking at two ideologies here. One is a quite deliberately formulated program by Bush, but also by some of his predecessors and particularly by some of the men surrounding Bush — the members of the Project for a New American Century, for example — a deliberately formulated program to project US power in all parts of the world. And that is a clear ideological and practical attempt which is being opposed by many, perhaps most of the politically involved people of the world, who are reacting in a whole lot of ways which Tony, I think slightly misleadingly, conflates as anti-Americanism. Now, it's not just a reaction. We're not just talking about negative campaigning here. There is a huge trend in global democracy movements, for example, of people who are saying the most effective counterweight to a new imperialism on the part of one nation is international co-ordination, internationalism — or global justice, as we prefer to call it — built

around such ideas as a massive reform of the global financial institutions — getting rid of the World Bank and the International
Monetary Fund, replacing them with something much closer to the
International Clearing Union which John Maynard Keynes proposed
in 1944; a massive reform of the World Trade Organization, ensuring that it oversees fair trade rather than unfair trade; a massive
reform of the United Nations so that it's no longer dominated just
by the five permanent members of the UN Security Council, which,
in turn, tend to be dominated by the demands of the United States.
In other words, a large and positive countermovement with quite a
strongly formulated ideology of its own. And I think it's misleading, first of all, to say that everyone's just being anti-American for
reasons of their own without recognizing that they're reacting to a
very powerful ideological trend. And secondly, to suggest that they
do not have alternative proposals.

TONY JUDT

Well, I thought that we were being invited to speculate at such a level
of grandiose generality that it was okay to say things like that. If
George can say the French Revolution was sort of spurred in part by
the 1788 famine, I can say that anti-Americanism is a global mobiliz-
ing ideology. But he's right. There are many things that come under
the heading. I didn't mean to suggest that it's some sort of free-
floating, abstract sort of collective global resentment of something
that doesn't actually exist. Of course, much of what he says about
American foreign policy is true. But the reaction to America — and
this is the point I was making — has become sufficiently common
and sufficiently widespread that, even though there are very different interests in play in France and Malaysia, let's say — and, indeed,
contradictory interests in play in some cases — there's still a common
sense that what they are concerned with is the same: aggression,
dangers, American insouciance, American imperialism, etc. And that
is rhetorically similar to the sort of anti-capitalist radicalism of, let's
say, the generation from 1930 to 1970. And in that sense, I think
it's likely to act as a sort of an umbrella for many different forms of
localized mobilization. And no more than anti-capitalism can anti-

Americanism itself be a sort of new form of left-wing politics. And in that sense, I think Margaret is much closer to the mark with the notion that we're going to get a recovery of something that's going to look more like social democracy, and the reason for that, it seems to me, is prudential rather than ideological.

People have forgotten that the chief reason for the rise of the welfare state in its homelands in western Europe was prudential rather than ideological. It was a fear of the return of the conditions of the 1930s and with that the return of the politics of the 1930s that generated the post-war consensus on the need for the state to play some kind of securing role in society. I think the generation of the eighties and nineties forgot that quite literally because it had no reason to remember it in its experience. We're going to remember them for all the reasons that we've talked about here so far, but also because the rise of a new political Right in places like Antwerp or in Denmark or in Austria or in France and other places as well, driven by all kinds of things we haven't talked about, is going to make it much more important to think about ways to protect democratic forms, and that, in turn, is going to lead us back to some of the reasons we got to social democracy in the first place.

GEORGE MONBIOT

I think there's a lot of truth in what Tony says, but there are a couple of other caveats I would like to throw in. The first is that there's another strong trend of thought on which this big global movement is drawing, and that is the absolute need, quite irrespective of what US power is doing — although, of course, that's a very major factor — for a much better and more intense level of international co-ordination because of the international or, rather, global nature of some of the problems we confront, problems such as climate change, the proliferation of weapons of mass destruction, the proliferation of international debt. And so there is a sense that, quite irrespective of what our opponents are doing, though obviously that's a very major factor, we have to internationalize, we have to start looking for some of our politics at the global level rather than just the national level.

The other thing I'd like to say is that I would love to share the optimism which Tony and Margaret have about the return of the welfare state, and I think that, all other things being equal, there would be a lot of truth in what they're saying. But I would just like to throw this into the discussion: if, indeed, we are going from a position of net energy surplus at the global level to a position of net energy deficit, then we are necessarily heading towards prolonged, possibly more or less permanent global recession, and the question I would like to raise is this. Is it possible to have humanitarianism, is it possible to have a welfare state, is it possible to have peaceful relations between class factions, economic factions, within a nation, and between nation-states themselves in a situation of net energy deficit, when we're quite likely to be fighting like cats in a sack for the remaining resources?

MARGARET MacMILLAN

Well, you think of the 1930s when, yes, we were fighting like cats in a sack, but there were also huge strides made in the United States, for example, towards welfare for those less fortunate. I mean, think of the whole New Deal. Also, just to go back to this issue of global democracy, which sounds wonderful but I'm not sure what it actually amounts to, a number of single-issue groups are forming or have already formed and are loosely clumped together because they share a common anti-Americanism, whatever that may mean. But that seems to me not to translate into global democracy. I mean, democracy involves political parties, it involves mediation, it involves deals. I like the idea that people around the world can communicate — and the Internet, of course, makes this so much more possible — and deal with single issues, but it still doesn't get away from the fundamental fact that some nations have more power than others. And to say that we will remodel the United Nations and we will make the WTO about fair trade rather than free trade — both of which terms, of course, can be interpreted in many ways — it can't happen without the powerful nations of the world. We may not like it that some nations are more powerful than others, but they have got to be taken into account. The United States has got to be taken into account. I think also we should be careful not to caricature the United States. The present Bush administration has done many things that many of us don't like, but it's not all the United States. It doesn't represent all the American people. It doesn't represent all the many great traditions of the United States. And there are people within the United States who are very concerned about this present administration. So, to see the United States — I know you didn't mean this, George — but I think there is a danger in talking about the United States as if it is a single malevolent force motivated by a single will. I don't think it is, and I think we have to remember that, and we have to work with it if we're going to try and deal with some of the issues you're talking about.

GEORGE MONBIOT

I don't think that's the case, either, and of course I recognize there are some fantastic, brilliant, innovative movements within the United States with whom, indeed, we are working. But I would point you to some of the real and practical things which are happening right now. I was at the World Social Forum in Mumbai in January at which there were people from a hundred and seventy-six nations. And among the many things on which a lot of people are beginning to agree is the need, for instance, to establish, from the bottom up, at a grassroots level, a world parliament in which we can begin to establish forms of representative democracy at the global level. Also, the need to start applying cruel and unusual measures against the powerful which might actually hurt them. And one proposal I would throw into the discussion is the idea that the indebted countries, the indebted Third World countries, can effectively collectivize their debt and threaten the First World with a collective default unless they get what they want. So they say, for example, "Either you re-form the global financial system or we will, all at once, drop our debt and effectively cripple the global financial system." So by recognizing that, of course, all treaties have the threat of force behind them, there is a genuine attempt to try to mobilize global forces behind some quite specific ideas, which I think perhaps this discussion has so far missed.

ANTHONY GERMAIN

Sounds to me as though you're answering the question that Margaret MacMillan asked — namely, what is global democracy?

GEORGE MONBIOT

Yes. And I would put forward several proposals which I think go some way towards answering that. First of all, a directly elected world parliament built by the world's people, not handed down from above. Secondly, and of course, this is talking at the theoretical level at the moment, the abandonment of the UN Security Council, the vesting of its powers in the General Assembly, the democratization of the General Assembly so we don't have a situation where Tuvalu has the same number of votes as India, the scrapping of the World Bank and IMF and their replacement, as I say, with something like an international clearing union, and a complete reformulation of the World Trade Organization so that, first of all, it commits the poor countries to follow the same routes to development as the rich countries and, second, so that it becomes a licensing authority for global trade — so that a multinational company cannot trade internationally unless it is following the International Labour Organization's guidelines and several others. So there is out there a clearly formulated list of demands, a clearly formulated ideology which we should not dismiss.

TONY JUDT

Well, all I can say about that is that in the 1950s there was a clearly formulated set of demands and a clearly formulated bunch of ideologies that Marx, at one point, dismissed as utopian socialism, and they were widely regarded as the correct and logical and applicable solution to the problems of rampant early capitalism and all its injustices. And maybe they would have been and maybe they wouldn't have been, but the fact is it didn't happen, and it won't happen this time, either, and for much the same reasons. And they're the reasons Margaret gave. You have to begin with politics. You can't dismiss the politics of where you live, the world in which you find yourself. It's so politically convenient to say, "Well, we'll simply start from somewhere else and imagine an alternative world." And even if that were a legitimate starting point, I wouldn't imagine the world you've come up with.

I think the notion of a world parliament is simply silly. I think the notion of changing the World Trade Organization is very rational, but combining all of those things is simply going to devalue the sensible solutions because they'll be associated with the silly ones. It's not silly in any moral sense, it's silly in a purely practical sense. The world is extraordinarily, complexly networked already in ways that we don't normally talk about that are both intergovernmental and non-government and semi-informal and semi-voluntary, and these forms of networks are the ways in which communications and ideas and protests and also innovations in administration and in regulation and so on happen. A world parliament would simply be something like, on a very large scale and therefore even more impractical, the various European parliaments and talking shops and councils and so on that were imagined after World War II and that had no impact whatsoever on the actual coming of the European Community and Union but existed in a kind of virtual parallel European talking-shop universe. And there's nothing wrong with them, but they didn't create whatever it is that's virtuous about the network of European countries and peoples today, and they wouldn't create a world network. And the chief reason is that so long as power resides in countries like the United States, it will not be possible simply to bypass them. You can wish them away but you won't be able to wash them away. And we have to accept that we must begin with the domestic politics of the real existing states.

GEORGE MONBIOT

There's a fundamental contradiction here, because you say we're dealing with all this through these informal networks of NGOs and citizens' groups and the rest of it, but you can't deal with it through a world parliament. Well, it strikes me that if you can deal with it through the informal networks, you can also deal with through formal networks. Not alone, of course — backed up by the informal networks and the rest of it. But let me put this to you. Already this

movement, this global justice movement, commands moral authority. It may seem a peculiar concept, but it does. When the World
Social Forum — this gathering of the great unwashed of the world
— convened in 2003, one of the most powerful men on earth, James
Wolfenson of the World Bank, applied to go and speak there. And
he applied for a very simple reason: he recognized that it had more
legitimacy than the World Bank did, which is controlled exclusively
by the rich nations, because it drew most of its membership from
the poorest nations. And as if to show where power really lies in
this circumstance, the World Social Forum told him to go to hell,
he couldn't come and speak. Now, it strikes me that if already we
are effectively getting them to come to us when we have as yet no
claim to represent directly the world's people, a self-convened forum
which was directly elected, which was directly representative of the
world's people, would swing quite a lot of moral weight, just as,
indeed, the self-convened forum called the Tribunes of the Plebs did
in early Rome and created the basis for a hold, effectively, over the
established structures of power.

ANTHONY GERMAIN

It seems to me that perhaps one factor that you're not giving enough
weight to is nationalism and the fact that nations and the state tend
to speak for their own people. Where does nationalism fit in?

MARGARET MacMILLAN

Nationalism, which we all thought was dead at the end of the 1980s,
came back with a bang and seems to me to be something that is going to be a very disruptive force. And I also worry about the other
sorts of things that are out there: fascism, ultra-nationalism. There
are already very unpleasant nationalist movements all over the world,
as we know. The intolerance that people show towards those who
aren't like them, of the same religion — I mean, we're already seeing
religious-based movements. I worry that, for all the globalization,
there is also that other side, the underside, the dark side of globalization, where you have people turning to these movements which
promise them security and safety, even if they don't promise them

an international sort of world to live in. Also, the revival, which I find very worrying, of the belief in prophecies and the supernatural. I mean, there's some frightening survey in North America of how many people actually believe in astrology. It's enormous. And maybe they only believe in it because it's something that's in the daily newspapers and they don't take it very seriously, but it seems to me there's a whole dark and irrational side of human behaviour which is very frightening. And again, I wish I could believe that what happens at the grassroots is always good, but what happens at the grassroots is often very bad and very nasty.

TONY JUDT

I just wanted to say something by way of a concrete example here to back up Margaret. The Netherlands used to be, by all measures, the most globalized, the most pro-European, pan-European, open, liberal society in Europe. In the course of the last fifteen years, we've seen in the Netherlands a trend that has moved so far back that it is now one of the most anti-European, most inner-regarding, self-regarding, worried societies in the western, the wealthy world. The Pym Fortuyn moment was very symbolic of this. Here you had a very tolerant, open society complaining, in Rotterdam, that there were too many intolerant people coming in who would spoil their nice, closed, tolerant world, and, as a result, they became extremely intolerant of the intolerant Muslims, as they saw them. The Netherlands has now become one of the least globalized mentally, as it were, of the European Union members. And this is something. If it can happen there, it can certainly happen very fast in other places. I also want to say that if there were a world parliament based on one-person-one-vote, then a very significant number of people voting here in this country, in the United States, would, I'm afraid, vote for the kind of people George would not want to see in his parliament.

GEORGE MONBIOT

Well, that's a hazard of democracy — that's what democracy's all about. And the whole point of democracy is that you don't prescribe what sort of people turn up in the parliament and what sort of policies they advocate. And, you know, this is how democracy works. There's a clash of political positions, and hopefully the majority position, moderated by the needs of the minorities, comes out on top. There's a lot of truth in what Tony and Margaret are saying. There's a huge backlash taking place at the same time. The one trend does not cancel out the other. We have these two trends existing in parallel: a trend towards what used to be called "internationalism" — I prefer to call it global justice, as it doesn't depend on nation-states — and at the same time a trend towards this ultra-nationalism, this very ferocious backlash, often backed by new or newly invigorated fundamentalist religions. And what we see is that this idea of the clash of civilizations, which Samuel Huntingdon so infamously promulgated, is becoming almost self-fulfilling. It's a self-fulfilling prophecy. When he wrote the book it wasn't true, but partly as a result of his book and the ideology which surrounds it, it's becoming true.

ANTHONY GERMAIN
When you talked about this notion of a world parliament, you talked about some of the dangers of having a one-person-one-vote system, but you assumed, of course, that people would bother to vote. Where is the engagement of citizens from Canada, the United States, Britain? When we actually talk about politics driving ideology, have people basically resigned from being engaged?

TONY JUDT
If you take the historical picture, you'll see that the history of active political engagement by enfranchised masses is a very short one. It goes, certainly in the West, from the 1890s, let's say, through the 1930s, and there was already the beginnings in the fifties of a sort of disenchantment with politics, a stepping away from the public sphere into private life, into economic life — people no longer bothering to vote, no longer joining parties, no longer taking part in labour or union activities and so forth. The sixties are a misleading blip in this respect because, in fact, the trend begins in the late forties and has continued unbroken through the present. And we should not

too readily assume that the future is a future of politicized citizens. Citizens are not necessarily politicized. The bulk of human history consists of non-political, non-civic, non-citizen communities of subjects, and I'm not sure that we're going to see a return to the mass politics, the organized politics of the twenties and thirties.

MARGARET MacMILLAN

Well, I'm not even sure we even want to see that, because mass politics sometimes led to good things, but Nazi Germany and fascist Italy had mass politics, and people were deeply engaged, and look where it led. George, I'm afraid you will think that I'm now speaking on behalf of the World Bank and the IMF, but if democratic politics is to work, you need an engaged elite, you need people who actually see their responsibility as participating in politics. And I think that has been the strength of democracies, that they've had people who needn't have got involved — people with money, with influence, with positions in society — but who do have enough commitment to the system to get involved. Now, this is not entirely a good thing. I know there are many objections to it, but this is really what political parties are: they are engaged political elites, not necessarily in financial terms but in other sorts of terms. And I think you would get that if you had your world democracy movement, your world politics, your world parliament. You'd have the same thing. I mean, even the forum you talked about — grassroots, maybe, but there were people there representing organizations, and you have to have organizations, you have to have people leading, and you have to have people prepared to get engaged.

GEORGE MONBIOT

I don't deny that for a moment, and nor do I deny what both of you have been saying about the decline of democratic participation and that this is a very serious problem. In fact, I've often found, when advocating the idea of global democracy, that people buy the global bit. They absolutely accept that if national democracy's the best way to run a nation-state, then why shouldn't we have global democracy when it comes to global power as well. It's just the democracy bit they're not so sure about. And they're not so sure about it because patently it has not delivered. And while I agree with what Margaret says, there's also, obviously, a clash here, because when the elites take over politics, they take over politics for their own purposes, not for the purposes of the masses. A question I'd like to put is, without these mass movements, how do you think that we will see a revival of the welfare state? It's certainly not in the interests of the elite.

TONY JUDT

That's historically inaccurate and logically untenable. It doesn't follow that just because elites get involved in the public sphere they're doing it on behalf of some presumptive classes or class of people.

GEORGE MONBIOT

It's certainly the case at the moment.

TONY JUDT

Excuse me, it's not certainly the case at the moment, and a lot depends on which elite you're looking at. There are, after all, very different elites which have competed for power with very different purposes in mind, and the fact of the matter is that one reason the Bush administration is so profoundly unpopular in the circles in which I move is that there are other elites here in the States who think that it's disastrous, not only for their interests but for the interests of a large number of people who, if they're made sufficiently angry, will be bad news for everyone.

GEORGE MONBIOT

Absolutely. But that doesn't mean at the moment that it's operating in the interests of the people.

TONY JUDT

I didn't say it was operating in the interests of the people. I agree that it's not necessarily operating in the interests of the masses or the people, but nor does it function on behalf of some describable, specific group of persons who can be thought of as elite.

GEORGE MONBIOT

And on behalf of a group of military figures and military funders — it's clear.

MARGARET MacMILLAN

No, it's not clear. Sorry to be un-Canadian and disagree with you so vehemently here, but I do think it's unfair. I mean, you're sounding as if the United States is run by Opus Dei out of *The Da Vinci Code*. It's not. There's not a coherent elite. There are many elites. There are many people with different points of view, and to assume that you're bound by your class background is the same mistake that Marx made, and, of course, he didn't apply it to himself. I mean, he came from an upper-class or relatively upper-class background but was able to see beyond it. And people can. Think of the people who made the Great Reform Bill work in England in 1832. They were seeing beyond their particular interests. There is such a thing as the common good.

GEORGE MONBIOT

All democracy movements that we've seen in Britain have been backed by large popular movements, and it's the same around the world. De-colonization, the struggles for freedom have been struggles against the elite by the masses, and we have a situation in the United States now where the demands of the elite, define it how you will — in this case, I would define it as principally a corporate elite — are plainly at variance with the demands of the common man and the common woman, and we're only going to see the demands of the common man and the common woman taking a central place in politics once again with mass political participation.

MARGARET MacMILLAN

But your view of politics is a morality play. I mean, you've got the common man and the common woman on one side, who are good and decent and upright and don't want to use too much gas, and on the other side you have the corporate elite who are sitting there, swilling away champagne. This is not the way the world works. Let us recognize that the world is more complex.

TONY JUDT

In the United States, the common man, woman, whoever they are, are among George Bush's strongest supporters, even while they may be misled by all kinds of ideological hegemonies and other things into believing that Bush operates in their interests. The fact is, they are so misled, and the chief hope against the kinds of people whom George so dislikes is probably other elites, because I fear that, in terms of the masses, Bush — having observed him quite close up — is very effective at convincing them that he speaks for them. I think democracy may be more dangerous than George supposes.

GEORGE MONBIOT

Well, it's not at all clear which elites are going to stand up for the needs of the common man and the common woman. It's certainly clear that the Democrats under John Kerry aren't going to do so. When the Republicans say, "Jump," Kerry says, "Off which high building?" And what we have plainly is a mass divorce between a whole number of different elites and some very basic needs, such as the need for universal health care, the need for serious investment in education, the need for environmental protection — these are not being reflected by any powerful, identifiable elite.

TONY JUDT

You're absolutely right about that, but you have to remember that, again, when such reforms as those you describe and others, like the coming of the welfare state in the thirties and forties and fifties in Europe, came about, they came about because elites — I hate the term, but since you put it on the table — but educated persons chose to take a particular position on public policy and in public affairs, mobilized opinion around their own set of, at that point, quite elite beliefs about the way a country ought to be run and the way policy out to be made and the way taxes ought to be spent, and that became popular politics. It's not the other way round.

GEORGE MONBIOT

I think you have a very top-down view of history.

TONY JUDT

I do, indeed.

GEORGE MONBIOT

For instance, let's take a look at housing after the Second World War. In the closing stages of the Second World War in Britain, there was a mass squatters movement. There were over a thousand mass squats, many of which involved several thousand people. There were probably hundreds of thousands involved in this movement, taking over derelict buildings, taking over old Army and Air Force buildings, occupying them, demanding housing. And it was only when that reached a sufficient head of steam that you saw the government responding with mass housing, a publicly funded housing project. It did not come from the top down. It came very plainly from the bottom up. And one of the problems we have with history is that it's so reluctant to record the grassroots movements which push politicians over the edge.

MARGARET MacMILLAN

I've got to defend history here — historians for the past twenty or thirty years have been looking at grassroots movements. But I think the point here is not that it's either grassroots or coming from the top down. Politics is a whole process of pressures and compromises and working it out. And yes, pressure comes up from below, but the pressure from below is not always the sort of result you want. And I don't see how occupying buildings — it may call attention to an issue, but I don't see how that's democratic. I mean, that's direct action which may be necessary, but your definition of democracy, it seems to me, is that it's all right to take direct action and do what you feel is right because you're morally justified, but that isn't what politics is about.

GEORGE MONBIOT

Actually, my definition of democracy is my definition of mass movement.

ANTHONY GERMAIN

How optimistic are each of you for the future?

MARGARET MacMILLAN

I think I was more optimistic when I started. I don't know now. I see mass movements washing around the world, and goodness knows what the results will be. I mean, I am optimistic. I do think that there are many hopeful signs, and I think many of the international movements that are taking place, such as the push for an international criminal court of justice, are very important. That's been one of the most positive developments since the end of the Second World War, and the more we are linked together the more we are likely to be able to salvage this planet. And I agree with George. We have very large issues, although I don't share his pessimism about gasoline prices, about the running out of oil. I think we've been there before: the Club of Rome issue, that very pessimistic report in 1975. I have some faith in the resilience of human society and the resilience of human beings and our capacity to deal with crises. But I agree there are crises coming down the pipeline, and we're going to have to deal with them.

TONY JUDT

I agree with Margaret, but I draw more pessimistic conclusions. I think that the domestic politics of the States, which play the most important roles in international affairs, are liable to take, as we might see it, a turn for the worse in the next thirty years, and as a consequence of that, I don't think they will perform the kind of responsible role that they should in the direction that both Margaret and George indicate. So I'm pessimistic. I'm a sort of negativist liberal. I think that our chief task is going to be to make sure that the wrong kinds of people don't get in control of states, rather than that the right kinds of people do get in control of mass movements.

GEORGE MONBIOT

Well, I'm probably a little more pessimistic still. I think that the past one hundred and fifty years of general economic growth is a historical anomaly — largely as a result of the ever-expanding availability of cheap fuel, which is plainly coming to an end. In fact, T. Boone Pickens, the Texan oil billionaire, said this month that we have reached the peak of oil production already this year. And if that's the case, then it's very hard to see how this fractional reserve banking system on which the whole of capitalism is built can be sustained at current levels or possibly, in the long run, can be sustained at all. And that being so, it could well be that the economic and ecological space which has permitted so much co-operation between elites and the masses — yes, between other nations, between people of all descriptions — may no longer be sustainable. And if that's the case we're in a lot of trouble, and that's why I think we have to start looking at these very big, plausible, global ideas as a potential way out of this mess.

"The Next Ideology," originally heard on The Current, *was rebroadcast on* Ideas *on October 18, 2004.*

Global Interdependence

SYLVIA OSTRY

Interviewed by

MICHAEL ENRIGHT

Raised in Winnipeg, educated at the finest schools and possessed of a mind that is acute, quick, thoughtful and deep, Dr. Sylvia Ostry has been a senior public servant, an international advisor, an acclaimed scholar and a prolific writer. She has participated in some of the most important economic gatherings of our time and deserves no small amount of the credit for their achievements. She teaches and writes, researches and advises Canadian and international organizations about where the world is headed and how that could or should change. "Globalization" is a slippery term. Standing for a host of virtues and sins, it is sometimes seen to be about jobs, sometimes about culture, sometimes about freedom. It can be a rallying cry for nationalism, an argument about economic inevitability, a plea for justice, a banner for anti-Americanism, or a wistful remembrance of times gone by.

MICHAEL ENRIGHT

John Ralston Saul wrote a piece in *Harper's* magazine in which he said that globalization is dead. He said that since 1995 the signs of decline have turned a confused situation into a collapse — that globalization, for all its promise, had failed to deliver, that the nation-states had not collapsed, that there were still strong elements of sovereignty and that the whole thrust of globalization hadn't made the impact that all of its proponents said it would. Is he right? Is this the end of globalization?

SYLVIA OSTRY

Well, I think that there's been a very lively debate between those who have three cheers for globalization and those who think it's the source of all evil. But to say that it's collapsed is rather breathtaking. The nation-state is certainly affected by — I hate the word "globalization" — but by the much tighter integration among countries which is fed by greatly increased trade, greatly increased financial flows, very significant foreign direct investment and, most of all, the revolution in information and consumer technology. And it has been true that that growing, much tighter, deeper integration affects the room to manoeuvre of all the nation-states, even the United States, the most powerful.

There are those who would like to see that cut off. There is a movement in the anti-globalization group that dreams of some beautiful past Eden in which only communities exist and there's very little trade and so on. That's impossible, but that's one of the dreams they pursue. The other option, which Saul doesn't seem to be talking about, is recognizing that globalization has very serious bad effects on many countries and to do something about it through international policy co-operation, and that's what's happening, although it's stumbling, I'm afraid.

MICHAEL ENRIGHT

You don't like the word "globalization." The term you used in a couple of papers that you've written is the term "deepening integration." What is being integrated and how deeply? What are we talking about here?

SYLVIA OSTRY

I'm talking about what started in the post-war period, which was to try to undo some of the disastrous effects of the 1930s in terms of the enormous increase in protectionism which led to the Great

Depression and all the nasty things that happened after that, including the Second World War. I think it was Raymond Aaron who said that the post-war system was built by leaders walking backwards into the future, because the impetus for it, "Never again," was not just for the post-war system but also for European unification.

That was the beginning. The barriers were reduced and trade flows increased enormously. Then, in the 1970s, as a consequence of the OPEC shock, you got an enormous increase in financial flows. In the eighties, you had the beginning of a massive flow of foreign direct investment, a surge which began in the middle eighties and is continuing, although it's shifting its location and source. All these things tighten the linkages between countries. If you want to cut off trade flows, you will pay a very heavy price. You will also pay a very heavy price for financial flows in terms of crises. We've had a series of very serious exchange rate and financial crises, particularly in the nineties. Foreign direct investment, I've always felt, is a much more intensive integration. You have a firm in the country, which begins to affect a whole range of things that trade doesn't — it's much more penetrating. And now, with information and communications technology, the phrase that's used is a "fusion of the global market." We're now beginning to realize how powerful the tool of greatly enhanced communications is. The thing I'm most interested in now is how it has facilitated non-state actors. It's obviously done that for business because you have the creation of production networks around the world, but I'm thinking of the non-governmental organizations.

MICHAEL ENRIGHT

Leaving aside the impacts of technology and the infusion or the movement of capital, let me stick with trade for a moment. Is globalization simply the enhancement of the idea of free trade between and among nations, and if it is, there is evidence it's not working, because we talk free trade and then we protect. So, in that sense, it's not working as it should, is it?

SYLVIA OSTRY

I don't think, just as a correction, that anybody, even the most ide-alist of those post-war leaders, believed it was possible to have true free trade. So when the trade institution was set up, it had so many holes that I've called it "termites in the basement." It had a number of loopholes because it was very clear that trade has good and bad results and that the people who get hurt by the adjustment which will increase the standard of living don't want trade. I mean, they're not interested. So there were many loopholes to try to mitigate, reduce the impact.

I was involved in the last big round, the Uruguay Round of trade talks under the GATT, the General Agreement on Tariffs and Trade, which turned into the World Trade Organization. It had a number of unintended consequences, but it really was a transformation to a world of deeper integration because it began to penetrate beyond the border into domestic policies, of which trade and services, intellec-tual property and investment were far more intrusive — not that we fully understood the implications of that. And that deeper integration is something which now affects the trading system because it created a divide between North and South, with the South arguing that it had not benefited to the same extent as the North had from the trad-ing system. If you look at the poorest countries, their benefits were zero — they actually lost from the Uruguay Round, on account of the decline in the price of commodities, the much greater difficulty of abiding by these more complex rules and so on. So it created a North-South divide which persists and is getting more important.

And because the Uruguay Round was heavily influenced by multi-national corporations — most of all, Americans — in getting these new issues in, it gave a tremendous boost to anti-globalization NGOs. It's not the only thing, but post-Uruguay Round they were really helped by being on the Internet. They really became far more power-ful by tapping into an anti-trade, anti-globalization view that already existed in many countries. At the famous meeting in Seattle you saw the NGOs and the demonstrators and the protest movement and the anarchists. What I'm finding now is that the brand of dissent which was working in the marches and the protests has been seriously damaged. There was too much violence, and there's growing evidence that extremists were attempting to capture the demonstrations.

MICHAEL ENRIGHT

You have referred elsewhere to the "dissent industry" — that, in fact, it is in the interests of some organizations to be in the business of dissent.

SYLVIA OSTRY

Yes, if you're a policy entrepreneur and you want to influence policy, it is clear that you can raise the issues and the agenda if you're on TV, and the media are very much attracted by the more violent portions of it. I'm saying that the dissent industry's success, if you want to call it that, at Seattle and post-Seattle, has very much diminished because of the violence, and there is evidence — for example, in Genoa — that anarchists perhaps were used by the police. The anarchists, the Black Bloc and some of the others, can't give up a free lunch: if somebody's organizing a demonstration, they might as well go. We saw it in Quebec City. But then you had 9/11 and the association of the anti-globalization movement — they've given up that name — with terror has made the mainline groups say, "We don't want to do that, we're much more interested in being inside the tent, assisting and aiding governments, than outside the tent."

MICHAEL ENRIGHT

When you talk about anti-globalization in some of your writings, you use the terms "alienation" and "anomie." In what context? How do they apply?

SYLVIA OSTRY

Well, that's the part that intrigues me so much. Somebody said that the only thing that was left from Marxism that was not in the dustbin of history was his concept of alienation — that the workers in industry have become commodified, they are like commodities. Unlike pre-capitalism, where there was a degree of community and integration — that's part of the reason for all the yearning for the past — these were commodities. And he talked about alienation and argued that it would lead to a revolution. Durkheim, a French sociologist, saw the concept of anomie as de-linking the worker from what he was doing and the output, but he didn't think there'd be a revolution. He said that the alienation was from society as a whole, its values, its objectives. A whole school was set up — I think it was at the University of Chicago — to talk about anomie as a source of criminal activity, because if you've rejected society, but you want to achieve the goals that it's talking about — lots of money — and you can't do it by legal means, well, what's wrong with doing it by criminal means?

Polling data suggest that there is lack of confidence in the institutions of democracy. People don't have confidence in their political leaders. They don't have confidence in parliaments. They don't have confidence in all the institutions that are the infrastructure of democracy.

MICHAEL ENRIGHT

It goes back to the idea that the nation-state is too small to solve the big problems and too big to solve the small ones.

SYLVIA OSTRY

That was Daniel Bell who said that. But I also look at [Joseph] Schumpeter, who says — I think in the most penetrating way — that the Achilles heel of capitalism is the lack of a moral core. He has this wonderful phrase that the stock exchange is a poor substitute for the Holy Grail. It's a kind of cynical phrase. And I say, even more cynically, but today the stock exchange is the Holy Grail. I think the disaffection, particularly of the young people, with the system as a whole has certainly fed these movements, and I'm still pursuing this.

There was a fascinating article in *The New York Times* about young Japanese born after the economic bubble there burst and their rejection of everything about Japanese society. I mean, it's really frightening — no connection with the society. The reason I mention it is that I was at a meeting and two Japanese friends of mine were there and I was asking them about the cult that attacked the Tokyo subway, and they said their children are tempted, that they're looking for things, something, to commit to. And you know, that cult recruited some of the best students from Japanese universities. I think it's dangerous because why can't you work inside the system? Why, if you want to make all these changes, can't you do it by going into the political system?

MICHAEL ENRIGHT

Nobel Prize-winning economist Amartya Sen says that some people view globalization as global westernization. That it has overtones of colonialism and conquest and all of that — that, in fact, it's not an economic thrust as much as a political, social, cultural thrust. Is there anything to that?

SYLVIA OSTRY

Oh, absolutely. That's why I don't like using the word, because there are many facets of it. So I try to be more objective on the tightening interdependence. But that's part of an ongoing debate in which the pro-globalists have argued that cultures reflect preferences, and if people prefer American culture, then what are you talking about? And there are those who say that, actually, individual cultures are not only being preserved, they're growing more vigorously. I don't know. But there's no question that the role of the media has an effect on cultural preferences.

I have a wonderful story about when we tried to suggest a global cultural exception in the Uruguay Round. The French were in favour, but the American, a good friend of mine, said, "Sylvia, what is the difference between yogurt and Canada?" And I said, "I don't know, what is the difference?" And he said, "Yogurt has an active culture." I laughed, and then I said, "You are the only people in the world who don't understand that culture is not just a commodity." It is a commodity, there's no question, but it is more than that.

MICHAEL ENRIGHT

In terms of globalization and its implementation, is it a zero-sum game? In order to enhance the wealth of the North or the West, does it follow that somebody else has to lose wealth?

SYLVIA OSTRY

Not at all, and there's no evidence of that. There's strong evidence that, by and large, the trade was beneficial. It did increase growth and so on — not in the poorest countries, which are a special problem, but in a whole range of middle-income countries. What it does show is what I said: there are winners and losers, and the need to compensate the losers is overwhelming. It's very interesting that, in order to get what they call "fast track" through in the United States — that is, to allow Congress to vote up or down on the trade, give more room to manoeuvre for the executive — they had to introduce the idea of an adjustment program. Whether they'll use it or not, I don't know. But the business of outsourcing is a very interesting issue, because there's fear among the people I know in Washington that if really protectionist actions are taken against countries like India or China, that could be a very serious development. And the argument is, yes, the world is changing. Those countries are going up the value-added ladder. What are you going to do — stop them? Who stopped you in the nineteenth century? The debate is there.

MICHAEL ENRIGHT

In Canada, there is a sort of fear of outsourcing commingled with selfishness — I want the jobs in Moncton; I don't want them in Peshawar. And aren't we supposed to be thinking about the Third World? Aren't we supposed to be more generous to them? Someone has to win, someone has to lose. Or can you have both?

SYLVIA OSTRY

You can have both. I think that there's been a major change, and I don't know the outcome yet. At the last ministerial meeting of the World Trade Organization in Cancun, I had a feeling of *déjà vu* because this group called the G-21, led by Brazil and including India and China, said, "Unless you can do something on agriculture, the ballgame's over." And another group, called the G-90, from the poorest countries, said, "We are not going to discuss the issues you've put forward, like competition policy and investment and so on. The ballgame's over." The reason I had *déjà vu* is that I was at the Montreal ministerial in 1988, and the last night we were up all night waiting for the Europeans and the Americans, who had been up all night in another room dealing with agriculture. At six o'clock in the morning they came in, and we perked up and said, "Okay, tell us what happened." And they said, "Nothing happened, we couldn't reach agreement, so we'll just write a memorandum, a communiqué." And the Brazilians, with a group of Latin Americans, said, "No agreement on agriculture? We take everything else off the table."

And so I said I had *déjà vu* because the Brazilians and the Indians and the Chinese — you can't tell where the Chinese are — had formed a group which, in fact, said, "We're a power bloc; you can't run the system any more," which is an astonishing thing. Africans had so many NGOs in their delegation that we'd never seen anything like it. Who was running the African thing? But that's a changed world, and if you're going to try and restore a global system of rules, you have got to recognize the Africans, the ones that depend on commodities. They put on a demonstration, the countries did, on the first day, which was fantastic. Talking about the poverty-stricken farmers who grow cotton and the subsidies of the rich world that are destroying them. They'll all starve to death. And instead of responding by saying, "Okay, we'll provide compensation, and we're going to do something about cotton subsidies," they did nothing. They gave a long lecture on commodity diversification and what have you. Total non-response. If you're going to do that and if you can block the system, what kind of system will you have?

MICHAEL ENRIGHT

You hear the term "adjustment" a lot; everyone uses it. Well, those adjustments involve living, breathing human beings. What does that mean in terms of globalization — that things are going to be really, really bad and then they're going to get really, really good? Is that the message?

SYLVIA OSTRY

No. I think that at the meeting that preceded Cancun — which launched what's called the Doha Round, because the meeting was in Doha, Qatar — the North-South divide that started in the Uruguay Round appeared to have an enormous impact. It wasn't really called a round but a "development agenda," with the usual items — agriculture and so on — but it laid enormous emphasis on technical assistance, capacity-building and so forth to help the poorest countries. By capacity-building, I mean the idea that they don't have the infrastructure, they don't have the capabilities in their countries to take advantage of trade. The Big Two, the US and the Europeans, appeared to have bought the idea that development was absolutely crucial, that there was too much disparity between the poorest countries and the other countries, and that part of the function of the WTO would be to improve the possibilities, the capabilities of the poorest countries.

So what happened? The answer is, by and large, zilch. So I think that the backlash at Cancun was hardly surprising. The idea that you cannot run the system from Brussels and Washington was made very clear. The question is, what will happen?

A frightening thing was the reaction of the Americans at Cancun. Their rage didn't surprise me; they were very angry. But they threatened the other countries. Not just the trade people but the people from other parts of the American government and the big business groups that were there — they said they'd do bilateral deals, but only with countries who were accommodating.

And so I don't know what will happen. If the WTO, which is a global institution, becomes marginalized and you have unilateralism and bilateralism, then surely the Europeans would be tit-for-tat, and then you're facing not a very pleasant world.

MICHAEL ENRIGHT

Young people have now come to be suspicious of, or certainly doubt the capacity of, institutions, political, commercial or whatever, to do anything. You've just given an example of their inability to do something. You're as suspicious of the institutions as the young people?

SYLVIA OSTRY

Well, certainly, as somebody who's interested in trade, I am astonished. I mean, I was in the Uruguay Round, and each time we thought it was going over the edge we managed to retrieve it. In Montreal we were so smart. We said, "No, the meeting hasn't been concluded." We just temporarily stopped it, and we'll meet again in April in Brussels. And the press bought that. Then there was another one in 1990 and they were near the edge and so on. They finally got an agreement and the agreement was the Big Two: the Americans at Blair House and the Europeans. I don't know if the powerful countries and also the G-21 — Brazil and India and China — could form a consensus which wasn't based on received doctrine and which recognized how complex the system was, which said it's not just trade, there's got to be development, we've got to have compensatory mechanisms. I think the Cold War was the glue that held the West together, and the present situation is an acid that is eroding the West. So I don't know what's going to happen.

MICHAEL ENRIGHT

You've worked at every level of public service in this country and have done so many things and have known everybody. When you were beginning in the sixties, there was a sense that there was a nobility about the federal civil service — call it the public service — or there was a feeling that these men and women were acting in a kind of noble way. And there was the idea that an impact could be made, that you could do something, you could change things, that the institutions that you were involved with did work.

SYLVIA OSTRY

It's very depressing. I think the erosion of the public service — I mean, of the ethos of the public service and the belief that things could be done and so on — begins at the end of the Trudeau era. And then it's accelerated by changes in the Mulroney era, when power was shifted from the bureaucrats to the political people in the ministerial office, which made it very difficult. And then there are now more alternatives, so that the concept of a life career in the public service is a very alien idea. So there's a kind of vicious circle. Some of the most outstanding people, like Bob Bryce and a number of others, really unbelievable people, were recruited at the end of the Great Depression. They had no alternative. They came in and, I mean, I knew Bryce. It was astonishing. I remember a meeting at a Bank of Canada seminar. John Kenneth Galbraith was there, and he said that Keynes had said that his best pupil ever was Bob Bryce. And that Bryce was sent by Keynes to Harvard to carry Keynesian ideas. But he's not the only one; they were an extraordinary group, and I think we're being naive if we think we can get that.

MICHAEL ENRIGHT

You were at the centre of many debates in the Trudeau era. And these debates sometimes happened in public. People talked about issues and policies and things. That does not happen now, does it? The globalization issue is not a debate, it's an argument. The government says one thing, the people march in the street. It's back and forth and back and forth.

SYLVIA OSTRY

What you're talking about is a decline in the system of democracy. What I've been saying on anomie was not a rejection of the system but of the way it worked, the institutions and so on. There's a survey, called Latino Barometro, of the values of Latin America, and you see the alienation there. It is not a rejection of the system. But if the system degrades and a vicious circle develops, with the destruction of the only other systemic view, which was Marxism, there's only one other system, apart from democracy, and that's fascism. There are only two systems. I say fascism because I don't know another word. But if, in fact, there's discontent and alienation and you don't do anything positive, will there not be a desire for some kind of order?

MICHAEL ENRIGHT

But that means the man on the horse.

SYLVIA OSTRY

I don't know. But in order to be optimistic — I mean, I don't think it's impossible that the trading system could be restored, but then you've got to ask about the larger system, and there you have the two builders of the system now growing further apart. That is, the transatlantic alliance is eroding.

MICHAEL ENRIGHT

Have you toyed with the idea that the trading system can't be restored? And what does that mean, if it can't?

SYLVIA OSTRY

I believe there are two systems. One is a system of rules, which is the global system, and the other is a system in which the powerful decide what will be done. And I think that if you turn to that, you're in an anarchic situation and it becomes impossible to forecast what would happen. But I have some optimism.

MICHAEL ENRIGHT

The United States can choose to play the game or not, because it has all of the power. Where do we fit into this in Canada? Are we going to get ground between the Big Two here? Is there some way for us to function, to grow and to still remain a humane, decent society?

SYLVIA OSTRY

I have argued that, given the situation today, there is, in fact, a role for middle powers like Canada. During the Uruguay Round, we, with other middle powers, set up a group which excluded the big powers — the United States, Europe and Japan. And we had people from each region, Latin America, Asia — not Africa, because they were just ignored. And it was we who finally put together the draft of the meeting for Punta del Este in Uruguay that became the launch of the Uruguay Round. I have argued that there's an opportunity now, because what is needed is some kind of mediation among the blocs, between the G-21, the Africans, the Big Two, and so on. And that could be a useful role for Canada. We have credibility with southern countries. We have not done enough in Latin America, in my view. I think we're a logical intermediary between Latin America and the United States. I mean, nobody knows the United States better than we do.

We have to maintain our linkages and we may have to increase them. But that doesn't mean we can't search for a role which would allow us to begin a process of saying these blocs will serve no purpose except to destroy the World Trade Organization. Why do you want to do that?

MICHAEL ENRIGHT

After all your work in all of this, are you, at the end of the day, optimistic about the world economy? If you look at the scale of the gap between the poor and the rich and the possibility of the whole thing collapsing in some kind of recession, how can you be optimistic?

SYLVIA OSTRY

Well, I don't think that the disparities between the rich and the poor are a threat to the world economy. They are a profoundly moral issue, and the issue of equity has been ignored. I don't happen to think that you can dismiss it, but I think that the one thing that is bothering people is the American current account deficit and the growing dependence on countries like China. I'm not sure the Americans understand the implications — I'm not sure anybody does — of what is genuinely a power shift to a Third World country, and so the uncertainty and the possibility of greater and greater friction by the middle of the century is a very serious one. Do we have the leaders who are walking forward into the future?

"Global Interdependence" was broadcast in The Enright Files *series as "The World of Sylvia Ostry" on April 5, 2004.*

Acknowledgements

Diligent efforts have been made to secure appropriate permissions to publish the material included in this book. Please contact Goose Lane Editions if errors have inadvertently been made.

The following broadcast transcripts are published with the permission of the Canadian Broadcasting Corporation: *The American Stake in Europe and the European Stake in the United States* (Nexus Lecture, 2001), Richard Holbrooke; *America Unbound*, Ivo Daalder and James Lindsay; *Anarchism in the Mid-Twentieth Century*, George Woodcock; *Common Culture, Multiculture* (Education Debates), Charles Taylor, Bernie Farber, and Bob Davis; *Community and Its Counterfeits*, John McKnight; *Debating the Welfare State*, William Kristol and Bob Rae; *Dictatorships and Democracies*, Ronald Wintrobe; *The Empty Society* (Massey Lectures, 1966), Paul Goodman; *How the World Has Changed*, Ursula Franklin, Robert Fulford, and Janice Stein; *A Polemicist's Journey*, Tariq Ali; *The Next Ideology*, Margaret MacMillan, Tony Judt, and George Monbiot; *Remembering Rwanda (The Enright Files)*, Roméo Dallaire and Gerry Caplan; *The Ethics of Intervention (Taking a Stand)*, Dr. James Orbinski; *Global Interdependence, The Enright Files*, Sylvia Ostry.

The following selections appear by permission of the authors or their agents: *The Public Good in Canada*, Michael Bliss; *We the People: A Prescription for*

Ending the Arms Race (Jacob Bronowski Lecture, 1984), Helen Caldicott; *What Has Changed: The Impact of 9/11 on the Middle East* (Frum Lecture, 2003), Bernard Lewis; *The Legitimacy of Violence as a Political Act*, Hannah Arendt, Noam Chomsky, Robert Lowell, and Conor Cruise O'Brien.

Material reprinted from books or material appearing in slightly different form in books is published with the permission of the following publishers: "The Secular Messiahs," *Nostalgia for the Absolute*, copyright © 1974 George Steiner. Reprinted with the permission of House of Anansi Press, Toronto. "On Religion and Language," *Northrop Frye in Conversation*, copyright © 1992 David Cayley. Reprinted with the permission of House of Anansi Press, Toronto. "Apocalypses: Prophecies, Cults and Millennial Beliefs Through the Ages," *Apocalypses*, Eugen Weber. Copyright © 1999 by Eugen Weber. Published by Random House Canada.